Effective Management of Student Employment

D1193315

Effective Management of
Student Employment

∽

Organizing for Student Employment in Academic Libraries

David A. Baldwin
> Director, Fine Arts Library
> University of New Mexico

Frances C. Wilkinson
> Director, Acquisitions and Serials
> University of New Mexico

Daniel C. Barkley
> Director, Government Information
> University of New Mexico

2000
LIBRARIES UNLIMITED, INC.
Englewood, Colorado

To all of the student employees I've worked with at Upper Iowa College Library, Boise State University Library, University of Wyoming Libraries, and the University of New Mexico General Library—thanks. **—Dave**

For Arianne Barnhill Brown, Ruth Richardson Scales, Michael Brown, Darhla Gilson, and Jennifer Lizut, five extraordinary student employees. You brought out the best in me as a supervisor. **—Fran**

To every student assistant whom I've had the pleasure of supervising—thank you. To the staff of the Government Information Department at UNM, thank you for your patience, tolerance, and support. **—Dan**

Libraries Unlimited, Inc.
P.O. Box 6633
Englewood, CO 80155-6633
1-800-237-6124
www.lu.com

Library of Congress Cataloging-in-Publication Data

Baldwin, David A. (David Allen), 1946-
  Effective management of student employment : organizing for student employment in academic libraries / David A. Baldwin, Frances C. Wilkinson, Daniel C. Barkley.
    p. cm.
  Includes bibliographical references and index.
  ISBN 1-56308-688-3
  1. Academic libraries--United States--Personnel management.   2. Student library assistants--United States.   I. Wilkinson, Frances C.   II. Barkley, Daniel.   III. Title.

Z675.U5 B279   1999
023--dc21   99-046277

CONTENTS ∾

List of Figures, Job Descriptions,
Tables, and Tests xv

Introduction xvii

1—THE STUDENT EMPLOYEE—A PERSPECTIVE 1

Today's Academic Libraries 1
The Role of Student Employees 2
History of Student Employment 4
    Student Employment in the 1930s 4
    Student Employees as Potential Librarians 5
    Student Employment in Recent Years 6
Size of the Student Workforce 7
Student Workers and Regular Staff 8
Work-Study Versus Non-Work-Study Student Employees . . . 9
Why Do Students Work? 9
Supervising Student Employees 11
    Why Is Good Supervision Important? 12
    The Rewards of Student Employee Supervision 13
Looking Ahead 14
Notes 14
Bibliography 15

2—THE STUDENT EMPLOYEE SUPERVISOR 17

The Role of Student Employee Supervisor 17
Definition of Supervisor 18
    Getting Things Done Through Others 18
Who Are the Student Employee Supervisors? 19
    The Best Worker May Not Be the Best Supervisor . . . 20
    Personal Qualities of Good Student
        Employee Supervisors 21
    Types of Persons Who Should Not Be Supervisors . . . 22
    Student Employee Supervisor Attitudes 22
Moving from a Staff to a Supervisory Position 23
    Seven Transition Stages 25

2—THE STUDENT EMPLOYEE SUPERVISOR (continued)

Problems Faced by New Student Employee Supervisors . . . 26
    Expectations for Student Employee Supervisors 27
    Common Mistakes New Supervisors Make 28
    What Employees Don't Like About
        Their Supervisors 28
    Why Student Employee Supervisors Fail. 31
Preparing to Become a Student Employee Supervisor 31
The Student Employee Supervisor 32
Notes. 32
Bibliography 33

3—BASICS FOR SUPERVISORS 35

Becoming a Supervisor. 35
Leadership 35
    Your Leadership Potential 37
Authority and Accountability. 40
    Assessing Your Degree of Accountability 41
Managing Change and Time 44
    Identifying Time Wasters 46
    Time Management Guidelines 46
Dealing with Stress 48
Determining Your Potential 49
    Tips on Getting Noticed and Promoted 50
    Learn from Your Mistakes 51
    Behavior to Avoid 52
    Getting Along with Your Supervisor 52
    Writing Better Reports 53
Summary 53
Notes. 54
Bibliography 54

4—ORGANIZING FOR STUDENT EMPLOYMENT— JOB DESCRIPTIONS 57

Organizing Function of Management 57
Organizing a System for Student Employee Positions 57
    Job Design and Analysis 58

Purpose of Job Descriptions 59
    Features and Uses of a Good Job Description 60
Guidelines for Preparing Job Descriptions. 61
    Job Descriptions for the Library 61
Student Employee Job Descriptions. 62
    Grade I Student Positions. 62
    Grade II Student Positions 62
    Grade III Student Positions 63
Sample Student Employee Job Descriptions 63
Job Matching. 108
Student Employment Application Form 108
Summary 111
Bibliography 111

5—UNDERSTANDING STUDENT FINANCIAL AID. 113
Federal Aid for Student Employment 113
Federal Student Aid Programs. 115
Independent Student Definition for Eligibility
   Determination 115
    Cost of Attendance 120
    Expected Family Contribution (EFC) 122
Financial Aid Administrator. 123
Federal Pell Grants 123
Federal Family Education Loan (FFEL) Program 124
William D. Ford Federal Direct Loan Program 125
Campus-Based Student Financial Aid Programs 127
Federal Supplemental Educational Opportunities
   Grant Program 127
The Federal Work-Study (FWS) Program. 128
    Employment Conditions and Limitations 130
Work-Colleges Program. 133
Federal Perkins Loan Program. 134
State Student Incentive Grants Program 134
National Early Intervention Scholarship and
   Partnership Program 135
The Robert C. Byrd Honors Scholarship Program. 136
Counseling the Student on Financial Aid. 137
Internet Sites of Interest 138
Notes 141
Bibliography 142

6—HIRING STUDENT EMPLOYEES 145

Hiring and Firing. 145
Referral of Student Workers. 145
Recruiting Student Workers 147
    Interviewing Techniques. 149
Legal Implications of Employment Decisions 153
    The Supervisor's Responsibility 154
    Nondiscriminatory Interviewing 155
Reference Checks. 155
Communicating the Hiring Decision 156
Bibliography 157

7—STUDENT EMPLOYEE COMPENSATION 159

Differentiated Pay 159
Student Employee Allotments. 161
Wages and Salaries 163
Fair Labor Standards Act (FLSA) 164
    Exempt Versus Nonexempt 166
    Minimum Wage. 167
    Overtime 167
    Jury Duty, Witness Duty, and Voting Time 167
    Child Labor Laws 168
    Payment of Wages 168
Equal Pay Act 169
Overview of Laws Governing the Workplace 169
Notes 172
Bibliography 172

8—ORIENTATION AND TRAINING OF STUDENT EMPLOYEES 175

Training Is Everything 175
Why Provide Orientation? 176
    Orientation and the New Student Employee 176
Training and Development Are Not the Same 179
    Role of the Student Employee Supervisor
      in Training 180
    Should Supervisors Do All the Training? 180

What Do You Train For? 181
Four-Step Method for Training 181
    Step 1. Preparation of the Learner 181
    Step 2. Presentation of the Operation. 182
    Step 3. Performance Tryout 182
    Step 4. Follow-up 183
Extending the Training 183
Job Instruction Training (JIT) 184
Tips for Improving Training. 186
Active Versus Passive Learning 187
Implementing Your Training Program 188
Developmental Training 189
    Developmental Training Methods 190
Supervisor Training Checklist. 191
Notes 192
Bibliography 192

9—SUPERVISION TECHNIQUES FOR STUDENT EMPLOYEE SUPERVISORS

9—SUPERVISION TECHNIQUES FOR
    STUDENT EMPLOYEE SUPERVISORS 195
Managing and Being Managed 195
Hierarchical Library Organization 196
Team Management. 196
    Participative Management 196
Five Functions of Management 197
About Authority 198
Responsibility 201
About Making Decisions 202
About Communication 204
Group Effort 206
Giving Direction 206
    Guidelines for Giving Direction 207
    Getting Cooperation. 208
Motivation 208
    Coaching 209
About Counseling 210
Supervisory Principles 213
Notes 213
Bibliography 213

10—STUDENT EMPLOYEE PROBLEM RESOLUTION 215

Student Employee Problems 215
   The Student Employee Who Complains 216
   The Unmotivated Student Employee 217
   The Student Employee with Low Morale 218
   The Disloyal Student Employee 219
   The Student Employee Who Violates Library Rules . . . 220
   The Student Worker with Absenteeism Problems . . . 221
   Time, Telephone, and Dress Policies 223
   The Student Who Is Dishonest 223
   The Student Employee Who Violates
      University Rules 224
   The Student Employee with Personality Problems . . . 225
   The Student Employee with Personal Problems . . . 227
   Dealing with Rumors in the Workplace 227
   The Student Employee Who Procrastinates 228
   The Student Worker Who Resists Change 228
   Dealing with Stress 229
   Dealing with Insubordination 229
   Dealing with the Older Student Employee 230
Problem Resolution 230
Bibliography 231

11—PERFORMANCE APPRAISAL 233

How Am I Doing? 233
Praises and Raises 234
Job Evaluation Versus Performance Appraisal 234
How Formal Should the Performance Appraisal Be? . . . 236
Questions to Be Answered in an Appraisal 237
How Often Should Student Employee
   Appraisals Be Done? 237
Sequence of Activities in Performance Appraisal 237
   Set Performance Standards 238
   Communicate Standards 238
   Observe Employees Performing Work 239
   Collect Data 239
   Have Employees Complete Self-Appraisal 239
   Use the Information Gathered 240
   Evaluate the Employee 240
   Provide Feedback 241

The Appraisal Meeting 241
    Validity and Reliability 245
    Making Nondiscriminatory Appraisals 246
    Confidentiality of Appraisals 246
    Good Evaluations Don't Always Result in
        Advancement or in More Money 247
    What Happens to the Appraisal Forms? 247
    Follow Up the Appraisal 248
    Appraisal Formats 248
Don't Wait for the Annual Review 251
Positive Approach to Performance Appraisal 251
Notes 252
Bibliography 252

12—EMPLOYEE/EMPLOYER RIGHTS AND RESPONSIBILITIES 255
Employee/Employer Rights 255
Legal Rights 255
Right to a Safe Work Environment 256
Right to a Nondiscriminatory Workplace 256
Sex Discrimination 257
Sexual Orientation 258
Disabled Workers 259
Age Discrimination 261
National Origin Discrimination 261
Religious Discrimination 262
Right to a Harassment-Free Workplace 263
Last-Resort Termination Rights 264
Privacy Rights 264
Union Participation Rights 266
University-Granted Rights 267
    Right to an Appeal and Grievance Process 267
    Common Types of Grievances 269
    When a Grievance Is Filed Against You 269
    Right to Equitable Compensation 270
Employee Responsibilities 270
Ethics for Supervisors 271
    Library Ethics 272
    Managerial Ethics 273
Notes 274
Bibliography 275

13—PROGRESSIVE DISCIPLINE AND TERMINATION PROCEDURES . . . 277

Discipline and Discharge. 277
Termination of Employment 278
    Resignation 278
    Release 279
    Relieved. 279
    Layoff. 279
    Discharge 279
Reasons for Termination. 280
Reducing the Number of Problem Employees. 283
    Corrective Discipline 283
    Predischarge Rights of Public Employees 284
    Steps to Take Before Terminating an Employee . . . 285
How to Terminate an Employee 286
    The Impacts of Termination 287
    Mistakes Made in Terminations. 288
Constructive Discharge 289
Gross Misconduct. 289
Notes. 290
Bibliography 290

14—QUESTIONS ASKED BY NEW SUPERVISORS 293

How Is This Book Different?. 293
    Will I Have to Change to Become a Supervisor? . . . 294
    Why Do Beginning Supervisors Feel Underpaid?. . . 294
    How Much Should I Depend on Other
      Supervisors? 295
    Where Else Can I Turn for Help? 295
    How Important Is Education to Advancement? . . . 295
    How Do I Cope with Too Much Work? 296
    How Can I Get Everything Done?. 296
    What Should I Do When I Get Discouraged? 296
    How Can I Be Sure I Want to Be a Supervisor? . . . 297
    Where Will I Be in Five Years? 297
    How Do I Know When I Have Developed a
      Leadership Style?. 297
    In a Few Words, What Is the Best Advice for
      Supervisors? 298
Bibliography 298

Glossary of Financial Aid Terms 299
   Acronyms 299
   Definitions 301
Index 327

LIST OF FIGURES, JOB DESCRIPTIONS, TABLES, AND TESTS ✑

Figures

Student employment application 109
Federal on-budget funds for education, by agency:
Fiscal Year 1997 114
Job Instruction Training from the 1945 Bureau of
Training. 185

Student Job Descriptions

Copy Assistant I 65
Copy Assistant II 66
Copy Assistant III. 67
Office Assistant. 68
Fiscal Services Assistant. 69
Personnel Assistant 70
Mail Room Assistant 71
Circulation Desk Assistant I 72
Circulation Desk Assistant II. 73
Circulation Desk Assistant III 74
Page 75
Shelver I 76
Shelver II. 77
Shelving Student Supervisor. 78
Interlibrary Loan Assistant. 79
Reserve Desk Assistant 80
Government Documents Assistant I 81
Government Documents Assistant II 82
Government Documents Assistant III 83
Reference Assistant I 84
Reference Assistant II 85
Reference Assistant III. 86
Map Room Assistant 87
Media Center Assistant 88
Special Collections Assistant. 89

Manuscript Archives Assistant. 90
Photo Archives Assistant 91
Acquisitions Assistant I 92
Acquisitions Assistant II. 93
Acquisitions Assistant III 94
Cataloging and Classification Assistant I 95
Cataloging and Classification Assistant II. 96
Cataloging and Classification Assistant III 97
Preorder Searching Assistant 98
Gifts Assistant 99
Serials Assistant I 100
Serial Assistant II 101
Serials Assistant III. 102
Bindery Assistant 103
Exchange Program Assistant 104
Systems Assistant I 105
Systems Assistant II 106
Systems Assistant III 107

Tables

ARL Library Data Tables 1996–97 7
Eligibility Requirements for Federal Student
    Financial Aid 119
Pay Rate Structures for Student Employees 160
Number of Hours That Can Be Worked in 20 Pay
    Periods 162
Purpose of the Performance Appraisal Process. 235

Tests

Test of Leadership Potential 38
Supervisory Responsibility Survey 42

INTRODUCTION ✄

In his introduction to the 1991 publication of *Supervision of Student Employees in Academic Libraries*, the author stated that although there were a number of excellent library administration books in print, as well as entire libraries of business management and employee supervision books, none paid much attention to the employment of thousands of students by academic libraries. Nor did those books acknowledge that university students are an important employee group, that they are a critical part of the library's workforce, or that very few of those charged with supervision of these employees have adequate supervisory training or experience. There were virtually no books written specifically for the library student employee supervisor. Although there have been a few additions to the literature in this field, none is as complete as the 1991 publication. After reviewing the literature, it was determined that a revision and expansion of the handbook would be useful.

Two areas were identified as needing more attention: a system of job descriptions for students and funding for student employment. Libraries must pay close attention to the development of appropriate job descriptions for student employees. Frances C. Wilkinson, Director of Acquisitions and Serials at the University of New Mexico General Library, has been instrumental in developing this library's student job descriptions, which provide student employees with meaningful duties and responsibilities and are the basis for differentiated pay. Professor Wilkinson headed the Student Employment Advisory Committee, which provided the structure for student jobs at the University of New Mexico General Library. Although written for a research library, the student employee job descriptions could be used by libraries of all types. This revision also pays particular attention to the area of funding for student employment. Daniel C. Barkley, Director of Government Information at the University of New Mexico General Library, is especially well qualified to address the topic of student financial aid. Professor Barkley clearly describes the numerous financial aid programs available to students and how they may qualify and apply for assistance.

The student workforce and their supervisors have been taken for granted for a long time. They are, after all, only student workers and anyone can supervise them. Library administrators are beginning to realize how important this group has become to the library and that student employee salaries comprise a significant portion of the operating budget. Library personnel, for the most part, enjoy working in an academic environment with young people and with others who are interested in bringing information and people together. Many student employee supervisors began their library careers as student workers who, as they gained experience, were given more responsibility, including the supervision of fellow students. As staff members, they became supervisors of student employees, and then supervisors of other staff. How were these skills developed? Did the library staff you know come to the job with supervisory training and experience? Were they given on-the-job training? Were they given any training at all? How systematic is the training given to all supervisors, let alone supervisors of student employees? Most have become good supervisors through trial and error.

This book is designed to provide a foundation in the principles of supervision and to serve as a handbook for the day-to-day problems that arise in supervising student employees in academic libraries. This book emphasizes humane treatment of employees; it will confirm much of what you have already known and will, we hope, provide you with new information.

The first three chapters describe the role of student employees in the academic library, the role of the student employee supervisor, and basic principles of supervision. The next chapter describes how to organize for student employment; it includes student job descriptions and explains why they are needed. Because federal student financial aid is an important part of student employment, information is provided on various federal aid programs in chapter 5. Chapter 6 deals with the hiring of student employees. A thorough discussion of student employee compensation is found in chapter 7. Orientation and training of student employees are discussed in chapter 8; supervision techniques are described in chapter 9. Chapter 10 provides suggestions for resolving the most common problems encountered by supervisors. Performance appraisal is covered in chapter 11 and employee/employer rights are described in chapter 12. Chapter 13 deals with corrective discipline and termination procedures. The final chapter provides answers to questions commonly asked by new student employee supervisors. A glossary of financial aid terms is provided to assist the student employee supervisor in dealing with student financial aid.

If you supervise student employees or aspire to such a position in your library, this guide is written for you. Your comments and suggestions on the content would be much appreciated.

THE STUDENT EMPLOYEE— A PERSPECTIVE

> *Do not follow where the path may lead. Go instead where there is no path and leave a trail.*
>
> —George Bernard Shaw

TODAY'S ACADEMIC LIBRARIES

More changes have been made in academic libraries in the past 30 years than in all of previous history. Those changes have been brought about, in large part, by the baby boomers—the generation born after World War II, and by dramatic technological advances made in recent years. The administrators, faculty, and staff in today's academic libraries are of all ages and include many who were college students in the 1960s. This mix, together with the ever-changing group of student employees, makes the academic library a challenging, interesting, and exciting place to work. Most notable are changes brought on by the development of international bibliographic databases and the development of the Internet. We have seen a dramatic shifting of work assignments from professional to nonprofessional, clerical, and student staffing. Duties performed by librarians not that long ago have gradually been assigned to part-time student employees, making student employment supervision an even more important staff responsibility.

All positions have been impacted by automation. Librarians are required to focus their efforts upon improving access through database development/management and the interpretation of information for users. They must also devote time to library and university committee work and to professional activities. Library faculty have to meet requirements for tenure and promotion, including publication. Clerical, technical, and professional staff now perform high-level technical and public service duties that were once the librarian's responsibilities. As a result of the upward shifting of job responsibilities, student employees are being asked to assume more complex technical and service responsibilities. Student employees play an important role in the ability of today's academic library to respond to technological change. Job responsibilities of staff at all levels are affected by online systems and the increase of user demand. Today's technical services staff are required to perform complex acquisitions, cataloging, and processing as well as to master terminal/system operations. Improved access has resulted in increased demands for assistance in not only finding but also interpreting information. Reference and information desks must be staffed by knowledgeable personnel to assist library users in using the library's systems and resources effectively. Interlibrary loan staff must respond to greater numbers of requests and staff in the circulation department are often required to be skilled in the use of an automated circulation system.

Only with librarians, staff, and student employees working together can libraries respond effectively to the information explosion, the technological challenge, the research and information needs of faculty, staff, students, and members of the community.

Success hinges on the effective use of a large segment of the library's staff resources—student employees. Student employees are a very real part of any college or university library workforce. They represent approximately 24 percent of university libraries' staffing and 26 percent of all staff in college libraries. In academic libraries, the number of student employees often exceeds the number of regular staff. Because of their importance, academic libraries need to place a high priority on the effective management of student employment.

THE ROLE OF STUDENT EMPLOYEES

Visit any college or university library and you will find students working at circulation, information, reference, special collections, documents, or periodicals desks. You can observe students assisting patrons, shelving materials, or working as security staff. Stop by the director/dean's office and you will likely be greeted by a student employee. In the nonpublic areas, you will find student assistants engaged in a wide variety of technical and clerical tasks. If you happen by late in the evening or at night, you will be hard put to find a nonstudent staff member on duty, except perhaps in circulation or reference areas.

Do student assistants run the library? No, but the library would not run as efficiently without them; they are a critical part of the staffing of today's academic library. Do students do only the work that staff won't do? No, they perform technical and demanding work as well as provide the coverage needed for long hours of access to collections and services. Indeed, students perform all manner of job duties formerly reserved for "regular" staff employees.

Student workers primarily carry out circulation services; these include charging, discharging, and file maintenance. The most experienced students receive additional supervisory and training responsibilities. Student workers accomplish almost all reshelving and stacks maintenance; they also manage periodicals and newspaper collections and assist patrons in using them. Managing microform files and equipment along with assisting patrons in their use are typically student workers' duties.

In reference departments, student assistants usually handle all the filing and the more senior student workers provide ready reference either at information desks or with librarians and staff at the reference desk. In branch libraries and government publications units, student employees are involved in all public and technical service activities; often student workers are given responsibility for overseeing operations during night and weekend hours. Academic libraries without the benefit of campus security patrols in their buildings often rely on student workers to make regular rounds in the stacks and study areas. These student assistants, identified as library security staff, enforce policies relating to food/drink and noise; Campus or local police are usually summoned to deal with illegal activities.

Technical service operations are also dependent upon student employees for many tasks. Acquisitions departments depend on students with language skills for pre-order searching of monographs and serials. Students quickly learn automated acquisitions systems and perform many of the same functions as staff. Routine receiving activities and serials check-in are usually assigned to student workers. Many bindery and preparation operations which are handled by student workers. Cataloging departments use student assistants for many of the more routine cataloging activities such as catalog maintenance for automated and manual files. Student assistants with language abilities can be indispensable to cataloging departments.

Clerical tasks in all departments have become the responsibility of student employees in most libraries. The dean/director's office staff is supplemented with student hours as are library personnel, facilities, and fiscal services offices. There are very few clerical or manual tasks that cannot be assigned to student assistants. Former student employees remember, with varying degrees of fondness, their experiences in dismantling and building shelves, shelfreading, shifting books, and moving entire library collections.

Student employees bring to their library jobs a wide range of talents and skills, which, if properly identified and matched with jobs, can provide meaningful employment for the students, valuable contributions to the operation of the library, and lifelong friendships among students and staff. Reliance on students as employees in American academic libraries can be traced back to the early 1800s.

HISTORY OF STUDENT EMPLOYMENT

In a report of the Librarian's Conference in 1853, G. B. Utley noted, regarding staffing, that some university librarians had student assistants only and others didn't have any help at all.[1] During the late 1800s, universities experienced rapid growth in science and technology programs, resulting in the need for research by faculty and students; libraries expanded their collections, services, and staff to meet the demand. Brown University Librarian Harry Lyman Koopman reported that in 1893 the staff consisted of himself, an assistant librarian, and one student helper. By 1930, the staff had grown to 25 and the student assistants to 17.[2]

Student Employment in the 1930s

Mary Elizabeth Downey in a paper delivered at ALA (American Library Association) Midwinter in 1932 commented on the conflicting attitudes of librarians on student employees:

> So far as the attitude of college librarians is concerned, our problem naturally resolves itself into two sides: on the one hand are those who do not see how the library can be run without the aid of student assistants, and who feel that a greater amount of work can be done satisfactorily with them. This type of librarian gets a real kick out of seeing a boy come to college not knowing how to use his

hands and legs, to say nothing of his head, to see him develop into a well-rounded adult, and from the feeling that his work in the library is somewhat responsible for the transformation. On the other hand are college librarians who do not know how to organize and manage such help, who do not have teaching ability, and so strenuously object to being bothered with student assistants. They feel that teaching and supervising the work of students has no part in their work as librarian and that none of it should be delegated to those not having come through a library school.

Ms. Downey, in addition to providing a long list of duties that may be performed by students, also reported that suitable work for students may include "emptying waste baskets; sweeping, dusting, and mopping floors; washing woodwork, shelves and windows; and even painting woodwork and floors in unsightly quarters to make them more sanitary and attractive. Sometimes men students, who cannot do clerical things well, are suited to this very necessary work." For their work, Ms. Downey suggests a rate of 25 to 30 cents an hour for freshmen, 30 to 35 cents for sophomores, 35 to 40 cents for juniors, and 40 to 45 cents for seniors.[3]

Student Employees as Potential Librarians

In addition to being the source of cheap labor and expediters of library processes and procedures, student employees were sometimes viewed as potential librarians. In 1956, Wilson and Tauber noted in *The University Library*, "Through his activities in the library the student assistant sometimes discovers his interest in librarianship as a profession, and his training can be directed by the librarian to that end."[4] The same is true today. More than 30 percent of professional librarians were at one time student employees in libraries. Many academic libraries provide encouragement and guidance to promising student employees who are interested in pursuing librarianship as a career. Special programs are in place in some academic libraries and library schools to encourage minority students to become librarians.

Student Employment in Recent Years

In recognition of student capabilities, libraries in recent years have treated student employees as coworkers, almost like colleagues. Keith M. Cottam, in a 1970 article based on his work at Brigham Young University, discusses the value of student employees:

> It is doubtful that any library, as a major resource for teaching and learning, can reach a maximum level of service without full utilization of the capabilities, opinions, talents, and background of capable, part-time student employees as well as of its full-time staff. Librarians are in the business of education and in developing people for the future of the profession . . . [and] should apply the widest possible latitude to their utilization of student assistants if they aspire successfully to accomplish their goals.[5]

The debate continues today about the cost effectiveness and efficiency of student employees in academic libraries and what kinds of responsibilities should be assigned to them. The title of Andrew Melnyk's 1976 article, "Student Aides in Our Library (Blessings and Headaches)," reflects that attitude. Emilie C. White comments on students contributions to the library:

> At the very least, students constitute a labor reserve for the monotonous and repetitious tasks that are necessary for successful library operation. Their willingness to perform largely time-consuming, routine chores in the midst of their own intellectual accomplishments has contributed significantly to the professional posture of academic librarianship.[6]

Student employees today are not required to mop floors or paint woodwork in the library for thirty cents an hour. Today's academic libraries employ many of their institutions' students to augment their permanent staff positions in order to accomplish their missions.

SIZE OF THE STUDENT WORKFORCE

Students are employed on all of America's college and university campuses by various departments and for all types of jobs. The employers of the largest number of students on most campuses are food services and libraries.

Student workers comprise a significant portion of academic libraries' staffing. An examination of Association of Research Libraries (ARL) statistics for 1996–97[7]shows that in the 110 university member libraries there are 8,470 FTE student employees (see table 1.1). Generally, smaller college and university libraries have a larger ratio of students to staff.

In ARL university libraries, librarians comprise 27 percent of all staff. Professional, technical, and clerical staff make up 49 percent and students account for 24 percent. The median number of students employed in ARL university libraries is 69; with an average of 17 hours per week, or 0.425 FTE for each student, an estimated 19,929 students work in ARL university libraries.

Table 1.1. ARL Library Data Tables 1996–97

	Summary Data: Personnel						
	Professional Staff (FTE)	Professional % of Total FTE Staff	Support Staff (FTE)	Support Staff % of Total FTE Staff	Student Assistants (FTE)	Students % of Total FTE Staff	Total Staff (FTE)
University Libraries (110)							
Median	73	26.8%	130	47.8%	69	25.4	272
High	415	35.1	593	50.2%	208	17.6	1,182
Low	23	20.7%	54	48.6%	1	0.9%	111
Totals	9,294	27.1%	16.885	49.2%	8,141	23.7%	34,320
Non- University Libraries (11)							
Median	113	46.1%	106	43.3%	9	3.7%	245
Totals	2,708	36.3%	4,423	59.3%	329	4.4%	7,460
Grand Totals	12,002	28.7%	21,308	51.0%	8,470	20.3%	41,780

STUDENT WORKERS AND REGULAR STAFF

The contribution of student assistants to the successful operation of college and university libraries is extremely important. Student employees have much in common with regular staff. Working closely with regular full-time and part-time staff, students perform many of the same tasks and often work without staff supervision at nights and on weekends. Students are expected to abide by the policies of the library and to follow its procedures. Student assistants often participate in departmental staff meetings and have the opportunity to make suggestions for improvements.

Student workers differ from regular staff in their work schedules, job duties, benefits, funding sources, and their planned impermanence. Some universities prohibit student employees from working more than 20 hours per week, partly because of the desire to provide employment for more students and partly because it is felt that full-time students should devote their attention to academic pursuits. Students' work schedules must also be arranged around class schedules, which change each semester. Students applying for work are often selected because they can work the desired hours in a department's schedule.

Job duties for students are dependent both on the department's needs and on available staff, but they are typically of the lowest level in the department. Student workers do not earn vacation or sick leave and are not eligible for the benefits provided to staff. The funding sources for student assistants are normally college work-study or a separate library student employment budget. It is known beforehand, when students are hired, that they are temporary employees. Freshmen students may stay with the library throughout their undergraduate careers; more often than not, they do not stay that long.

Not all regular staff are model employees and the same is true of student employees. Nearly all the problems associated with regular staff are also found in the student employee workforce. Just as with regular staff, not all student assistants are productive employees; they often lack the commitment expected of other staff or are simply unable to work and keep up their grades. Student employees are not immune to any of the potential problems in the workplace. We will discuss how to deal with these problems in a later chapter.

WORK-STUDY VERSUS NON-WORK-STUDY STUDENT EMPLOYEES

We should also dispel, once and for all, the myth that non-work-study students are better employees than work-study students and therefore deserve better pay. It is true that fewer upperclassmen qualify for work-study awards because of grants, loans, or scholarships, which reduce their financial needs. Often students begin as work-study qualified students, become invaluable to the department, and then have their work-study awards reduced or eliminated. Those students are either lost to the library or must be paid from other funds.

Many non-work-study students are more experienced than beginning work-study students and are viewed as better employees. In some libraries, non-work-study students are permitted to work more hours than work-study students, who must stay within their award amounts. Some supervisors prefer not to be bothered with tracking work-study students' awards and definitely do not want to lose needed help near the end of the year because awards have been exhausted. The most significant difference, however, between work-study and non-work-study student employees is the account from which they are paid.

A salary scale that pays work-study and non-work-study at different hourly rates should be avoided if at all possible. We will discuss pay rates in the chapter on organizing for student employment.

WHY DO STUDENTS WORK?

Most people work first for the money with which to pay for the necessities of life and for the pleasure money can buy, and second for the satisfaction work can provide—being with other people or gaining satisfaction from accomplishment. A college student's first priority is to gain an education and a degree that will lead to a career. Student workers generally use the money they earn to help pay for food, shelter, and college expenses as well as to support families. Until students' paychecks become sufficient to cover basic living expenses, job satisfaction and collegiality in the work place will not be the primary reason students work. That is not to say that supervisors should not strive to provide for job satisfaction, only that they should recognize that job satisfaction is not the reason students seek employment in the library.

How many people are truly happy with their jobs? A study published in 1974 showed that nearly 90 percent of all employees were satisfied, if not happy with their work.[8] Studies show that blue-collar workers are more dissatisfied with their work than white-collar workers and young people are more dissatisfied than older workers. Job satisfaction tends to increase with age.

Different people gain satisfaction from different things. Factory workers place the most importance on wages. Some workers feel that comfortable working conditions, good hours, or good transportation are most important. Generally, the more education a person has, the greater his or her need for challenging and interesting work. Satisfaction in the workplace is also a function of how many hours a person works. A student working half-time or less is most concerned with money but wants to be challenged by the work. Concerns about working conditions are more important to full-time staff members than to student employees who normally work half-time or less.

Work is a unique activity in that it requires conformity through rules and procedures; they specify that one must report to a supervisor and that one's performance becomes a matter of written record. Because students may be working in this type of formal situation for the first time, adjustments must be made; recognition by supervisors of these concepts will help new student employees. In addition, incoming freshmen will most likely be experiencing an entirely new sensation of freedom and lack of structure in their lives. When students arrive on campus, no one tells them when to go to class, when to go to work, or when to study. The real challenge for an 18-year-old freshman is not the course work. The challenge is to manage all of the hours of the day and week. They must attend classes, study, do homework, maintain a work schedule, and remember to eat and sleep, all the while resisting a myriad of temptations to do everything else. Library employment can provide an anchor for students, a place where people care about them, and a constant amid the whirlwind of other activities. Recognition of the place of work in their students' lives is part of the information supervisors must possess to supervise student employees effectively.

Are libraries just providing a way for students to obtain spending money? No, libraries require that essential work be accomplished by students and in the process libraries provide positive work experiences for many students for whom this is their first job. No, there is no time to study on the job; but the supervisor is humane and remembers what it was like to be a college student. Library staff must require that student assistants perform essential work but at the same time realize why students seek employment on campus in the first place. Allowances must be made to permit students to accomplish their first objective—the degree. A discussion of the seemingly perpetual problem of student employee requests for time off or rescheduled work time is included in the chapter on student employee problem resolution.

Academic libraries have a right to expect that student employees will perform their assigned duties, practice good work habits, and contribute to the library's mission. Student employees are expected to maintain a schedule, come to work on time, and adhere to the library's policy on reporting absences. Expectation is a two-way street. Employees have a right to expect fair treatment in return for their contributions to the library. The rights of the employee and the employer are detailed in chapter 11.

The student employees' primary contact with the library organization is the student employees' supervisor. Much of what student employees learn and think about the library will be a direct result of their relationships with the supervisor.

SUPERVISING STUDENT EMPLOYEES

In academic library organizations it is most efficient to assign student employee supervision responsibilities to a staff member in the department. The department head often delegates student employee supervision to a position that does not have responsibility for "regular" staff supervision. In many cases, there are two or more student employee supervisors in a single department. For example, in acquisitions, there may be separate units for searching, receiving, gifts, and serials. Each of these units has a group of student assistants reporting to a supervisor.

Job descriptions for many staff positions include the supervision of student assistants. Attrition in these staff positions, especially at the lower levels, sets the stage for a relatively high number of new supervisors each year, many without prior supervisory experience. Assuming there are 10 student assistants reporting to each supervisor, ARL libraries have approximately 1,915 staff members with student supervisory responsibilities.[9] Generally, student supervisors work with fewer than 10 students each.

A supervisor plays many roles. Some are well defined, others are not. Supervision is without doubt a people-oriented activity. One study found that supervisors spend two-thirds of their time relating to other people. One of the roles supervisors play is that of a connecting bridge between management and operations. The supervisor has the responsibility of communicating and interpreting library policy and procedures to student employees, making recommendations, and communicating employee concerns to management. Supervisors serve as role models to workers in interpreting and carrying out activities that help the library achieve its goals. A study performed in industry showed that supervisors spend much more time with those they supervise—55 percent—than with those holding the same or higher-level positions in the organization.

In addition to the bridging role of supervisors, they perform all of the managerial functions: planning, organizing, staffing, leading and motivating, and controlling. Planning includes determining the goals and objectives of the unit and strategies for achieving them. It includes such activities as examining alternative uses of staff, thinking, gathering data, and evaluating procedures. Organizing involves creating a structure for accomplishing unit objectives. The supervisor identifies the tasks to be performed, groups those tasks into jobs, and establishes relationships between people and jobs. Staffing is the process of selecting, training, evaluating, and rewarding employees. By leading and motivating, the supervisor directs the work of student employees so that their tasks are performed correctly and efficiently.

The final managerial function of supervisors is controlling; this is the process by which actual performance is compared to planned performance. Controlling involves monitoring the work being accomplished and taking corrective action if necessary.

Managerial functions are not discrete or independent activities. The objectives set in planning are used in controlling. Organizing, staffing, leading, and motivating are continuous activities. Although most supervisors of student workers don't think about the names of these functions, all supervisors perform the whole range of managerial functions. Supervisors of student employees plan and organize the work to be done by students; not only do they hire, train, evaluate, and reward workers, they monitor the results as well. Because supervisors of student employees have their own job responsibilities in addition to supervision, they lead and motivate by example.

Why Is Good Supervision Important?

It is assumed, because most library staff members were at one time student employees or at least college students, that student employee supervision is not difficult. It is also assumed that there could be no problems, because, after all, they are only students. You hire them, you train them, and if they don't like it, they quit. Why worry?

They are students who will inevitably quit anyway because college isn't supposed to be forever.

This assumption is simply not valid today. Because libraries are so dependent on the work done by student employees, it is critical that supervision be taken seriously. Through careful selection, thorough training, and skillful supervision, libraries can maximize their investment in students while giving them meaningful work experiences. The need for proper training and support by student employee supervisors also makes good sense because pay rates for students are such that they can be expected to produce.

Are student employees worth the hassle? Absolutely. Are good supervisory techniques and skills needed to make the experience worthwhile? You bet! Should students expect to develop and practice good work habits through library employment? Yes. Should libraries expect their supervisors of student employees to practice sound supervision and management principles while giving students valuable work experiences? Yes, absolutely.

The Rewards of Student Employee Supervision

The effort exerted in student employee supervision is not without its rewards. Library staff members, whether they supervise or not, value their associations with students over the years. Supervisors watch students mature and become self-confident; they take pride in student accomplishments long after students depart from the library. The student supervisory experience translates well to staff supervision, permitting staff members to advance to higher level positions. How many librarians and professional, technical, and clerical staff members do you know who were library student employees? How many of those people will tell you that the primary reason they are in their present positions is because of positive student work experiences? The student employee position in a library is often the experience which starts people on the track to library careers. Good supervision gives students the correct message—library careers are viable options.

Student employee supervision is a skill that can be acquired, providing the supervisor wants to learn, gets along with people, and knows student employees' jobs. It is an important responsibility and it can be rewarding. Although a poor supervisor will most certainly be remembered, a good one will be thought of fondly for providing a meaningful work experience. If successful supervision is your goal, the information in this handbook can be adapted to your own situation.

LOOKING AHEAD

Either you have already become a student employee supervisor or you have decided that you would like to be one. Although it is true that not everyone has the aptitude for supervision and that skills come more naturally to some people than to others, remember that many of the skills can be learned. Supervision is a difficult yet rewarding job that can be performed well by those who are willing to work at it. If you are willing, this book is designed for you. In the next 12 chapters, we will review the basic principles of supervision and relate them to student employees in libraries. Suggestions and advice are offered throughout to help you improve your knowledge and skills in supervision and to help you apply what you know to your student supervisory responsibilities.

NOTES

1. Elizabeth W. Stone, *American Library Development, 1600–1899* (New York: H. W. Wilson Company, 1977), 115–16.

2. Harry Lyman Koopman, "The Student Assistant and Library Training," *Libraries* 35 (March 1930): 87.

3. Mary Elizabeth Downey, "Work of Student Assistants in College Libraries," *Library Journal* 57 (May 1, 1932): 417–20.

4. Louis Round Wilson, and Maurice F. Tauber, *The University Library*, 2d ed. (New York: Columbia University Press, 1956), 57.

5. Keith M. Cottam, "Student Employees in Academic Libraries," *College and Research Libraries* 31, no. 4 (July 1970): 248.

6. Emilie C. White, "Student Assistants in Academic Libraries: From Reluctance to Reliance," *The Journal of Academic Librarianship* 11, no. 2 (May 1985): 97.

7. Association of Research Libraries, *ARL Statistics 1996–97* (Washington, D.C., Association of Research Libraries, 1998), 38–45.

8. Department of Labor, Manpower Administration, *Job Satisfaction: Is There a Trend?* Research Monograph no. 30 (Washington, D.C., 1974), 4.

9. Association of Research Libraries, 38–45.

BIBLIOGRAPHY

Association of Research Libraries. *Student Assistants in ARL Libraries*, SPEC Kit 91. Washington, D.C.: Association of Research Libraries, 1983.

Baird, Brian J. "Motivating Student Employees: Examples from Collections Conservation." *Library Resources & Technical Services* (October 1995): 410–16.

Boyer, Ernest L. *College: The Undergraduate Experience in America.* New York: Harper & Row, 1988.

Brown, Helen M. "Conditions Contributing to the Efficient Service of Student Assistants in a Selected Group of College Libraries." *College and Research Libraries* 5 (December 1943): 44–52.

Camp, Mildred. "Student Assistants and the College Library." *Library Journal* 59 (December 1, 1934): 923–25.

Cottam, Keith M. "Student Employees in Academic Libraries." *College and Research Libraries* 31 (July 1970): 246–48.

Crawford, Gregory Alan. "Training Student Employees by Videotape." *College & Research Libraries News* (March 1988): 149–50.

Downey, Mary Elizabeth. "Work of Student Assistants in College Libraries." *Library Journal* 57 (May 1, 1932): 417–20.

Downs, Robert B. "The Role of the Academic Librarian: 1876–1976." *College and Research Libraries* 37 (November 1976): 491–502.

Evans, Charles W. "The Evolution of Paraprofessional Library Employees." *Advances in Librarianship* 9 (1979): 64–102.

Floyd, Barbara L., and Richard W. Oram. "Learning by Doing: Undergraduates as Employees in Archives." *The American Archivist* (summer 1992): 440–52.

Fuller, F. Jay. "Evaluating Student Assistants as Library Employees." *College & Research Libraries News* (January 1990): 11–13.

Gregory, David James. "The Evolving Role of Student Employees in Academic Libraries." *Journal of Library Administration* (winter 1995): 3–27.

Heron, Alexander R. *Why Men Work.* Stanford, CA: Stanford University Press, 1948.

Holley, Edward G. *The Land-Grant Movement and the Development of Academic Libraries.* College Station, TX: Texas A & M University Libraries, 1977.

Kathman, Michael D., and Jane McGurn Kathman. "Integrating Student Employees into the Management Structure of Academic Libraries." *Catholic Library World* (March 1985): 328–30.

———. *Managing Student Employees in College Libraries.* Chicago: Association of College and Research Libraries, 1994.

Kaufman, Diane B., and Jeanne M. Drewes. *Using Student Employees to Focus Preservation Awareness Campaigns: Promoting Preservation Awareness in Libraries.* Westport, CT: Greenwood Press, 1997.

Kendrick, Curtis L. "Cavalry to the Rescue: The Use of Temporary Employees in Place of Student Assistants." *College & Research Libraries News* (April 1989): 273–74.

Koopman, Harry Lyman. "The Student Assistant and Library Training." *Libraries* 35 (March 1930): 87–89.

Lyle, Guy R. *The Administration of the College Library.* 4th ed. New York: H. W. Wilson, 1974.

McHale, Cecil J. "An Experiment in Hiring Student Part-Time Assistants." *Libraries* 36 (October 1931): 379–82.

Melnyk, Andrew. "Student Aides in Our Library (Blessings and Headaches)." *Illinois Libraries* 58 (February 1976): 141–44.

Metz, T. John. *Student Employees Enhance Internet Expertise for a Liberal Arts College Library: The Internet Initiative.* Chicago: American Library Association, 1995.

Riley, Cheryl, and Barbara Wales. "Introducing the Academic Library to Student Employees: A Group Approach." *Technical Services Quarterly* (winter 1997): 47–59.

Rosen, C. Martin, et al. "Student Employees and the Academic Library's Multicultural Mission." *The Reference Librarian* (1994): 45–55.

Shores, Louis. "Staff Spirit Among Student Assistants." *Libraries* 34 (July 1929): 346–48.

———. *Origins of the American College Library, 1638–1800.* New York: Barnes & Noble, 1935.

Smith, Jessie J. "Training of Student Assistants in Small College Libraries." *Library Journal* 34 (April 1, 1930): 306–9.

Stone, Elizabeth W. *American Library Development, 1600–1899.* New York: H. W. Wilson, 1977.

U.S. Department of Labor. Manpower Administration. *Job Satisfaction: Is There a Trend?* Research Monograph no. 30. Washington, D.C., 1974, 4.

White, Emilie C. "Student Assistants in Academic Libraries: From Reluctance to Reliance." *Journal of Academic Librarianship* 11, no. 2 (May 1985): 93–97.

Wilson, Louis Round, and Maurice F. Tauber. *The University Library.* 2d ed. New York: Columbia University Press, 1956.

Worthy, John. "A Graduate Assistant at the University of Florida." *Library Association Record* 67 (November 1965): 395–96.

Wright, Alice E. *Library Clerical Workers and Pages Including Student Assistants.* Hamden, CT: Linnet Books, 1973.

Chapter Two

THE STUDENT EMPLOYEE SUPERVISOR

> *Even if you're on the right track, you'll get run over if you just sit there.*
>
> —Will Rogers

THE ROLE OF STUDENT EMPLOYEE SUPERVISOR

The student employee supervisor in an academic library occupies a unique and important position. The supervisor of student employees' job description likely includes the words, "supervises student employees." In fact, the supervisor of student employees has responsibility for hiring, training, scheduling, assigning duties, disciplining, evaluating, counseling, and above all, assuring that student workers contribute to the accomplishment of the unit or department's objectives and the objectives of the library.

Because the supervisors of student workers have much in common with supervisors in industry, the same basic principles of industrial supervision may be applied in the academic library. Although the supervision of student employees shares much in common with industrial supervision, it also has important differences. First, the types of employees supervised are quite different from those in industry. Nearly all the student employees are postsecondary students who typically work half-time or less; they seldom work all year, they are not considered regular or permanent employees, and they usually aspire to a career that is different from their work in the library. Recognizing that there are differences between student employees and those employees in business and industry, let us examine the student employee supervisor's role.

DEFINITION OF SUPERVISOR

By definition, "anyone at the first level of management who has the responsibility for getting the 'hands-on-the-work' employees to carry out the plans and policies of higher level management is a supervisor."[1] The Taft-Hartley Act of 1947 defines a supervisor as

> . . . any individual having authority, in the interest of the employer, to hire, transfer, suspend, lay off, recall, promote, discharge, assign, reward, or discipline other employees, or responsibility to direct them, or to adjust their grievances, or effectively to recommend such action, if in connection with the foregoing the exercise of such authority is not of a merely routine or clerical nature, but requires the use of independent judgment.[2]

The word *supervisor* derives from a Latin term that means "look over." Early on, the supervisor was the person in charge of a group of workers and was a foreman or "fore man," at the lead of a group, setting the pace for the rest. Today's supervisor is a leader, one who watches over the work, and a person with technical/professional skills.

Getting Things Done Through Others

The most common definition of management is "getting things done through other people." Unfortunately, the emphasis is placed on "through other people." The primary task of any employee is "getting things done." As a staff member, a supervisor knows that getting things done is the most important part of the job. Because there is clearly more work than one person can accomplish, it is necessary to employ additional workers. Therefore, as a student employee supervisor, you must not only accomplish your own work but you must get things done through student employees.

Doing a job and getting someone else to do it are entirely different propositions. Simply telling someone to do something properly very seldom works; the employee must be *motivated* to do the job properly as well as have prerequisite knowledge and skills. If the work is not done properly, the supervisor must teach and apply techniques that will show student workers how to apply themselves.

Every student employee has different needs, skills, attitudes, and motivations. The student employee supervisor needs to deal with each employee differently while dealing with all employees fairly. There is no universal technique that will work with every student employee. What works today with one student may have no effect tomorrow and what works on one student worker may have a negative effect on another. The purpose of this handbook is to provide a foundation of supervisory principles and suggestions on how to get student workers to help you accomplish work.

WHO ARE THE STUDENT EMPLOYEE SUPERVISORS?

In most organizations, supervisors rise from the ranks and are usually employees with seniority who have worked at different jobs within the organization. These supervisors normally have more education than those they supervise.

The student employee supervisor either advances within the library to a position with student employee supervisory responsibilities or, when hired, takes a position that includes student supervision. It is not true in libraries that the most experienced employees become student employee supervisors. The most experienced staff become supervisors of other regular staff, not student employees. Student supervision is a valuable training ground for future staff supervisors.

As a rule, most student employee supervisors are not senior members of a unit or department. Typically, student employee supervisors report to senior staff in the department or to the unit or department head, usually a librarian. In libraries with clerical, technical, and professional staff classifications, student employee supervisors will be found in all classifications, with the majority at the technical level. Some student supervision is provided by librarians and occasionally by senior student employees.

Student employee supervisors may be chosen on the basis of seniority, proficiency, favoritism, demonstrated leadership, experience, or educational background. It is not unusual, and is often desirable, to select someone on the staff for a supervisory position. The successful transition to a student employee supervisory position demands a great deal of effort from the employee and requires psychological, social, and educational support from management.

Persons who will become good supervisors of student employees can be identified quite easily from among existing staff; they must demonstrate good job skills, communicate well, get along with coworkers and management, and show a positive attitude. All the attributes of a good staff member are needed to become a good supervisor. Above all, prospective supervisors must like their work, their students, and themselves.

The Best Worker May Not Be the Best Supervisor

The best worker, however, is not necessarily the best student employee supervisor. The skills required of an effective student employee supervisor are different from those required of a skilled worker. Selecting the best worker to be a student employee supervisor is a common—and dangerous—practice. Because of the money, prestige, or status, good workers often accept supervisory positions without realizing that the skills required of a good worker are not the same as those required of a good supervisor.

Because they do not possess or develop the necessary supervisory skills, they perform poorly. When student supervisors don't enjoy the work, some quit and others may receive poor evaluations, possibly leading to termination; others may stay in student employee supervisory positions they dislike because they do not want to lose face.

People should go into supervisory positions because they want challenge and satisfaction. If these are not your reasons for seeking student employee supervisory responsibility, no amount of pay, prestige, or status will compensate for the stress and other problems associated with work you dislike.

In selecting an applicant for a student employee supervisory position, you must look for someone who communicates well, who likes people, who demonstrates good job skills, and who shows energy and enthusiasm.

Personal Qualities of Good Student Employee Supervisors

What are the personal qualities of good student employee supervisors?

1. *Energy and good health.* Supervision is a demanding activity and requires that individuals not only be able to handle a variety of activities but be physically and emotionally up to the task.

2. *Leadership potential.* Student employee supervisory responsibilities require the ability to get people to work for and with you to accomplish the objectives of your unit.

3. *Ability to get along with people.* One of the most important qualities management looks for in a student employee supervisor is the ability to get along with others. Getting others to carry out their responsibilities depends greatly on their feelings toward their supervisor.

4. *Job know-how and technical competence.* The supervisor must know the job in order to be effective in training and problem solving. Student employee supervisors usually have their own job duties and responsibilities in addition to supervision and must be proficient in those duties.

5. *Initiative.* The student employee supervisor should recognize when to make adjustments to the work flow or improvements to procedures. Initiative is required for awareness of current and potential problems.

6. *Dedication and dependability.* Workers who sense that their supervisor is not dedicated to the job/employer will display the same attitude. The example set by the supervisor will be followed by the employees. For example, a supervisor who is regularly absent will find employees will also be absent often.

7. *Positive attitude toward management.* Workers will mirror the feelings of the student employee supervisor.

These characteristics are desirable in any employee but are most important in student employee supervisors. If your supervisors don't exhibit all of these positive attributes, training and staff development can be provided to enhance them.

Types of Persons Who Should Not Be Supervisors

There are definitely types of persons to avoid when filling student employee supervisor positions. If selecting a person from your staff, avoid the negative employee, the rigid employee, the unproductive employee, and the disgruntled employee. The attitude of a negative employee will be contagious among student employees. The rigid employee will be unable to deal with student employees effectively. The unproductive employee will find it difficult to motivate others to work hard. The employee who is unhappy with the work, the supervisor, the organization, or life in general, will not be effective in dealing with student employees who may mirror those feelings.

Student Employee Supervisor Attitudes

Attitude is important to good supervision. Student employee supervisors have the proper attitude if they agree with the following statements:[3]

1. Supervisors must manage with a high degree of integrity and lead by example.

2. Supervisors must keep their word to employees.

3. Supervisors must earn the respect, trust, and confidence of employees.

4. Supervisors must strive to help employees develop to their full potential.

5. Supervisors must give credit to employees who do a good job.

6. Supervisors must accept higher level management decisions and directives and support them to employees.

7. Supervisors must not discuss personal feelings about management with employees but should discuss disagreements privately with management.

8. Supervisors must be responsible for the performance of their employees.

9. Supervisors must be objective in judging the actions of employees.

10. Supervisors must decide matters involving employees on the bases of facts and circumstances, not on personal sympathies.

11. Supervisors must accept the responsibility for rehabilitating rather than punishing employees whenever possible.

12. Supervisors must be prepared to support employees in cases where employees are in the right.

13. Supervisors should attempt to allow employees to retain as much control over their own work as possible.

14. Supervisors must work to maintain a climate in the workplace that allows employees to express their feelings and concerns openly and without fear of reprisal.

MOVING FROM A STAFF TO A SUPERVISORY POSITION

The transition from worker to supervisor is difficult for any staff member. The new student employee supervisor must realize that "doing" and "supervising" require entirely different skills. The supervisor has, in effect, a contractual arrangement with student workers. You, as the student employee supervisor, have a right to expect certain things from them and they have the right to expect certain things in return. You represent management and represent your student employees to management. It is a delicate balance that must be achieved if supervision is to be successful. Without question, supervision is one of the most difficult responsibilities any employee can assume.

Because most new supervisors of student employees are selected from among present staff members in the department, it is important to remember that the move represents a significant change for everyone involved. Here are five major differences between being a subordinate and being a supervisor:

1. *Managing others' time.* Supervisors must set time schedules for others to meet, as well as manage their own time.

2. *Satisfaction becomes more abstract.* A supervisor's satisfaction is often indirect. It comes from taking pride in helping others succeed rather than from completing the job alone.

3. *Shift in job evaluation.* Performance is judged not just by one's boss but by one's subordinates as well—top down and bottom up.

4. *Long-term problems.* A supervisor must deal with problems that may persist for weeks, months, or even years.

5. *Key resources are people.* Because a supervisor must get things done through others, people are a very important resource. Learning the capabilities of each person helps a supervisor make good use of this resource.

The step from employee to supervisor is a large and important one for both the individual and the organization; much time and thought goes into selecting the right person for the job. Because the same careful attention is seldom given to helping this person develop into a productive member of management, new supervisors are often left to "sink or swim." Many changes accompany a promotion from subordinate to supervisor.

1. *Perspective.* Most employees are concerned primarily with doing a good job and planning how to get ahead. Supervisors, however, must keep the big picture in mind and consider the impact of decisions on the department and the library.

2. *Goals.* A supervisor's primary concern is to meet the organization's goals. By contrast, the employee's focus is on meeting personal goals (such as becoming more skilled at the job).

3. *Responsibilities.* A supervisor must supervise and speak for a group of people in addition to completing technical and administrative tasks. A supervisor must also accept responsibility for decisions instead of criticizing others.

4. *Satisfaction.* Because a supervisor does less of the actual work, satisfaction comes from watching others succeed rather than from the work itself.

5. *Job skills.* Although becoming technically competent is important, supervisors must also become proficient at communicating, delegating, planning, managing time, directing, motivating, and training others. Many of these are new skills, which must be developed.

6. *Relationships.* If one is promoted to a supervisory position, new relationships with former peers, other supervisors, and the new boss must be developed. People quickly change how they behave toward the new supervisor, whether or not the supervisor changes his or her behavior toward them.

Seven Transition Stages

The new supervisor does not make an overnight transformation from thinking and behaving like a subordinate to thinking and behaving like a boss. Instead, he or she passes through several predictable stages. While people seldom move neatly from one stage to the next, they generally experience all seven stages:

1. *First stage: Immobilization.* The new supervisor feels overwhelmed by the changes. This may be typified by: "This job is a lot bigger than I thought. Everyone is making demands. How can I possibly do everything?"

2. *Second stage: Denial of change.* This phase allows the individual involved time to regroup and to fully comprehend the change. "This job is not so different from your other job. Let's see, first I'll take care of this and then I'll begin to work on that."

3. *Third stage: Depression.* Awareness sets in regarding the magnitude of the changes that must be made in one's habits, customs, relationships, etc. "Why did I ever leave my other job? I wish I could afford to quit. I hate my job!"

4. *Fourth stage: Acceptance of reality.* Feelings of optimism return and the person is ready to let go of the past. "Maybe this isn't so bad. Forget about that old job. I'm doing fine."

5. *Fifth stage: Testing.* This is a time of trying out new behaviors and ways of coping with the new situation. "If I meet with staff every Thursday and try this schedule, I think I can manage."

6. *Sixth stage: Search for meanings.* Concern shifts to trying to understand both how and why things are different now. "Now I feel comfortable in this job. It is different but not really that bad."

7. *Seventh stage: Internalization.* In this final stage, the new supervisor incorporates the new meanings into behavior. "I like my job and I'm good at what I do."

PROBLEMS FACED BY NEW STUDENT EMPLOYEE SUPERVISORS

One of the biggest problems facing new student employee supervisors is their lack of preparation for the job. An employee is often selected for promotion to a management position because of performance as a specialist. Those skills and abilities are often quite different from those needed by a supervisor. As a result, the new supervisor must develop new skills.

Organizations normally expect new supervisors to step into the job and function right away. This expectation exists even though statistics show that most organizations offer little help or support to them. Often, formal supervisory training is not provided to the new supervisor until after six to twelve months on the job. The "sink or swim" philosophy is prevalent.

Finally, the new student employee supervisor often lacks an immediate peer group. Former peers no longer regard the new supervisor as one of them. Other supervisors are hesitant to consider this person a part of their group until the new supervisor has demonstrated the ability to think and act like management. This leaves the new supervisor belonging to neither group at a time when support from others is badly needed.

New supervisors of student employees must be willing to learn, change, adapt, and ask for help; they must have realistic expectations about what supervision is like. These newcomers can expect expertise from a previous job to be helpful in some, but not all, situations. They can expect to make mistakes because they are an unavoidable part of learning a new job. It takes a lot of hard work to gain the loyalty and support of other people and new supervisors must recognize that. The new supervisor must realize that new behaviors are needed and that the change takes time.

Practicing supervisors must also recognize that it takes time for new supervisors to become effective and that they need help and support. Because the process of becoming a good supervisor is ongoing, one never stops learning.

Expectations for Student
Employee Supervisors

Supervising people is undoubtedly the most difficult and complex activity of managers. Student employee supervisors are the direct link between the managerial structure and the operational structure of an organization. To employees, the supervisor represents "the organization." Workers' feelings about the organization, management, and their jobs are directly affected by their relationships with their immediate supervisors. Management's assessment of a unit's effectiveness is based on the productivity of the employees reporting to supervisors. Student employee supervisors are in a unique position because their ability to accomplish work through others has a direct impact on the organization's accomplishing its mission.

Many people in technical and staff positions fail to recognize or to appreciate the demands placed on student employee supervisors. Medical research has shown that supervisory positions carry with them tremendous stress. Although it is true that some people work better under stress and that channeling stress into productive activity can be satisfying, stress can also contribute to heart attacks, ulcers, and medical depression. To be able to supervise successfully requires considerable training and skill development.

In the past, supervisors had far less complex roles, partly because they enjoyed more authority. The controls and penalties imposed on employees for not following a supervisors' directives were much more severe. Today's student employee supervisor may still gain cooperation through the use of indirect force, but often feels frustrated by policies, rules, and regulations imposed by management. In some organizations, even though the supervisor has the power to discipline student employees, it is not unusual for decisions to be overruled by management, further frustrating supervisors.

Because student employee supervisors are the link between workers and management, they are sometimes called upon to represent both the employees' interests and those of management. If they were to represent only employees' views, they would find themselves at odds with management. If they represented only management, they would diminish their effectiveness in gaining and keeping employees' cooperation. Successful student employee supervisors must continually work to meet both organizational and individual needs. Is it any wonder that today's student employee supervisors feel confused, frustrated, and torn between two groups?

Libraries expect that student employee supervisors will recruit, hire, and train student employees in addition to performing other duties requiring technical expertise. Many supervisors are given the responsibility without training. The practice of hiring a new student employee supervisor to begin work after the incumbent has left further exacerbates the problem. The new student employee supervisor, whether new to the library or given new responsibilities, must recognize that the development of supervisory skills takes time and effort.

Common Mistakes New Supervisors Make

We have all seen the mistakes supervisors can make. Here are some of the most common:

1. *Overcontrolling.* The new supervisor (or the experienced one, for that matter) may believe that it is necessary to show everyone who's boss.

2. *Undercontrolling.* One who refuses to make decisions in an attempt to make everyone happy is headed for trouble.

3. *One-way communication.* The supervisor may be guilty of just giving orders without listening or of just listening without providing leadership.

4. *Half-way delegation.* Some supervisors are good at delegating responsibility without the authority to act. This too, leads to problems for all concerned.

These are only some of the mistakes that new supervisors make (and some experienced ones, too). Mistakes *will* be made, but it is part of the responsibility of practicing supervisors to help new supervisors develop an effective management style.

What Employees Don't Like About Their Supervisors

One way to learn how to be a good supervisor is to think about all of the supervisors you have had and what it was about them that you would have changed if you could. By considering the traits, actions, and skills of supervisors you have known, you know what to avoid in your own supervisory style. The following are some of the things employees don't like about their supervisors.

Supervisor Traits

1. *Too sensitive.* Employees don't like to tiptoe around their supervisors for fear of upsetting them; nor should they be afraid of saying the wrong thing to a supervisor who takes everything personally or who is in a bad mood.

2. *Indecisive.* Indecisive supervisors can survive in an organization but will not win the support of employees.

3. *Opinionated.* Supervisors who will not listen to any kind of reasoning but always have their minds made up will find that employees soon stop making suggestions.

4. *Autocratic.* Supervisors must understand that, if they do not allow their employees to participate in decisions, a lot of good talent is wasted.

5. *Vulgar language.* Crude language impresses no one and is to be avoided at all costs.

6. *Unstable personality.* Employees shouldn't have to guess which supervisor came to work that day. Unpredictable changes in a supervisor's personality cause problems.

7. *Dishonest.* Supervisors need to recognize the importance of honesty in the workplace and make it easy for employees to be honest.

Supervisor Actions

1. *Shows favoritism.* Even when other employees are treated fairly, they resent it if another employee is given favorable treatment. Problems like this may lead to discrimination charges, even though in most cases prejudice is not involved.

2. *Does not listen.* Good supervisors are anxious to hear what employees think about the job and encourage them to talk. Nothing is more frustrating that to talk to a supervisor who does not listen.

3. *Can't accept bad news.* Supervisors must be willing to listen to bad news and not punish the bearer. It won't take long for employees to realize that the supervisor wants to hear only good news and will ignore problems that need attention.

4. *Ridicules employees.* A supervisor who ridicules or makes sarcastic remarks to employees may not even be aware of doing so. Ridiculing an employee in front of peers is unforgivable. Supervisors must be aware of how their words affect employees. They must be tactful at all times.

5. *Makes uninformed decisions.* Employees respect supervisors who make decisions based on information.

6. *Does not trust employees.* Supervisors must trust employees and employees must be able to trust their supervisors.

7. *Makes impossible promises.* Employees know when the supervisor makes promises that cannot be kept. If this happens often, the supervisor's credibility is destroyed.

8. *Breaks reasonable promises.* Employees also know when the supervisor's promises can be kept but are not. Supervisors must either honor a promise or be able to explain why it has been broken.

Supervisor Skills

1. *Poor time management.* Supervisors with poor time management skills will waste their employees' time as well as their own.

2. *Disorganized.* Employees want supervisors who are organized and can get things done.

3. *Failure to exert authority.* Employees respect supervisors who know how to use their authority. Employees want leaders.

4. *Poor planning.* Supervisors who fail to plan anything in advance waste employees' time. Poorly planned meetings, for example, are terrible time wasters.

5. *Poor communicator.* Supervisors must develop good communication skills.

Why Student Employee Supervisors Fail

Supervisory styles cover the full spectrum, from the *laissez-faire* supervisor to the authoritarian. The supervisor who lacks self-confidence or feels uncomfortable in the supervisory role tends to let the unit run itself. The dictatorial or authoritarian supervisor tends to over-supervise. Few good supervisors are found at either extreme but are most often found in the middle of the spectrum.

When a student employee supervisor doesn't succeed, the manager must look at the specific situation to determine the exact reasons. Possibly the failure can be traced to lack of support from the boss or to lack of training or encouragement. Most failures, however, can be attributed to one of the following six supervisory pitfalls:

1. Poor personal relations with student employees, management, or other supervisors.

2. Lack of initiative or emotional stability on the part of the supervisor.

3. Unwillingness or inability to understand the management point of view.

4. Failure to spend the necessary effort or time to improve skills.

5. Lack of skill in planning and organizing the work of student employees.

6. Unwillingness or inability to adjust to changing conditions.

PREPARING TO BECOME A STUDENT EMPLOYEE SUPERVISOR

Many people begin their careers in libraries in public service or technical service positions without supervisory responsibilities. The aspiring student employee supervisor would do well to begin with the first function of management: planning.

1. Develop a career plan based on a realistic appraisal of your interests, aptitudes, and abilities.

2. If you are in a library with a career development program, take advantage of it.

3. Talk to student employee supervisors to learn more about what they do.

4. Talk to your supervisor to learn about opportunities for supervisory responsibilities.

5. Participate in supervisory and management training courses offered by the university.

6. Complete your college education. Most supervisory positions require a bachelor's degree. Being a student will help you relate to those you will be supervising.

7. Remember that advancement depends on successful performance. Although successful performance of your job will not guarantee advancement and will not guarantee that you will be a successful supervisor, good supervisors advance from the ranks of good workers, not bad ones.

THE STUDENT EMPLOYEE SUPERVISOR

The importance of the student employee supervisor's role is underestimated in many libraries for a number of reasons. In library school, librarians often do not receive the level of training in management that is required to manage large organizations; they usually develop their skills through post-graduate workshops and on-the-job experience. Many supervisors have no formal training whatsoever; such training is therefore not expected of staff who supervise students. Students are clearly on the bottom rung of the library staffing ladder.

By understanding the importance of student employee supervision and developing supervisory skills, the student employee supervisor can make a valuable contribution to the operation of the library and help students gain life-long job skills. Yours is a critical role in the organization.

NOTES

1. Lester R. Bittel, *What Every Supervisor Should Know* (New York: McGraw-Hill, 1980), 3.

2. *Labor Management Relations Act, 1947, U.S. Statutes at Large* 61, pt. 1 (1947): 138.

3. Adapted from Louis V. Imundo, *The Effective Supervisor's Handbook* (New York: AMACOM, 1980), 12–14.

BIBLIOGRAPHY

Abboud, Michael J., and Homer L. Richardson. "What Do Supervisors Want from Their Jobs?" *Personnel Journal* (July 1972): 308–12.

Bailey, Martha J. "Requirements for Middle Managerial Positions." *Special Libraries* 69 (September 1978): 323–31.

Baker, H. K., and S. R. Holmberg. "Stepping Up to Supervision: Being Popular Isn't Enough." *Supervisory Management* 27 (January 1982): 12–18.

Bedeian, Arthur G. *Management*. Chicago: The Dryden Press, 1986.

Benson, Carl A. "New Supervisors: From the Top of the Heap to the Bottom of the Heap." *Personnel Journal* (April 1978): 176.

Bittel, Lester R. *What Every Supervisor Should Know*. New York: McGraw-Hill, 1980, 3.

———. *Practical Management for Supervisors*. Westerville, OH: Macmillan/McGraw-Hill, 1993.

Bullock, Gwendolyn A. *Performance Standards Handbook: A Reference for Managers and Supervisors*. Washington, D.C.: U.S. Office of Personnel Management, 1981.

Carroll, Stephen J., and Dennis Gillen. "Are the Classical Management Functions Useful in Describing Managerial Work?" *Academy of Management Review* 12, no.1 (January 1987): 38–51.

Certo, Samuel. *Principles of Modern Management*. 3d ed. Dubuque, IA: Wm. C. Brown, 1985.

Daughtrey, Anne Scott, and Betty Roper Ricks. *Contemporary Supervision: Managing People and Technology*. New York: McGraw-Hill, 1988.

Donnelly, James H., James L. Gibson, and John M. Ivancevich. *Fundamentals of Management*. 6th ed. Plano, TX: Business Publications, 1987.

Flamholtz, Eric G., and Yvonne Randle. *The Inner Game of Management: How to Make the Transition to a Managerial Role*. New York: AMACOM, 1987.

Fulmer, William E. "The Making of a Supervisor." *Personnel Journal* (March 1977): 140–43, 151.

Ianconnetti, Joan, and Patrick O'Hare. *First-Time Manager*. New York: Macmillan, 1985.

Imundo, Louis V. *The Effective Supervisor's Handbook*. New York: AMACOM, 1980, 12–14.

James, Muriel. *The Better Boss in Multicultural Organizations: A Guide to Success Using Transactional Analysis*. Walnut Creek, CA: Marshall, 1991.

Lucas, Robert W. *Training Skills for Supervisors*. Burr Ridge, IL: Irwin, Professional Publishing, 1994.

The Supervisor's Handbook: A Quick and Handy Guide for Any Manager or Business Owner. Hawthorne, NJ: Career Press, 1993.

U.S. Office of Personnel Management. *Addressing and Resolving Poor Performance: A Guide for Supervisors*. Washington, D.C.: U.S. Office of Personnel Management, Office of Workforce Relations, 1998.

Weiss, W. H. *Supervisor's Standard Reference Handbook*. 2d ed. Englewood Cliffs, NJ: Prentice-Hall, 1988.

Chapter Three

BASICS FOR SUPERVISORS

A good leader takes a little more than his share of blame; a little less than his share of credit.

—Arnold H. Glasgow

BECOMING A SUPERVISOR

This chapter includes discussions about the basic qualities and skills required of good supervisors as well as the process of becoming a supervisor, and suggestions on how supervisors can be successful. Leadership is one of the most important skills/qualities successful supervisors must develop.

LEADERSHIP

Leadership is a basic requirement for good supervision. There are many definitions of leadership as evidenced by the number of books on the subject. Leadership is simply the ability to get others to follow you and do the things you want them to do; it is also a knack that may be developed with hard work or that may come naturally. Successful leaders possess the following qualities:

1. A belief in their ability to lead.

2. A sense of mission.

3. The willingness to put the organization's well-being above their own egos.

4. Honesty.

5. Courage.

6. Sincerity.

7. Dependability.

8. Job knowledge.

9. Common sense.

10. Sound judgment.

11. Energy.

12. The willingness to work hard.

There are three basic kinds of leadership:

1. Autocratic leadership is a technique whereby the leader makes the decisions and demands that workers follow instructions without question.

2. Democratic leadership involves those supervised. The leader consults with workers and lets them help set policy.

3. With free-rein or participative leadership, the leader exercises minimum control, allowing workers to exercise their own judgment and sense of responsibility to accomplish the necessary work.

Different kinds of leadership can be successful with different employees. An autocratic style works best with a situation in which the student employee supervisor has real authority and a personality that can exert strong control. Autocratic leadership works best for assembly line-type situations. Participatory or democratic leadership works best with situations in which the supervisor's authority is unclearly defined, the procedures are subject to change with the situation, and employees are required to use creativity and initiative.

The leadership style practiced by student employee supervisors is dependent largely on the situation. Usually, participative or free-rein leadership is most effective with student employees who are typically cooperative, self-reliant, and want to exercise their own judgment. It is up to the supervisor to communicate to employees the idea that they are to "do as I do, which is the same as do what I say." Leaders are responsible for setting good examples for employees to adopt and follow.

The style of leadership, however, is less important than the leaders themselves. The qualities of leadership in employees are sought by all organizations for their student employee supervisors and managers. Good leadership is essential for good supervisors of student employees in academic libraries.

Your Leadership Potential

The following scale (on page 38) is designed to help you measure your leadership potential.[1]

Text continues on page 40.

Test of Leadership Potential

Directions: Record the number that indicates where you fall, from 1 to 10, on the scale. Interpretation of the results follows the scale.

I can develop the talent and confidence to be an excellent speaker in front of groups.	10......5......1	I could never develop confidence to speak in front of groups.
I have the capacity to build and maintain productive relationships with workers under my supervision.	10......5......1	I'm a loner. I do not want the responsibility of building relationships with others.
I intend to take full advantage of all opportunities to develop my leadership qualities.	10......5......1	I do not intend to seek a leadership role or to develop my leadership skills.
I can develop the skill of motivating others. I would provide an out-standing example.	10......5......1	I could never develop the skill of motivating others. I would be a poor example to follow.
I can be patient and understanding with others.	10......5......1	I have no patience with others and could not develop it.
I could learn to be good at disciplining those under me—even to the point of terminating a worker after repeated violations.	10......5......1	It would tear me up to discipline a worker under my supervision. I'm much too kind and sensitive.

| I can make tough decisions. | 10......5......1 | I do not want decision-making responsibilities. |

| It would not bother me to isolate myself and maintain a strong discipline line between workers and myself. | 10......5......1 | I have a great need to be liked. I want to be one of the gang. |

| I would make an out-standing member of a "management" team. | 10......5......1 | I hate staff meetings and would be a weak or hostile team member. |

| In time, I would be a superior leader—better than anyone I have known. | 10......5......1 | My leadership potential is so low it is not worth developing. |

TOTAL SCORE _____

Interpretation of your score:

The total number of points possible is 100. If you circled any number less than five, you should re-examine your career objectives. Perhaps supervision is not an activity you should seek until you can honestly circle a five or higher on every question.

If your score is:

> 100: Are you sure this is an honest appraisal?
>
> 90–99: You will enjoy supervision.
>
> 80–89: You have great supervisory potential.
>
> 70–79: You should be a good supervisor.
>
> 60–69: Are you sure supervision is your goal?
>
> 50–59: Supervision will not be easy for you!
>
> 0–49: Supervisory responsibilities will make you miserable!

To be effective, supervisors must have authority with which to carry out their responsibilities.

AUTHORITY AND ACCOUNTABILITY

Authority is the legitimate exercise of power. Authority is given to student employee supervisors by the library by virtue of having given them supervisory responsibility. Authority and responsibility are usually handed down to student employee supervisors from their immediate supervisors. These supervisors in turn receive their authority from those above them. Authority and responsibility are handed down from the top, beginning with the highest levels: the university president to the vice presidents to the dean/director of the library, and so on. As the authorities and responsibilities come down the line to the student employee supervisor, they become more specific. For instance, although the dean/director has the authority to manage the personnel budget and a large staff, it is the supervisor's responsibility to supervise a group of student employees with specific jobs and duties.

Although authority and responsibility go hand in hand, they are quite different. Authority is the power you need to carry out your responsibilities as student employee supervisor. Responsibilities are those things for which you are held accountable by management.

Authority and power are not the same. Power does not require legitimacy. An armed robber has power but no authority. The robber has no legitimate right to rob but has a gun and the ability to make people follow instructions.

Authority carries with it the responsibility for using it wisely. The student employee supervisor has the authority and the attending responsibility to manage, which is accepted by employees. A student employee supervisor who, in the opinion of employees, exceeds supervisory authority will find that employees question or even resist that authority. Student employee supervisors must remember that their authority is retained only so long as its use is approved by the organization and accepted by the majority of employees supervised.

The student employee supervisor is held accountable to the boss for performing the supervisor's responsibilities. For example, you may be held accountable for assuring that the charging and discharging of books is done efficiently and accurately. You may delegate the responsibility for performing those activities to students who are accountable to you. When the boss complains that there are too many books waiting to be discharged, you have the responsibility to investigate and correct the problem if possible. The boss does not know why there are too many books but feels that there is a problem. You are accountable. There may be any number of explanations but you must solve the problem. You can delegate the responsibility but cannot delegate the accountability. The boss expects you to perform your responsibilities, which include the work student employees do.

Assessing Your Degree of Accountability

You can gain an idea of the degree to which you are responsible (or accountable) in your supervisory job by completing the Supervisory Responsibility Survey.[2]

Text continues on page 44.

Supervisory Responsibility Survey

DO YOU FEEL IT IS YOUR RESPONSIBILITY TO . . .

	YES	NO	DON'T KNOW
1. Request that additional employees be hired as needed?	___	___	_____
2. Approve new student employees assigned to you?	___	___	_____
3. Tell employees about upgrading and pay ranges?	___	___	_____
4. Prepare employee work schedules?	___	___	_____
5. Assign specific duties to workers?	___	___	_____
6. Delegate authority?	___	___	_____
7. Discipline student employees?	___	___	_____
8. Discharge student employees?	___	___	_____
9. Specify the number and level of student employees to do a job?	___	___	_____
10. Determine the amount of work to be accomplished by each employee?	___	___	_____

DO YOU FEEL IT IS YOUR RESPONSIBILITY TO . . .

	YES	NO	DON'T KNOW
11. Authorize overtime?	___	___	_____
12. Transfer student employees within your department?	___	___	_____
13. Lay off employees for lack of work?	___	___	_____
14. Grant leaves of absence?	___	___	_____
15. Explain to student employees how their pay is calculated?	___	___	_____
16. Start jobs in process?	___	___	_____
17. Stop jobs in process?	___	___	_____
18. Make suggestions for improvements in departmental procedures?	___	___	_____
19. Make recommendations on changes in departmental layout?	___	___	_____
20. Participate in setting up your departmental budget?	___	___	_____

If you are able to say YES to all the questions, you could honestly say that you have supervisory responsibilities. If you also have the authority and accountability for all of these activities, your supervisory role is very clear. If you responded NO to more than five of the 20 questions, your supervisory role needs to be clarified with your boss. If you answered DON'T KNOW to any of the questions, you also need to speak to your boss about your responsibilities. If you don't know whether an activity is your responsibility, you certainly don't know whether you should be performing that activity. You cannot have authority or accountability for any activity that is clearly not your responsibility.

Change occurs in all organizations whether supervisors plan for change or not. Change is brought about by changing technology, by library patron demands, by administrative policy, or by recognition of the need for improvement. An important part of an effective supervisor's job involves the ability to deal with and to manage change.

MANAGING CHANGE AND TIME

Change is any modification or alteration of the status quo. Student employees are, for the most part, amenable to change, but staff as a group tend to be less so. Different employees have different responses to change: these include rejection, resistance, tolerance, or acceptance. Outright rejection or acceptance is uncommon. Most often there is resistance or tolerance, which is usually the result of conscious thought. Employees make their decisions based on their assessment of the effect of the change on them.

Employees' resistance to change comes typically from fear for their jobs, dislike for change in the status quo, group pressure, lack of understanding, or plain shortsightedness. If managed properly, employees will not only tolerate the change, but will accept it. The four steps for managing change should be carried out sequentially:

1. *Define the change.* The supervisor must fully understand the change before introducing it to the workers.

2. *Identify the situational factors.* Will there be resistance? Who is likely to resist? How can that resistance be met? How much advance notice should be given?

3. *In cooperation with employees, develop a change strategy.* Explain the change, encourage participation in developing an implementation plan, provide support, and if necessary,

use persuasion to reduce resistance. If resistance is too great, the supervisor may have to exert whatever authority available to overcome it.

4. *Implement and monitor the change.* Implement the strategy and follow-up.

The acceptance of change by employees depends to a great extent on their perceptions of their supervisors. If they feel they are involved in the decisions made in the department and believe that changes are made for good reasons, the chances that change will be accepted will be greatly improved.

Many supervisors feel that they need more hours in each day to complete their work. If you often feel that at the end of the day you didn't really accomplish anything, it may not be the amount of work you do but the way you do it. The focus of time management is on working smarter, not harder. Supervisors are busy and that is why time management is so important to individuals.

There are three basic types of supervisor time: boss-imposed, subordinate-imposed, and self-imposed. Boss-imposed time is that time your supervisor requires of you; included are assignments and tasks performed for the boss. Subordinate-imposed time is that time those persons you supervise require of you; this is time used to help employees with their work. Self-imposed or personal time is that time remaining for you to manage as you wish; this is the time equal to the number of hours an individual works minus boss-imposed and subordinate-imposed time.

The supervisor can and should examine the amount of subordinate-imposed time spent. Are your employees delegating work to you? Are you working 12 hours a day so they can work less? Supervisors need to learn techniques that will help them avoid having to deal with all their employees' problems.

Self-imposed time is that time in which the supervisor accomplishes the work that must be done. In effectively managing that time, the supervisor must first keep subordinate-imposed time to a minimum and then use time management techniques to make the best use of personal time.

Identifying Time Wasters

To manage time, one must first know how it is presently spent. One way to accomplish that is to keep a time log. The log should be used to record exactly how time is spent. After keeping a log for a week or two, most supervisors are amazed by how much and how little is accomplished. The log will show a great number of activities but most supervisors find that little was actually accomplished. The following are the most common time wasters:

1. Telephone interruptions

2. Drop-in visitors

3. Unscheduled meetings

4. Crises

5. Personal disorganization

6. Failure to set priorities

7. Failure to delegate

8. Trying to do too much at once

9. Unclear lines of authority and responsibility

10. Inability to say no

11. Physical fatigue

12. Poor communication

Time Management Guidelines

Time management is a personal challenge. If you are sincere in your desire to manage time, it can be done. Success depends on desire and a plan of action. The following suggestions are designed to help you attack the time wasters in your workday and to gain control of your time:

1. Use a daily planbook to keep track of what needs to be done each day. Schedule a quiet time each day when you can work without interruption.

2. Establish priorities and work on the most important first. Focus first on doing the right things, *then* on doing things right.

3. Delegate work to subordinates.

4. If you are a morning person, work on your most important priorities in the morning. If you work better in the afternoon, plan to do them then.

5. Learn to say "no" graciously. Don't let others who don't manage their time waste yours.

6. Whatever you do, do it right the first time. This applies to tasks you perform yourself and to how you give directions to others.

7. Get organized. Clean up your desk and files. Throw out unnecessary papers.

8. Handle paper once. Avoid cluttering your desk with correspondence by acting on each piece of paper when you pick it up. If you can write a response, give it to someone to handle, forward it, or file it, do so.

9. Group tasks together. Handle your correspondence or make phone calls between 2 P.M. and 3 P.M., for example.

10. Break up large projects into smaller tasks and plan to do each task separately. For example, don't write a book, write chapters.

11. Make better use of bits of time. Don't start on a large project ten minutes before lunch. Do something you can complete.

12. Reduce interruptions by scheduling a quiet time or by turning your desk so that your back is facing the door. Visual interruptions are just as wasteful as drop-in visitors.

13. Recognize that although you can do a better job of managing personal time, you can't reach perfection.

14. Don't overdo time management to the point that you lose your friends, alienate your coworkers, or earn the nickname "time freak."

DEALING WITH STRESS

Stress is a feeling of anxiety, pressure, or tension and is experienced by everyone to some degree. Stress can be caused by everything from job-related incidents to everyday happenings; in the workplace, it is brought about by uncomfortable levels of noise, light, and temperature. Unclear job assignments, too much work, too much responsibility, interpersonal conflict, and the organizational environment can cause stress. Most of us also bring stress to the workplace from home. Students are also subjected to stressful situations through their coursework.

Everyone is affected by stressful situations in different ways. Most people work best under moderate degrees of stress; if there is too little, boredom results. With too much stress, individuals are likely to suffer from lack of memory, indecision, and poor judgment. Stress can be self-induced, but supervisors can help their employees and themselves to deal with it by recognizing that diet, physical fitness, and mental relaxation are important. The following are suggested remedies for stress:

1. Walk away from the source of stress. A walk around the block can release pent-up tension.

2. Talk it out with a friend or mentor.

3. Release your anger by exercising or by expressing it in writing and then destroying (don't forget this) your written words.

4. Don't procrastinate. Taking action can eliminate the stress caused by procrastination.

5. Short naps can effectively reduce tension.

6. Avoid irritating and overly competitive people if you can. Stay away from persons who appear free of stress yet produce it in others.

7. Take advantage of staff development programs or continuing education sessions that offer stress reduction techniques.

8. Seek professional counseling.

DETERMINING YOUR POTENTIAL

Most people wonder at one time or another if they have the potential to get better jobs than they presently have. What is it that indicates whether or not individuals have the potential to rise in an organization? What can individuals do to demonstrate their interest in advancement? Answers to the following questions provide indicators of potential for growth:

1. Do you enjoy your work? If you get satisfaction from your work, you are probably self-motivated and will not be content just to do the minimum required. Self-motivation is one key to success.

2. Are you given encouragement by your supervisor? If you are told either verbally and/or through evaluations that you are doing a good job, you have the potential to advance.

3. Do you enjoy solving problems? If so, you can demonstrate your potential by fully participating in departmental and library activities to the extent possible in your job. Persons who provide useful suggestions and ideas will get recognition.

4. Are you mature? Mature persons are usually practical in their viewpoints and demonstrate practical approaches to problems.

5. Are you stable? Stable persons can control their emotions and are able to handle stress effectively.

6. Do you read the professional literature? If you are interested in broader library issues and keep up with not only local but national library issues, you can demonstrate interests outside those of your job.

7. Do you join professional organizations? If you are interested in making a career in libraries at the staff or faculty level, you can demonstrate your interest by becoming a member of local, state, and national library organizations and by actively participating in those organizations.

Tips on Getting Noticed and Promoted

In today's libraries, the competition for more responsible and rewarding positions is great. Being in the right place at the right time for promotion is mostly luck and can't be counted on. If you want to advance, you have to do more than perform an excellent job. No matter how qualified you think you are for promotion, it is important that others share the same perception. You must be viewed as qualified and ready for promotion, your work must be recognized, and your accomplishments must be known. The following are suggestions on how you can be recognized for promotion:

1. Do an excellent job. There is no point in thinking about promotion if you do not perform your present job in an outstanding manner.

2. Behave like a professional and dress appropriately.

3. Acquire more knowledge/education. Learn by reading, by listening and asking questions, and by attending training sessions, workshops, and classes.

4. Make it known to your supervisor that you want to get ahead, but avoid giving the impression that you want to get ahead at the expense of others (including the supervisor).

5. Show your commitment to the organization. Complainers, moaners, and groaners don't often get promoted.

6. Show that you are a team player. Participate as fully as possible in departmental and library activities.

7. Be willing to admit mistakes and to *say* you don't know when you don't know.

8. Prove that you have a sense of humor and are able to laugh at yourself.

9. Always exhibit honest and ethical behavior.

10. Don't become indispensable. If you are indispensable, you can't be replaced or promoted. If you are indispensable, you are not delegating properly, not interacting with others, and not training anyone to fill in during your absences.

11. Participate in library committee activities.

12. Get yourself mentioned. If you do something newsworthy, let the editors of the library newsletter know about it.

13. Write for publication. If you have an area of expertise, write about it and get it published in library literature. If you don't have an area of expertise, develop one.

14. Converse with others at every opportunity. Offer your ideas and suggestions at committee meetings; get to know people outside your department.

Learn from Your Mistakes

It would be foolish to assume that good supervisors don't make mistakes. However, it is a fool who does not learn from them. Instead of simply dismissing a mistake by saying, "Everybody makes mistakes," why not take a few minutes to find out why the mistake was made? To learn from a mistake, you must analyze the situation to know what caused it. Ask yourself these questions:

1. What were you doing at the time?

2. What was the situation?

3. Were you under stress at the time?

4. Who else was involved?

5. Did you have incorrect or insufficient information?

6. Was the mistake the result of getting involved in the first place?

7. Was it the result of inattention or of not placing enough importance on the situation?

8. Was your timing wrong? Should you have dealt with the situation earlier, later, or not at all?

9. Were other persons involved? While the mistake may not have been yours alone, accept your share of the responsibility. Should you be more careful when working with these persons in the future?

10. Was the mistake the result of insufficient follow-up?

Learning from mistakes will help you prevent making more of them. It is all part of gaining experience.

Behavior to Avoid

It is as important to know what behaviors to avoid as it is to develop supervisory skills and knowledge. No matter how versed you are in supervision, good relationships with people must be developed. Any one of the following behaviors can prevent you from being the kind of supervisor you want to be:

1. *Being distrustful.* Showing people that you don't trust them by questioning their motives or not accepting their word.

2. *Being untrustworthy.* Demonstrating that your word and actions cannot be trusted by others.

3. *Being egotistical.* Talking about oneself too much.

4. *Being selfish.* Saying and doing things that indicate that you have little regard for other people.

5. *Being overly critical.* Finding fault with other people or criticizing unnecessarily.

6. *Being unwilling to accept blame.* Refusing to admit that you make mistakes.

7. *Being defensive.* Making excuses or trying to justify your actions when you are wrong.

8. *Being closed-minded.* Refusing to accept viewpoints which don't agree with yours.

Getting Along with Your Supervisor

To get along with your supervisor, put yourself in the shoes of those you supervise. How do you want your employees to view you? The following suggestions will help you get along better with your boss:

1. Provide support by keeping your supervisor fully informed. There should be very few "surprises."

2. Avoid wasting your supervisor's time. Don't go running to the boss for decisions that you should be making yourself.

3. Don't be a "yes" person all the time. If you don't agree with your supervisor, say so tactfully and be prepared to offer alternatives.

4. Avoid thinking you know more than your supervisor. Although you may indeed know more about certain aspects of the job, recognize that your boss is in that position for a reason.

5. Learn all you can from your supervisor if you wish to advance. That's how your boss became your boss.

6. Don't underestimate your supervisor's influence or ability to help you get ahead (or keep you where you are).

Writing Better Reports

Supervisors complain about having to write reports, yet writing good reports is extremely important. You can improve the quality of your reports by remembering the following:

1. *Be concise.* Eliminate superfluous and redundant words.

2. *Avoid jargon.* The acronyms and phrases unique to your department or to the library may not be understood by someone outside the field who may read the report. Spell out acronyms when you first introduce them.

3. *Write the way you talk.* Avoid stilted language.

4. *Always proofread your report.* Never allow a report to be distributed with misspelled words or typographical errors; this degrades you and those you work with.

5. *Don't procrastinate.* If you write a monthly report, do it monthly. No one wants to read a report six months old.

SUMMARY

In this and the other three chapters on supervision we have attempted to provide basic supervisory techniques and information beneficial to supervisors of student assistants. Please don't stop here. Make a habit of reading supervisory literature and talking with co-workers who supervise students and staff. There is simply no way to cover adequately all you need to know to do your job. We only hope that the information contained in these chapters will be useful to you and that you will continue learning about supervision any way you can. The following resources should be helpful.

NOTES

1. Adapted from Elwood E. Chapman, "A Self-Paced Exercise Guide," Supervisor's Survival Kit, 2d ed. (Chicago: Science Research Associates, 1980), 22.

2. Adapted from Lester R. Bittel, *Supervisory Responsibility Survey: What Every Supervisor Should Know* (New York: McGraw-Hill, 1980).

BIBLIOGRAPHY

Adair, John. *Effective Time Management.* London: Pan Books, 1988.

Argyris, Chris. "Managers, Workers, and Organizations." *Society* (January–February 1998): 343.

Arroba, T., and K. James. *Pressure at Work: A Survival Guide.* Toronto: McGraw-Hill Ryerson, 1987.

Lester R. Bittel, *Supervisory Responsibility Survey: What Every Supervisor Should Know.* New York: McGraw-Hill, 1980.

———. *Practical Management for Supervisors.* Westerville, OH: Macmillan/McGraw-Hill, 1993.

Bradley, Jana, and Larry Bradley. *Improving Written Communication in Libraries.* Chicago: American Library Association, 1988.

Brown, Nancy A., and Jerry Malone. "The Bases and Uses of Power in a University Library." *Library Administration and Management* 2 (June 1988): 141–44.

Bunge, Charles. "Stress in the Library." *Library Journal* 112 (September 15, 1987): 47–51.

Carr, Clay. *The New Manager's Survival Manual.* New York: Wiley, 1995.

Chapman, Elwood E. *Supervisor's Survival Kit.* 2d ed. Chicago: Science Research Associates, 1980, 22.

———. *Supervisor's Survival Kit: Your First Step into Management.* New York: Macmillan, 1993.

Drucker, Peter F. *The Effective Executive.* New York: Harper & Row, 1985.

Giesecke, Joan, ed. *Practical Help for New Supervisors.* Chicago: American Library Association, 1997.

Good, Sharon. *Managing with a Heart.* Naperville, IL: Sourcebook, 1997.

Gothberg, Helen M., and Donald E. Riggs. "Time Management in Academic Libraries." *College and Research Libraries* 49, no. 2 (March 1988): 131–40.

Hilgert, Raymond L., and others. *Supervision: Concepts and Practices of Management.* Cincinnati, OH: South-Western College, 1995.

Kaiser, Tamara L. *Supervisory Relationships: Exploring the Human Element.* Pacific Grove, CA: Brooks/Cole, 1996.

Levesque, Joseph D. *The Human Resource Problem-Solver's Handbook.* New York: McGraw-Hill, 1992.

Maurer, Rick. *Caught in the Middle: A Leadership Guide for Partnership in the Workplace.* Portland, OR: Productivity Press, 1996.

McCabe, Gerard B. *The Smaller Academic Library: A Management Handbook.* Westport, CT: Greenwood Press, 1988.

Mosley, Donald C., and others. *Supervisory Management: The Art of Empowering and Developing People.* Cincinnati, OH: South-Western College, 1993.

Rosenbach, William E., and Robert L. Taylor. *Leadership: Challenges and Opportunities.* New York: Nichols, 1988.

Ross, Catherine, and Patricia Dewdney. *Communicating Professionally.* New York: Neal-Schuman, 1988.

Weaver, Richard G., and John D. Farrell. *Managers As Facilitators: A Practical Guide to Getting Work Done in a Changing Workplace.* San Francisco: Berrett-Koehler, 1997.

Weiss, W. H. *Supervisor's Standard Reference Handbook.* 2d ed. Englewood Cliffs, NJ: Prentice-Hall, 1988.

White, Herbert S. "How to Cope with an Incompetent Supervisor." *Canadian Library Journal* 44 (December 1987): 381.

White, Herbert S. "Oh, Where Have All the Leaders Gone?" *Library Journal* 112, no. 16 (October 1, 1987): 68–69.

White, James. *Successful Supervision.* 2d ed. New York: McGraw-Hill, 1988.

ORGANIZING FOR STUDENT EMPLOYMENT—JOB DESCRIPTIONS

> *Strategy drives structure;*
> *structure facilitates strategy.*
>
> —Montague Brown

ORGANIZING FUNCTION OF MANAGEMENT

The organizing function of management involves the creation of a structure that provides stability for the unit or department. Tasks can then be identified and grouped into jobs and relationships among the jobs can be established to accomplish the objectives of the unit or department. In the academic library, the supervisor must know what has to be accomplished and have a well-developed plan for getting the work done; this plan should include job descriptions and a system by which new employees are matched to jobs.

ORGANIZING A SYSTEM FOR STUDENT EMPLOYEE POSITIONS

The recruitment, screening, and hiring of student employees for the library is described in detail in chapter 6. Before any of those activities can take place, however, it is crucial that a foundation for employment exist. On the basis of that foundation, the supervisor should be able to respond positively to the following questions:

1. Do you know what tasks you will have each of the student employees perform?

2. Are the duties of each position documented in the form of approved job descriptions?

3. Are all of the tasks to be performed by each student employee included in the job description? Have you made a decision on whether or not to include the statement, "Other Duties as Assigned"?

4. Do the job descriptions contain enough information to describe the job? Are they concise, accurate, and complete? Are terms consistently applied among job descriptions?

5. Can the tasks described be evaluated?

6. Have you documented the required and desired experience and qualifications for each position?

Job Design and Analysis

Each job must be specifically created and named before a student employee is selected to fill it. Creating jobs is an organizing task called *job design;* this is a process by which tasks to be performed are identified, methods for performing the work are delineated, and the relationships of these tasks to other jobs are described.

In determining the work to be accomplished, the job designer groups together a manageable number of similar tasks. In designing a job, it is important to keep the worker in mind. The following characteristics are important to student employees:

1. Jobs should provide for a variety of activities.

2. Completion of tasks should produce identifiable final results.

3. Jobs should be seen as significant to other workers.

4. Student employees want freedom in deciding the schedule and process for doing their jobs.

5. Workers want their completed tasks to provide feedback on how well the tasks have been performed.

Because student employees change jobs frequently, it is necessary to conduct ongoing job analysis; this is the process of gathering and studying information about existing jobs. Such data can be gathered by observing the worker on the job, by interviewing the worker, or by having the worker keep a log of tasks performed over a period of time. The job analysis process is designed to answer the following questions about each job to be performed:

1. What are the major duties and responsibilities?

2. What tools and procedures are used?

3. What knowledge, skills, and abilities are required?

4. What are the physical requirements of the job?

5. What are the environmental conditions of the job?

The data gathered from job design and job analysis are used to prepare or revise job descriptions.

PURPOSE OF JOB DESCRIPTIONS

A job description is a statement of the duties to be performed by the persons holding the described job. A job description has two purposes:

1. For the student employee or prospective student employee, the job description explains the duties and responsibilities of the position, as well as providing a written statement of what will be evaluated by the supervisor.

2. For the supervisor, the job description provides requirements and desired qualifications used in screening, interviewing, and hiring students for library positions and a method of evaluating the work performed.

The job description serves as the basis for all organizing activities. It provides information on what the personnel in a given unit or department should be doing and assists supervisors in organizing student employees on the basis of experience and expertise. Job descriptions permit the library to establish career ladders for student employees and to establish a system for differentiated pay.

Features and Uses of a
Good Job Description

A job description is a list of things for which the student employee is responsible. The following are some features of a good job description:

1. The job description contains factual statements about the job.

2. The job description is brief but concise.

3. The job description is easy to read and jargon-free.

4. The job description explains the environment in which the work is done.

5. The job description lists the requirements for the position.

6. The job description explains the supervision to be received and given.

7. The job description contains the criteria for evaluation.

The job description can be useful to both the student employee and the supervisor. The information contained in the job description can be used in the following ways:

1. The job description can stimulate supervisory discussion concerning the necessity of each job.

2. The job description can be used as part of a campus student employment recruitment program or job fair.

3. The job description can help the supervisor screen and hire student employees.

4. The job description can help the new student employee become familiar with the nature and scope of the job.

5. The job description can be used as part of an orientation program.

6. The job description can serve as the basis for establishing performance standards.

7. The job description can serve as the basis for evaluating and comparing positions within a unit, department, or library.

8. The job description can serve as a communication device between supervisor and employee for the discussion of job expectations and objectives.

GUIDELINES FOR PREPARING JOB DESCRIPTIONS

Most of the following suggestions for preparing good job descriptions emphasize brevity and clarity:

1. The sentence structure for job duties and responsibilities should be, object, and explanatory phrase. The implied subject is always the incumbent occupying the job. For example, respond to audiotaping requests in a timely manner.

2. The present tense is to be used throughout.

3. Avoid words that are subject to varying interpretations (e.g., some, great, occasionally).

4. Avoid proprietary names (e.g., Word, Excel, Access). These references are subject to change and inclusion in the job description will necessitate change.

5. Avoid sexist terminology. Construct sentences in such a way that gender pronouns are not required.

6. Job descriptions should be kept to no more than two pages; one is preferred.

7. Describe the position as it is now and not as it will exist sometime in the future. (Anticipated changes sometimes do not take place.)

Job Descriptions for the Library

Job descriptions can be useful organizational tools for student employee supervisors if they are carefully written and properly used. If you do not have them, you should. If you are writing or reviewing your student employee job descriptions, make certain the descriptions accurately reflect the jobs. If you are paying at different rates for different jobs, be sure you can justify the differential. Job descriptions should be revised and updated every year. Remember, job descriptions have no value if they cannot be understood or are too general. Inadequate descriptions can lead to serious complaints about inequitable compensation or poor managerial decisions.

STUDENT EMPLOYEE JOB DESCRIPTIONS

Because libraries require student employees to perform a variety of tasks with different levels of complexity, it is necessary to differentiate between jobs according to the knowledge, skills, abilities, and experience required—the substantive differences between jobs. Check with your campus student employment office to see if such a system already exists. If so, either it can be used as is or it can be modified to fit the library's needs, generally with the approval of the campus office. If not, you should develop a classification system for library student positions. A system can be developed by library personnel or by a committee of library supervisors. This chapter does not attempt to prescribe a system for how student job descriptions must be designed; rather, it provides one possible system for purposes of illustration. In this system, student positions are classed in one of three grades.

Grade I Student Positions

Entry level position, under general supervision and with a low degree of responsibility. Will perform routine duties which may include, but not be limited to, answering phones, typing/keyboarding, photocopying, running errands, sorting incoming and outgoing mail, filing, internal record-keeping, and shelving. May serve as a counter or desk attendant and provide basic referral and informational services. Must have the ability to understand and execute basic procedural operations of the individual department and to understand the organizational structure of the library.

Grade II Student Positions

Intermediate level position, under limited supervision and with a moderate degree of responsibility. Will provide specialized support to the individual department and, as appropriate, must be acquainted with the duties and responsibilities of Grade I. Will perform duties that may include, but not be limited to, automated record keeping; receiving, sorting, and distribution of library materials; preliminary processing of materials; basic duplicate and bibliographic searching; limited reference and information services. Must exhibit a capacity for limited decision making in consultation with area supervisors.

Grade III Student Positions

Advanced level position, under minimal supervision and with a high degree of responsibility. Will provide highly technical/specialized support to the individual department and, as appropriate, must be acquainted with the duties and responsibilities of Grade II. Will perform duties that may include, but not be limited to, specialized instructional, operational, technical, and security tasks, and/or involved in the training, monitoring, and supervision of other student employees. May handle cash and/or confidential records and may require knowledge of a second language.

SAMPLE STUDENT EMPLOYEE JOB DESCRIPTIONS

The following figures depict sample student employee job descriptions. They are divided into three broad categories—Administrative Services, Public Services, and Technical Services—and then further divided by department (see figures 4.1 to 4.43). Administrative Services includes Copy Center, the Director's Office, Fiscal Services, Human Resources, and the Mail Room; Public Services includes Access Services (Circulation, Interlibrary Loan, and Reserve), Government Documents, Reference (the Map Room and the Media Center), and Special Collections (Manuscript Archives and Photo Archives); Technical Services includes Acquisitions, Cataloging and Classification, Collection Development (Gifts), Serials (Bindery and the Exchange Program), and Systems.

Some job descriptions may be used in more than one category, for example, a version of the Director's Office Assistant job description in Administrative Services could be used in almost any department. The Page job description in Circulation could also be used in Special Collections. The job descriptions are listed under a department name for illustration purposes only. Each library is organized differently and the actual department that a given job description is located, if it is used at all, will vary by library.

In some cases where there is clear progression, job descriptions are presented in families, one for each grade level, for example, Reference Assistant I (Grade I), Reference Assistant II (Grade II), and Reference Assistant III (Grade III). In other cases, a job description may be presented at a single grade level, for example, Interlibrary Loan Assistant (Grade II) or Photo Archives Assistant (Grade III). The number of grade levels required in a given department will vary from library to library.

The job descriptions are designed for libraries that have an Integrated Library System—online public catalog; automated circulation; and automated acquisitions, serials control, and fund accounting—and for libraries that use a bibliographic utility, the Library of Congress classification system, have electronic reference resources, and use various personal computer software packages. However, they can be altered for libraries that use less automation and/or electronic resources, and other classification systems.

The format for the job descriptions includes the name of the department, section (if there is one), hiring supervisor (left blank in the sample descriptions), student job title, grade (I, II, or III), pay rate (left blank in the sample descriptions), degree of responsibility (low, moderate, or high), maximum supervision required (general, limited, or minimal), duties and responsibilities required (knowledge, skills, and abilities) and desired (knowledge, skills, and abilities). All the job descriptions are written to be as generic as possible while still serving as useful examples.

Text continues on page 108.

Administrative Services: Copy Assistant I

Department: *Administrative Services* _____

Section: *Copy/Media Center* _____

Hiring Supervisor: _____

Student Job Title: *Copy Assistant I* _____

Grade (check one): __√__ I ____ II ____ III **Pay Rate:** _____

Degree of Responsibility (check one):

____√____ Low _____ Moderate _____ High

Maximum Supervision Required (check one):

____√____ General _____ Limited _____ Minimal

Duties and Responsibilities:
Photocopying from books, microforms and prepared original documents. Do velobinding and folding. Fill coin-operated photocopiers with paper. General maintenance of copy center area and supply tables.

Required:
Manual dexterity. Reliability.

Desired:
Customer service skills.

Fig. 4.1. Student job description.

Administrative Services: Copy Assistant II

Department: *Administrative Services*

Section: *Copy/Media Center*

Hiring Supervisor: _____

Student Job Title: *Copy Assistant II*

Grade (check one): ____ I _√_ II ____ III **Pay Rate:** _____

Degree of Responsibility (check one):

_____ Low __√__ Moderate _____ High

Maximum Supervision Required (check one):

_____ General __√__ Limited _____ Minimal

Duties and Responsibilities:
Photocopying from books, microforms and prepared original documents. Operate cash register, make change, and handle money. Do velobinding and folding. Fill coin-operated photocopiers with paper. Take inventory. General maintenance of copy center area and supply tables.

Required:
Cash register skills. Good math abilities. Mechanical aptitude for minor equipment maintenance and repair.

Desired:
Customer service skills.

Fig. 4.2. Student job description.

Administrative Services: Copy Assistant III

Department: *Administrative Services*

Section: *Copy/Media Center*

Hiring Supervisor:

Student Job Title: *Copy Assistant III*

Grade (check one): ____ I ____ II __√__ III **Pay Rate:**

Degree of Responsibility (check one):

_____ Low _____ Moderate ___√___ High

Maximum Supervision Required (check one):

_____ General _____ Limited ___√___ Minimal

Duties and Responsibilities:
Photocopying from books, microforms and prepared original documents. Operate cash register, make change, and handle large sums of money. Do velobinding and folding. Fill coin-operated photocopiers with paper. Perform end-of-day closing procedures. Take inventory. General maintenance of copy center area and supply tables. Perform other special instructional, operational, technical, and security tasks as assigned. May work night shift without supervision. May train and/or coordinate and delegate photocopying assignments to lower graded student employees.

Required:
Cash register skills. Good math abilities. Mechanical aptitude for minor equipment maintenance and repair.

Desired:
Customer service skills.

Fig. 4.3. Student job description.

Administrative Services: Office Assistant

Department: *Administrative Services*

Section: *Director's Office*

Hiring Supervisor: _____

Student Job Title: *Office Assistant*

Grade (check one): ____ I ____ II _√_ III **Pay Rate:** _____

Degree of Responsibility (check one):

_____ Low _____ Moderate __√__ High

Maximum Supervision Required (check one):

_____ General _____ Limited __√__ Minimal

Duties and Responsibilities:

Provide specialized support and handle confidential material. Do data entry and word process draft versions of memorandums and reports. Maintain computer files. Assist in scheduling meetings via phone, e-mail, and mail. Coordinate meeting agendas, distribution, and room reservations. Answer phones, type/keyboard, photocopy, run errands and sort incoming and outgoing mail. May perform literature search on identified topics.

Required:

Typing skill, minimum 40 words per minute. Computer literacy. Knowledge of computer word processing, spreadsheet, and database software. Complex problem solving ability. Ability to interact tactfully and efficiently with students, staff, and faculty members. Must be able to handle confidential matters with tact and good judgment.

Desired:

Knowledge of computer desktop publishing and presentation software. Proofreading skills. Research and computerized literature searching skills.

Fig. 4.4. Student job description.

Administrative Services: Fiscal Services Assistant

Department: *Administrative Services*

Section: *Fiscal Services*

Hiring Supervisor:

Student Job Title: *Fiscal Services Assistant*

Grade (check one): ____ I ____ II _√_ III **Pay Rate:** _____

Degree of Responsibility (check one):

_____ Low _____ Moderate __√__ High

Maximum Supervision Required (check one):

_____ General _____ Limited __√__ Minimal

Duties and Responsibilities:
Process and file confidential information, including payroll and budget information. Prepare book bills for payment. Sort invoices for mailing to customers. Receive, sort and distribute some library supplies. Answer phones, type/keyboard, photocopy, run errands and sort incoming and outgoing mail. In the absence of supervisor, staff public desk.

Required:
Typing for accuracy more than speed. Computer literacy. Ability to use a calculator. Ability to interact tactfully and efficiently with students, staff, and faculty members.

Desired:
Knowledge of accounting principles. Knowledge of computer spreadsheet software.

Fig. 4.5. Student job description.

Administrative Services: Personnel Assistant

Department: *Administrative Services*

Section: *Human Resources*

Hiring Supervisor:

Student Job Title: *Personnel Assistant*

Grade (check one): _____ I _____ II __√__ III **Pay Rate:** _____

Degree of Responsibility (check one):

_____ Low _____ Moderate ___√___ High

Maximum Supervision Required (check one):

_____ General _____ Limited ___√___ Minimal

Duties and Responsibilities:
Prepare, process and file confidential employee records. Update records on personal computer and compute student pay rates. Answer phones, type/keyboard, photocopy, run errands and sort incoming and outgoing mail. In the absence of supervisor, staff public desk.

Required:
Typing skill, accuracy more important than speed. Computer literacy. Ability to interact tactfully and efficiently with students, staff, and faculty members. Must be able to handle confidential matters with tact and good judgment.

Desired:
Knowledge of computer word processing software. Ability to use calculator.

Fig. 4.6. Student job description.

Administrative Services: Mail Room Assistant

Department: *Administrative Services*

Section: *Mail Room*

Hiring Supervisor:

Student Job Title: *Mail Room Assistant*

Grade (check one): ____ I ____ II _√_ III **Pay Rate:**

Degree of Responsibility (check one):

_____ Low _____ Moderate ___√___ High

Maximum Supervision Required (check one):

_____ General _____ Limited ___√___ Minimal

Duties and Responsibilities:
Monitor security of the loading dock during daytime hours. Receive, sign for, and deliver book shipments and supplies. Prepare and package materials for shipment.

Required:
Manual dexterity. Ability to lift up to 40 lbs.

Desired:
Knowledge of procedures used by campus mail office, US Postal Service, Federal Express, and/or United Parcel Service.

Fig. 4.7. Student job description.

Public Services: Circulation Desk Assistant I

Department: *Access Services*

Section: *Circulation*

Hiring Supervisor:

Student Job Title: *Circulation Desk Assistant I*

Grade (check one): __√__ I ____ II ____ III **Pay Rate:** _____

Degree of Responsibility (check one):

___√___ Low _____ Moderate _____ High

Maximum Supervision Required (check one):

___√___ General _____ Limited _____ Minimal

Duties and Responsibilities:
Responsible for security and care of library materials and equipment. Perform basic circulation activities including check-out and discharge of books and process renewals on automated circulation system. File books in call number order in to-be-shelved area. Answer basic directional questions and make referrals. Answer phone.

Required:
Customer service skills. Manual dexterity. Reliability.

Desired:
Computer literacy.

Fig. 4.8. Student job description.

Public Services: Circulation Desk Assistant II

Department: *Access Services* _____

Section: *Circulation* _____

Hiring Supervisor: _____

Student Job Title: *Circulation Desk Assistant II* _____

Grade (check one): ____ I _√_ II ____ III **Pay Rate:** _____

Degree of Responsibility (check one):

_____ Low __√__ Moderate _____ High

Maximum Supervision Required (check one):

_____ General __√__ Limited _____ Minimal

Duties and Responsibilities:
Responsible for security and care of library materials and equipment. Perform circulation activities including check-out and discharge of books, place holds and call-ins, and process renewals on automated circulation system. Retrieve books from outside book drops. File books in call number order in to-be-shelved area. Answer directional questions and make referrals. Answer phone.

Required:
Customer service skills. Computer literacy. Ability to lift up to 40 lbs. Ability to interact tactfully and efficiently with students, staff, and faculty members.

Desired:
Knowledge of Library of Congress classification system. Familiarity with library collection and borrowing policies.

Fig. 4.9. Student job description.

Public Services: Circulation Desk Assistant III

Department: *Access Services*

Section: *Circulation*

Hiring Supervisor: _____

Student Job Title: *Circulation Desk Assistant III*

Grade (check one): ____ I ____ II __√__ III **Pay Rate:** _____

Degree of Responsibility (check one):

_____ Low _____ Moderate __√__ High

Maximum Supervision Required (check one):

_____ General _____ Limited __√__ Minimal

Duties and Responsibilities:
Responsible for security and care of library materials and equipment. Perform circulation activities including check-out and discharge of books and process renewals on automated circulation system. Place holds and call-ins on books, initiate requests for return of books from patrons, and contact patrons concerning the availability of recalled books. Search for missing books. Register patrons on automated circulation system. File books in call number order in to-be-shelved area. Answer patron questions regarding library fines and fees and make referrals. Answer phone. Perform other operational, technical, and security tasks as assigned. May assist with end-of-day building closing procedures. May train and/or coordinate and delegate circulation assignments to lower graded student employees.

Required:
Customer service skills. Computer literacy. Ability to interact tactfully and efficiently with students, staff, and faculty members. Knowledge of Library of Congress classification system. Familiarity with library collection and borrowing policies.

Fig. 4.10. Student job description.

Public Services: Page

Department: *Access Services*

Section: *Circulation*

Hiring Supervisor: _____

Student Job Title: *Page*

Grade (check one): __√__ I ____ II ____ III **Pay Rate:** _____

Degree of Responsibility (check one):

____√____ Low _____ Moderate _____ High

Maximum Supervision Required (check one):

____√____ General _____ Limited _____ Minimal

Duties and Responsibilities:
Locate and retrieve books from closed stacks. Reshelve books and read shelves. May shift books where shelving is tight as assigned.

Required:
Manual dexterity. Reliability.

Desired:
Knowledge of Library of Congress classification system.

Fig. 4.11. Student job description.

Public Services: Shelver I

Department: *Access Services*

Section: *Circulation*

Hiring Supervisor:

Student Job Title: *Shelver I*

Grade (check one): √ I ___ II ___ III **Pay Rate:** ___

Degree of Responsibility (check one):

___√___ Low _____ Moderate _____ High

Maximum Supervision Required (check one):

___√___ General _____ Limited _____ Minimal

Duties and Responsibilities:
Responsible for maintenance of stacks. Shelve, shelf read, and shift books where shelving is tight as assigned. Retrieve and reshelve books from study areas and photocopying areas.

Required:
Manual dexterity. Reliability.

Desired:
Knowledge of Library of Congress classification system.

Fig. 4.12. Student job description.

Public Services: Shelver II

Department: *Access Services* _____

Section: *Circulation* _____

Hiring Supervisor: _____

Student Job Title: *Shelver II* _____

Grade (check one): ____ I _√_ II ____ III **Pay Rate:** _____

Degree of Responsibility (check one):

_____ Low __√__ Moderate _____ High

Maximum Supervision Required (check one):

_____ General __√__ Limited _____ Minimal

Duties and Responsibilities:
Responsible for maintenance of stacks. Shelve, shelf read, and shift books where shelving is tight as assigned. Interfile loose-leaf updated pages and remove old ones. Retrieve and reshelve books from study areas and photocopying areas. Assist with the closing of the building as assigned.

Required:
Manual dexterity. Reliability. Knowledge of Library of Congress classification system.

Fig. 4.13. Student job description.

Public Services: Shelving Student Supervisor

Department: *Access Services*

Section: *Circulation*

Hiring Supervisor: _____

Student Job Title: *Shelving Student Supervisor*

Grade (check one): ____ I ____ II _√_ III **Pay Rate:** _____

Degree of Responsibility (check one):

_____ Low _____ Moderate ___√___ High

Maximum Supervision Required (check one):

_____ General _____ Limited ___√___ Minimal

Duties and Responsibilities:
Responsible for maintenance, security, and end-of-day closing procedures for one or more library stacks on one or more nights per week. Train and supervise lower graded student employees; make shelving, shelf reading, and shifting where shelving is tight assignments. May substitute for staff supervisor.

Required:
Manual dexterity. Reliability. Knowledge of Library of Congress classification system.

Desired:
Supervisory experience.

Fig. 4.14. Student job description.

Public Services: Interlibrary Loan Assistant

Department: *Access Services*

Section: *Interlibrary Loan*

Hiring Supervisor: _____

Student Job Title: *Interlibrary Loan Assistant*

Grade (check one): ____ I __√__ II ____ III **Pay Rate:** _____

Degree of Responsibility (check one):

_____ Low __√__ Moderate _____ High

Maximum Supervision Required (check one):

_____ General __√__ Limited _____ Minimal

Duties and Responsibilities:
Staff Interlibrary Loan Desk. Assist borrowers with ILL requests and policies. Receive, sort, and distribute incoming books and periodicals, and process materials for distribution to borrowers. Notify patrons when materials are ready to be picked up. Fax materials when necessary. Search computer databases. Retrieve books and periodicals to be loaned out. Photocopy articles. Process materials for mailing.

Required:
Customer service skills. Computer literacy. Knowledge of Library of Congress classification system.

Desired:
Knowledge of photocopying and faxing procedures.

Fig. 4.15. Student job description.

Public Services: Reserve Desk Assistant

Department: *Access Services*

Section: *Reserve*

Hiring Supervisor: _____

Student Job Title: *Reserve Desk Assistant*

Grade (check one): ____ I __√__ II ____ III **Pay Rate:** _____

Degree of Responsibility (check one):

_____ Low __√__ Moderate _____ High

Maximum Supervision Required (check one):

_____ General __√__ Limited _____ Minimal

Duties and Responsibilities:
Staff Reserve Desk. Check-out and discharge reserve materials. Explain Reserve policies to patrons and policies for placing materials on Reserve to faculty members. Perform all functions related to processing reserve materials including physical processing and entering records onto the reserve database. May staff Circulation Desk as assigned.

Required:
Customer service skills. Computer literacy. Ability to interact tactfully and efficiently with students, staff, and faculty members.

Desired:
Familiarity with library collection and borrowing policies.

Fig. 4.16. Student job description.

Public Services: Government Documents Assistant I

Department: *Government Documents* _____

Section: _____

Hiring Supervisor: _____

Student Job Title: *Government Documents Assistant I* _____

Grade (check one): _√_ I ____ II ____ III **Pay Rate:** _____

Degree of Responsibility (check one):

____√____ Low _____ Moderate _____ High

Maximum Supervision Required (check one):

____√____ General _____ Limited _____ Minimal

Duties and Responsibilities:
Shelve materials having different classification systems. Shelf read. Shift where shelving is tight as assigned. Answer phones, type/keyboard, photocopy, run errands, and sort incoming and outgoing mail.

Required:
Manual dexterity.

Desired:
Computer literacy.

Fig. 4.17. Student job description.

Public Services: Government Documents Assistant II

Department: *Government Documents*

Section: _____

Hiring Supervisor: _____

Student Job Title: *Government Documents Assistant II*

Grade (check one): ____ I __√__ II ____ III **Pay Rate:** _____

Degree of Responsibility (check one):

_____ Low __√__ Moderate _____ High

Maximum Supervision Required (check one):

_____ General __√__ Limited _____ Minimal

Duties and Responsibilities:
Receive federal depository shipments including unpack shipments of paper and microfiche publications, check shipping list and count, and check-in on database. Process materials including property stamp, label, and security strip materials. Pull materials for binding. Shelve materials having different classification systems. Shelf read. Shift where shelving is tight as assigned.

Required:
Manual dexterity. Computer literacy.

Desired:
Knowledge of Library of Congress and/or SuDoc classification systems.

Fig. 4.18. Student job description.

Public Services: Government Documents Assistant III

Department: *Government Documents*

Section: _____

Hiring Supervisor: _____

Student Job Title: *Government Documents Assistant III*

Minimal Grade (check one): ____ I ____ II __√__ III

Pay Rate: _____

Degree of Responsibility (check one):

_____ Low _____ Moderate ___√___ High

Maximum Supervision Required (check one):

_____ General _____ Limited ___√___ Minimal

Duties and Responsibilities:

Staff information desk and assist at reference desk. Use specialized paper and online indexes. Receive federal depository shipments including unpack shipments of paper and microfiche publications, check shipping list and count, and check-in on database. Process materials including property stamp, label, and security strip materials. Shelve materials having different classification systems. Shelf read. Shift where shelving is tight. May train and/or coordinate and delegate assignments to lower graded student employees.

Required:

Customer service skills. Manual dexterity. Computer literacy.

Desired:

Knowledge of Library of Congress and/or SuDoc classification systems. Supervisory experience.

Fig. 4.19. Student job description.

Public Services: Reference Assistant I

Department: *Reference* _____

Section: _____

Hiring Supervisor: _____

Student Job Title: *Reference Assistant I* _____

Grade (check one): __√__ I ____ II ____ III **Pay Rate:** _____

Degree of Responsibility (check one):

__√__ Low _____ Moderate _____ High

Maximum Supervision Required (check one):

__√__ General _____ Limited _____ Minimal

Duties and Responsibilities:
Staff information desk. Answer basic directional questions and make referrals. Answer phones, type/keyboard, photocopy, run errands, and sort incoming and outgoing mail. Shelve reference materials. Shelf read. Shift where shelving is tight as assigned.

Required:
Customer service skills. Manual dexterity. Reliability.

Desired:
Computer literacy. Knowledge of Library of Congress classification system.

Fig. 4.20. Student job description.

Public Services: Reference Assistant II

Department: *Reference*

Section:

Hiring Supervisor:

Student Job Title: *Reference Assistant II*

Grade (check one): ____ I _√_ II ____ III **Pay Rate:** _____

Degree of Responsibility (check one):

_____ Low __√__ Moderate _____ High

Maximum Supervision Required (check one):

_____ General __√__ Limited _____ Minimal

Duties and Responsibilities:
Staff information desk. Answer questions and make referrals. Answer phones, photocopy, run errands, and sort incoming and outgoing mail. Word process user guides and pathfinders. Process new materials. Pull materials for binding. Shelve reference materials. Shelf read. Shift where shelving is tight as assigned.

Required:
Customer service skills. Manual dexterity. Computer literacy.

Desired:
Knowledge of Library of Congress classification system.

Fig. 4.21. Student job description.

Public Services: Reference Assistant III

Department: *Reference* _____

Section: _____

Hiring Supervisor: _____

Student Job Title: *Reference Assistant III* _____

Grade (check one): _____ I _____ II _√_ III **Pay Rate:** _____

Degree of Responsibility (check one):

_____ Low _____ Moderate ___√___ High

Maximum Supervision Required (check one):

_____ General _____ Limited ___√___ Minimal

Duties and Responsibilities:
Staff information desk. Answer questions and make referrals. Answer phones, photocopy, run errands, and sort incoming and outgoing mail. Word process user guides and pathfinders. Process new materials. Pull materials for binding. Shelve reference materials. Shelf read. Shift where shelving is tight. May train and/or coordinate and delegate assignments to lower graded student employees. May assist with organizing and preparing materials for library instruction and public display areas as needed.

Required:
Computer literacy. Knowledge of Library of Congress classification system. Ability to interact tactfully and efficiently with students, staff, and faculty members.

Desired:
Supervisory experience.

Fig. 4.22. Student job description.

Public Services: Map Room Assistant

Department: *Reference* _____

Section: *Map Room* _____

Hiring Supervisor: _____

Student Job Title: *Map Room Assistant* _____

Grade (check one): ____ I __√__ II ____ III **Pay Rate:** _____

Degree of Responsibility (check one):

_____ Low __√__ Moderate _____ High

Maximum Supervision Required (check one):

_____ General __√__ Limited _____ Minimal

Duties and Responsibilities:
Staff Maps Desk. Answer questions and make referrals. Assist patrons, and check-in and out maps. File maps according to Library of Congress G-Schedule call numbering system. Preliminary processing of maps.

Required:
Customer service skills. Manual dexterity. Computer literacy.

Desired:
Geography or geology major.

Fig. 4.23. Student job description.

Public Services: Media Center Assistant

Department: *Media Center* _____

Section: _____

Hiring Supervisor: _____

Student Job Title: *Media Center Assistant* _____

Grade (check one): ____ I __√__ II ____ III **Pay Rate:** _____

Degree of Responsibility (check one):

_____ Low ___√___ Moderate _____ High

Maximum Supervision Required (check one):

_____ General ___√___ Limited _____ Minimal

Duties and Responsibilities:
Staff Media Center Desk. Answer questions and make referrals. Assist patrons, and check-in and out media. Monitor patrons using materials. Assist patrons with use of audio, video and other equipment. Research items requested by patrons. Fill recording requests as described by requester. Minor equipment maintenance and repair, clean and exercise tapes, sort and categorize materials, and label collections.

Required:
Customer service skills. Manual dexterity. Experience with audio and video taping equipment.

Desired:
Knowledge of music and films. Ability to read music scores.

Fig. 4.24. Student job description.

Public Services: Special Collections Assistant

Department: *Special Collections*

Section: _____

Hiring Supervisor: _____

Student Job Title: *Special Collections Assistant*

Grade (check one): ____ I ____ II __√__ III **Pay Rate:** _____

Degree of Responsibility (check one):

_____ Low _____ Moderate ___√___ High

Maximum Supervision Required (check one):

_____ General _____ Limited ___√___ Minimal

Duties and Responsibilities:
Staff Special Collections Information Desk. Monitors collection security. Answer basic reference questions and make referrals. Retrieve and shelve material. Shelf read. Shift where shelving is tight. Conduct search for missing items. Assist staff with processing of new materials. Perform preservation/conservation of monographic items including mending, boxing fragile monographs, and correcting minor errors in the spines of bound materials. May work night shift without supervision.

Required:
Manual dexterity. Knowledge of Library of Congress classification system. Ability to interact tactfully and efficiently with students, staff, and faculty members.

Desired:
Previous library experience.

Fig. 4.25. Student job description.

Public Services: Manuscript Archives Assistant

Department: *Special Collections*

Section: *Manuscript Archives*

Hiring Supervisor: _____

Student Job Title: *Manuscript Archives Assistant*

Grade (check one): ____ I ____ II __✓__ III **Pay Rate:** _____

Degree of Responsibility (check one):

_____ Low _____ Moderate ___✓___ High

Maximum Supervision Required (check one):

_____ General _____ Limited ___✓___ Minimal

Duties and Responsibilities:
Responsible for all phases for manuscript collection processing including security, determination of arrangement, preparation of inventory, providing appropriate preservation housing, background research and the preparation of biographical and scope notes for patron finding aids. May be responsible for patron photocopying.

Required:
Manual dexterity. Computer literacy. Complex problem solving ability. Previous library experience. Historical research skills.

Desired:
Word processing skills.

Fig. 4.26. Student job description.

Public Services: Photo Archives Assistant

Department: *Special Collections/Photo* _____

Section: *Photo Archives* _____

Hiring Supervisor: _____

Student Job Title: *Photo Archives Assistant* _____

Grade (check one): ____ I ____ II _√_ III **Pay Rate:** _____

Degree of Responsibility (check one):

_____ Low _____ Moderate ____√____ High

Maximum Supervision Required (check one):

_____ General _____ Limited ____√____ Minimal

Duties and Responsibilities:
Arrange and describe photography collections. Compile information in specialized format for data entry. File photographs. Assist researchers. Perform basic preservation/conservation of materials. Maintain collection databases. Maintain exhibit space; assist exhibitor with set up/taking down of exhibit materials and refurbish exhibit space as needed.

Required:
Manual dexterity. Computer literacy. Ability to interact tactfully and efficiently with students, staff, and faculty members.

Desired:
Photography, art, or art history major. Experience in a visual resource collection, library, or archive.

Fig. 4.27. Student job description.

Technical Services: Acquisitions Assistant I

Department: *Acquisitions* _____

Section: _____

Hiring Supervisor: _____

Student Job Title: *Acquisitions Assistant I* _____

Grade (check one): _√_ I ___ II ___ III **Pay Rate:** _____

Degree of Responsibility (check one):

___√___ Low _____ Moderate _____ High

Maximum Supervision Required (check one):

___√___ General _____ Limited _____ Minimal

Duties and Responsibilities:
Perform basic duplicate and bibliographic checking/searching for books to be ordered in manual files and online databases. Answer phones, type/keyboard, photocopy, run errands, and sort incoming and outgoing mail.

Required:
Manual dexterity.

Desired:
Computer literacy.

Fig. 4.28. Student job description.

Technical Services: Acquisitions Assistant II

Department: *Acquisitions* _____

Section: _____

Hiring Supervisor: _____

Student Job Title: *Acquisitions Assistant II* _____

Grade (check one): ____ I __√__ II ____ III **Pay Rate:** _____

Degree of Responsibility (check one):

_____ Low __√__ Moderate _____ High

Maximum Supervision Required (check one):

_____ General __√__ Limited _____ Minimal

Duties and Responsibilities:
Perform basic bibliographic checking/searching for books to be ordered in manual files and online databases. Receive book shipments including unpack shipments, check shipping list/invoice, and check-in on library's integrated library system. Process materials including property stamp and security strip materials. Answer phones, type/keyboard, photocopy, run errands, and sort incoming and outgoing mail.

Required:
Manual dexterity. Computer literacy. Ability to lift up to 40 lbs.

Desired:
Knowledge of library's integrated library system.

Fig. 4.29. Student job description.

Technical Services: Acquisitions Assistant III

Department: *Acquisitions* _____

Section: _____

Hiring Supervisor: _____

Student Job Title: *Acquisitions Assistant III* _____

Grade (check one): ____ I ____ II __√__ III **Pay Rate:** _____

Degree of Responsibility (check one):

_____ Low _____ Moderate ___√___ High

Maximum Supervision Required (check one):

_____ General _____ Limited ___√___ Minimal

Duties and Responsibilities:
Perform advanced bibliographic checking/searching for books to be ordered in complex manual files and online databases. Verify citations. Perform specialized technical tasks including the use of OCLC online database in searching routines and the creation of bibliographic/order records in the library's integrated library system. Answer phones. May train and/or coordinate and delegate assignments to lower graded student employees.

Required:
Manual dexterity. Computer literacy. Knowledge of library's integrated library system.

Desired:
Complex problem solving skills. Knowledge of OCLC online database.

Fig. 4.30. Student job description.

Technical Services: Cataloging and Classification Assistant I

Department: *Cataloging and Classification*

Section: _____

Hiring Supervisor: _____

Student Job Title: *Cataloging and Classification Assistant I*

Grade (check one): √ I ____ II ____ III **Pay Rate:** _____

Degree of Responsibility (check one):

____√____ Low _____ Moderate _____ High

Maximum Supervision Required (check one):

____√____ General _____ Limited _____ Minimal

Duties and Responsibilities:
Search and verify bibliographic records in library's integrated library system. Type, cut, and apply spine labels to books. Attach barcodes to books. Check books for errors in physical processing. Mark withdrawn items. File cards in withdrawn file and shelf list. Pull books from stacks as assigned. Answer phones, type/keyboard, photocopy, run errands, and sort incoming and outgoing mail.

Required:
Manual dexterity. Computer literacy.

Desired:
Knowledge of Library of Congress classification system.

Fig. 4.31. Student job description.

Technical Services: Cataloging and Classification Assistant II

Department: *Cataloging and Classification*

Section: _____

Hiring Supervisor: _____

Student Job Title: *Cataloging and Classification Assistant II*

Grade (check one): _____ I __√__ II _____ III **Pay Rate:** _____

Degree of Responsibility (check one):

_____ Low __√__ Moderate _____ High

Maximum Supervision Required (check one):

_____ General __√__ Limited _____ Minimal

Duties and Responsibilities:
Perform bibliographic searching for books and serials in OCLC online database. Search and verify name/series in OCLC online database authority files. Do withdrawal and transfer procedures. Do special projects relating to the maintenance of the library's integrated library system involving searching, updating, correcting and deleting records. Answer phones, type/keyboard, photocopy, run errands, and sort incoming and outgoing mail.

Required:
Computer literacy. Knowledge of Library of Congress classification system.

Desired:
Knowledge of OCLC online database.

Fig. 4.32. Student job description.

Technical Services: Cataloging and Classification Assistant III

Department: *Cataloging and Classification*

Section: _____

Hiring Supervisor: _____

Student Job Title: *Cataloging and Classification Assistant III*

Grade (check one): ____ I ____ II _√_ III **Pay Rate:** _____

Degree of Responsibility (check one):

_____ Low _____ Moderate ___√___ High

Maximum Supervision Required (check one):

_____ General _____ Limited ___√___ Minimal

Duties and Responsibilities:
Perform bibliographic searching for books and serials in OCLC online database. Search and verify name/series in OCLC online database authority files. Input corrections made by cataloger to CIP records and, after revision, produce the cataloging record. May perform 050 (Library of Congress) copy cataloging on OCLC online database with revision. May train and/or coordinate and delegate assignments to lower graded student employees.

Required:
Computer literacy. Knowledge of Library of Congress classification system. Knowledge of OCLC online database.

Desired:
Knowledge of MARC format. Reading knowledge of one or more foreign language.

Fig. 4.33. Student job description.

Technical Services: Preorder Searching Assistant

Department: *Collection Development*

Section:

Hiring Supervisor:

Student Job Title: *Preorder Searching Assistant*

Grade (check one): √ I ___ II ___ III **Pay Rate:**

Degree of Responsibility (check one):

√ Low _____ Moderate _____ High

Maximum Supervision Required (check one):

√ General _____ Limited _____ Minimal

Duties and Responsibilities:
Performs basic duplicate and bibliographic searching of preselection cata-
logs and lists for monographs and serials using various manual files and
online databases. Answer phones, type/keyboard, photocopy, run errands,
and sort incoming and outgoing mail. Assists with special projects as
assigned.

Required:
Manual dexterity.

Desired:
Computer literacy.

Fig. 4.34. Student job description.

Technical Services: Gifts Assistant

Department: *Collection Development*

Section: *Gifts*

Hiring Supervisor:

Student Job Title: *Gifts Assistant*

Grade (check one): ____ I __√__ II ____ III **Pay Rate:** _____

Degree of Responsibility (check one):

_____ Low __√__ Moderate _____ High

Maximum Supervision Required (check one):

_____ General __√__ Limited _____ Minimal

Duties and Responsibilities:
Receive, count and sort gift books by subject to appropriate selector/ bibliographer. Perform duplicate searching of gift serials on library's integrated library system. Type and install gift donor plates in books. Prepare lists of non-selected gift materials available to other libraries. May perform serials shelf check to verify holdings. Answer phones, type/keyboard, photocopy, run errands, and sort incoming and outgoing mail. Assists with special projects as assigned.

Required:
Manual dexterity. Computer literacy. Ability to lift up to 40 lbs.

Desired:
Knowledge of library's integrated library system. Word processing skills.

Fig. 4.35. Student job description.

Technical Services: Serials Assistant I

Department: *Serials*

Section:

Hiring Supervisor:

Student Job Title: *Serials Assistant I*

Grade (check one): _√_ I ___ II ___ III **Pay Rate:**

Degree of Responsibility (check one):

_√_ Low _____ Moderate _____ High

Maximum Supervision Required (check one):

_√_ General _____ Limited _____ Minimal

Duties and Responsibilities:
Receive, sort, and distribute serials and/or mail. Prepare serials invoices for paying including date stamping and making extra copies as needed. Process superseded serials. Perform basic duplicate and bibliographic checking/searching for serials to be ordered in manual files and online databases. Answer phones, type/keyboard, photocopy, run errands, and sort incoming and outgoing mail.

Required:
Manual dexterity. Ability to lift up to 40 lbs.

Desired:
Computer literacy.

Fig. 4.36. Student job description.

Technical Services: Serials Assistant II

Department: *Serials* _____

Section: _____

Hiring Supervisor: _____

Student Job Title: *Serials Assistant II* _____

Grade (check one): ____ I _√_ II ____ III **Pay Rate:** _____

Degree of Responsibility (check one):

_____ Low __√__ Moderate _____ High

Maximum Supervision Required (check one):

_____ General __√__ Limited _____ Minimal

Duties and Responsibilities:
Process serials and newspapers including check-in on library's integrated library system, property stamp, security strip, and label. Place serials in to-be-shelved area. Route serials as assigned. Pull older newspapers from shelves for storage or recycling. Perform basic bibliographic checking/searching for serials to be ordered in manual files and online databases. Answer phones, type/keyboard, photocopy, run errands, and sort incoming and outgoing mail.

Required:
Manual dexterity. Computer literacy. Ability to lift up to 40 lbs.

Desired:
Knowledge of library's integrated library system.

Fig. 4.37. Student job description.

Technical Services: Serials Assistant III

Department: *Serials* _____

Section: _____

Hiring Supervisor: _____

Student Job Title: *Serials Assistant III* _____

Grade (check one): _____ I _____ II _√_ III **Pay Rate:** _____

Degree of Responsibility (check one):

_____ Low _____ Moderate __√__ High

Maximum Supervision Required (check one):

_____ General _____ Limited __√__ Minimal

Duties and Responsibilities:
Process serials including check-in on library's integrated library system, property stamp, security strip, and label. Place serials in to-be-shelved area. Route serials as assigned. Process serials that are classed separately and analyzed. Perform advanced bibliographic checking/searching for serials to be ordered in complex manual files and online databases. Verify series. Perform specialized technical tasks including the use of OCLC online database in searching routines and the creation of bibliographic/order records in the library's integrated library system. Answer phones. May train and/or coordinate and delegate assignments to lower graded student employees.

Required:
Manual dexterity. Computer literacy. Knowledge of library's integrated library system.

Desired:
Complex problem solving skills. Knowledge of OCLC online database.

Fig. 4.38. Student job description.

Technical Services: Bindery Assistant

Department: *Serials*

Section: *Bindery*

Hiring Supervisor:

Student Job Title: *Bindery Assistant*

Grade (check one): ____ I __√__ II ____ III **Pay Rate:** _____

Degree of Responsibility (check one):

_____ Low __√__ Moderate _____ High

Maximum Supervision Required (check one):

_____ General __√__ Limited _____ Minimal

Duties and Responsibilities:
Pull material to be bound, mostly periodicals. Update records on library's integrated library system when books and serials are checked-out and check-in for binding. Pack and unpack bound items and process paperwork. Perform in-house mending procedures including pamphlet binding, making boxes for brittle books, etc. Correct minor errors in the spine labels of bound materials. Order missing pages, verifies material received, and tips-in pages. Verify completeness of theses and dissertations and send to be bound and/or to be microfilmed. Answer phones, type/keyboard, photocopy, run errands, and sort incoming and outgoing mail.

Required:
Manual dexterity. Computer literacy. Ability to lift up to 40 lbs.

Desired:
Knowledge of library's integrated library system.

Fig. 4.39. Student job description.

Technical Services: Exchange Program Assistant

Department: *Serials* _____

Section: *Exchange Program* _____

Hiring Supervisor: _____

Student Job Title: *Exchange Program Assistant* _____

Grade (check one): ____ I ____ II _√_ III **Pay Rate:** _____

Degree of Responsibility (check one):

_____ Low _____ Moderate ___√___ High

Maximum Supervision Required (check one):

_____ General _____ Limited ___√___ Minimal

Duties and Responsibilities:
Responsible for maintenance activities of the materials exchange program. Compose correspondence to institutions proposing, modifying, and terminating exchange agreements (frequently in foreign languages, especially Spanish). Prepare and mail exchange material. Receive exchange material from other institutions and route it for processing. May act as a liaison with library subject selectors/bibliographers and other departments. Search manual and online library files and databases. Special projects as assigned. Answer phones, type/keyboard, photocopy, run errands, and sort incoming and outgoing mail.

Required:
Manual dexterity. Computer literacy. Typing for accuracy more than speed. Reading and writing knowledge of one foreign language, preferably Spanish. Ability to interact tactfully and efficiently with students, staff, and faculty members.

Desired:
Library experience. Additional foreign language reading ability.

Fig. 4.40. Student job description.

Technical Services: Systems Assistant I

Department: *Systems* _____

Section: _____

Hiring Supervisor: _____

Student Job Title: *Systems Assistant I* _____

Grade (check one): __√__ I ____ II ____ III **Pay Rate:** _____

Degree of Responsibility (check one):

__√__ Low _____ Moderate _____ High

Maximum Supervision Required (check one):

__√__ General _____ Limited _____ Minimal

Duties and Responsibilities:
Clean personal computers, printers, and terminals on a periodic basis. Assist in setup of personal computers and peripheral devices. Answer phones, type/keyboard, photocopy, run errands, and sort incoming and outgoing mail.

Required:
Customer service skills. Manual dexterity.

Desired:
Computer literacy.

Fig. 4.41. Student job description.

Technical Services: Systems Assistant II

Department: *Systems* _____

Section: _____

Hiring Supervisor: _____

Student Job Title: *Systems Assistant II* _____

Grade (check one): ____ I __√__ II ____ III **Pay Rate:** _____

Degree of Responsibility (check one):

_____ Low __√__ Moderate _____ High

Maximum Supervision Required (check one):

_____ General __√__ Limited _____ Minimal

Duties and Responsibilities:
Receive, unpack, and inspect personal computers, printers, terminals, etc.
Assist in setup of personal computers and peripheral devices. Install software upgrades on personal computers. Provide assistance and do basic
troubleshooting for computer hardware problems. Maintain an inventory of
personal computers, printers, and terminals. Special projects as assigned.
Answer phones, type/keyboard, photocopy, run errands, and sort incoming
and outgoing mail.

Required:
Knowledge with personal computer software and hardware. Mechanical
aptitude for minor computer equipment maintenance and repair. Ability to
interact tactfully and efficiently with students, staff, and faculty members.

Desired:
Ability to troubleshoot personal computer hardware and software problems.

Fig. 4.42. Student job description.

Technical Services: Systems Assistant III

Department: *Systems*

Section: _____

Hiring Supervisor: _____

Student Job Title: *Systems Assistant III*

Grade (check one): ____ I ____ II _√_ III **Pay Rate:** _____

Degree of Responsibility (check one):

_____ Low _____ Moderate __√__ High

Maximum Supervision Required (check one):

_____ General _____ Limited __√__ Minimal

Duties and Responsibilities:
Set up personal computers and peripheral devices. Install software upgrades on personal computers. Provide assistance and do troubleshooting for personal computer hardware and software problems. Maintenance of library's World Wide Web site. Special projects as assigned. Answer phones.

Required:
Advanced knowledge of computer software, hardware, and peripherals. Ability to troubleshoot personal computer hardware and software problems. Mechanical aptitude for minor computer equipment maintenance and repair. Ability to interact tactfully and efficiently with students, staff, and faculty members.

Desired:
Ability to write HTML. Local area network experience.

Fig. 4.43. Student job description.

JOB MATCHING

Job matching is simply the process of bringing together the work and the people in such a way that the requirements of the work are matched with the skills and abilities of the persons available to do that work. Some student employees are good at detailed work such as those tasks required in academic library acquisitions and cataloging departments; some are well organized and can coordinate the activities of other student workers; some prefer the routine or physical work of shelving; and some like the challenges and diversity of a service desk. No one is good at everything, but most people have one or two skills or abilities that are higher than average. When the right student is matched with the right job, the library will function more efficiently and each student employee will have an opportunity to excel.

STUDENT EMPLOYMENT APPLICATION FORM

To match student applicants effectively to student jobs, it is necessary to have an application form that solicits the kind of information you need to screen applicants. A generic example (see figure 4.44) of such a form follows.

Text continues on page 111.

STUDENT EMPLOYMENT APPLICATION

Application will remain on file for the current semester only. Please PRINT clearly.

Date of Application: _____ Date Available to Begin Work: _____

_____

Last Name   First Name   Middle Initial   Social Security Number

Current Address: _____

Daytime Phone No.: _____ Best Time To Call: _____

E-mail address: _____

Cell Phone No./Pager: _____

Academic Major: _____ Minor: _____

Year in School (check one) FR _____ SO _____ JR _____ SR _____ Grad _____

Anticipated Graduation Date: _____ Amount of Award: _____

How many hours per week do you want to work? _____

Please list the times when you will be available to work. Notify this office of any changes.

Monday: _____

Tuesday: _____

Wednesday: _____

Thursday: _____

Friday: _____

Saturday: _____

Sunday: _____

Fig. 4.44 continues on page 110.

Library Experience: _____

_____

_____

_____

_____

Other Experience: _____

_____

_____

Skills (such as computer, language, office, etc.): _____

_____

_____

Preferred Position(s) at the Library:

1. _____

2. _____

3. _____

References (name, address, phone number[s]):

1. _____

2. _____

3. _____

Thank you.

Fig. 4.44. Student employment application.

SUMMARY

The organizing function is extremely important to supervision. You must know what you expect of student employees, just as they must know what you expect of them. The job description provides structure and lays the groundwork for everything that follows—compensation, training, and evaluation. Continuous re-evaluation of the tasks performed and of the work distribution is critical and should be done annually to keep job descriptions accurate and up-to-date.

BIBLIOGRAPHY

Boone, Morell D., Sandra G. Yee, and Rita Bullard. *Training Student Library Assistants*. Chicago: American Library Association, 1991.

Creth, Sheila. "Personnel Planning, Job Analysis, and Job Evaluation with Special Reference to Academic Libraries." *Advances in Librarianship* 12 (1982): 47–97.

Gael, S. *Job Analysis: A Guide to Assessing Work Activities*. San Francisco: Jossey-Bass, 1983.

Hill, Virginia S., and Tom G. Watson. "Job Analysis: Process and Benefits." *Advances in Library Administration and Organization* 3 (1984): 209–19.

———. *Job Analysis in ARL Libraries*. Washington, D.C.: Association of Research Libraries/Office of Management Services, 1987.

Kathman, Michael D., and Jane McGurn Kathman, comp. *Managing Student Employees in College Libraries*. Chicago: American Library Association, 1994.

Klingner, Donald E. "When the Traditional Job Description Is Not Enough." *Personnel Journal* 58 (April 1979): 243–48.

McCormick, Ernest J. *Job Analysis: Methods and Applications*. New York: AMACOM, 1979.

Mussman, K. "Socio-technical Theory and Job Design in Libraries." *College and Research Libraries* 39 (January 1978): 20–28.

———. *Personnel Classification Schemes*. Washington, D.C.: Association of Research Libraries/Office of Management Services, 1978.

Russell, Thyra Kaye. *Student Employment Programs in ARL Libraries*. Washington, D.C.: Association of Research Libraries/Office of Management Services, 1990. (SPEC Kit #168).

———. "Student Employment Manuals." *Journal of Library Administration* 21 (1995): 95–108.

Van Rijn, Paul. *Job Analysis for Selection: An Overview*. Washington, D.C.: U.S. Office of Personnel Management, Staffing Services Group, 1979.

Chapter Five

UNDERSTANDING STUDENT FINANCIAL AID

I ain't ever had a job.
I just always played
baseball.

—Satchel Paige

FEDERAL AID FOR STUDENT EMPLOYMENT

The majority of students employed in academic libraries will receive some type of federal or state administered financial aid. The predominant source of funding, administered by each university, is provided by the U.S. Department of Education (USDE) although there are other federal and state agencies which may also provide financial aid to eligible students (see figure 5.1).[1] Many of those programs, however, are geared towards students who qualify for academic or special scholarship programs. Currently, more than 9,800 (see figure 5.1) colleges and universities participate in one or more of the programs offered by the USDE; however, many colleges and universities still do not participate at all.[2]

Academic libraries generally vie for the distinction of being the largest undergraduate and graduate student employers on campus. Therefore it is essential that supervisors of student employees possess a fundamental understanding of their respective college or university's student financial aid system. It is especially necessary that supervisors understand some of the major financial aid programs, particularly those sponsored by the federal government, and how their students qualify for and receive their financial assistance.

In this chapter, many of the federal student financial aid programs offered by the USDE will be described. Although the basic provisions of each program have remained intact since the Higher Education Act of 1965 created them, the reader is advised that frequent revisions regarding funding, Expected Family Contributions (EFC) and other eligibility factors are made by the USDE and Congress regularly. Before advising student employees on federal student aid programs, consult your on-campus student employment office and its chief Financial Aid Advisor (FAA).

Note that there are several financial aid services which advertise themselves as "the source" to aid students and their parents in locating financial aid resources. Although many of these services are legitimate and can be of some value and assistance, particularly in locating private, corporate and endowment funds, caution should be used. Those services found exclusively on the Internet should be carefully scrutinized because they may provide information for a fee which, in some cases, can be found free of charge at other Internet sites. The motto when using any financial aid service is *caveat emptor*.

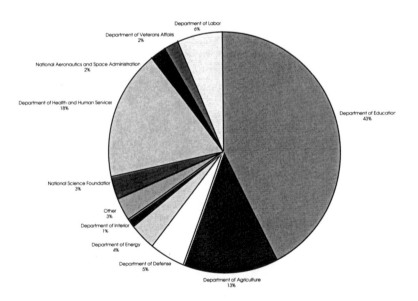

Fig. 5.1. Federal on-budget funds for education, by agency: Fiscal Year 1997.

FEDERAL STUDENT AID PROGRAMS

The U.S. Congress built the foundation of the current student financial aid program by enacting the Higher Education Act of 1965 (PL 89–329, 79 STAT 1219), specifically in Title IV of the Act. Throughout the past 30-plus years, numerous changes have been made through amendments to the original Act.[3] Currently, the Office of Postsecondary Education (OPSE), Student Financial Assistance Programs (SFAP) of the USDE administers the Federal Pell Grant Program, campus-based programs such as the Federal Perkins Loan (Perkins Loan) Program, the Federal Work-Study (FWS) Program, the Federal Supplemental Educational Opportunity Grant (FSEOG) Program, the William D. Ford Federal Direct Loan (Direct Loan) Program, which also includes the Federal Parent Loans to Undergraduate (PLUS) Program, the Federal Direct Stafford Loans Program, the Federal Family Education Loans (FFELs), which includes the Federal Stafford Loans, the Federal PLUS Loans, and the State Grant and Scholarship Program. For the 1997–98 fiscal year, the SFAP distributed approximately $42.8 billion in aid to over 7.6 million students.

Grants (Pell Grants and FSEOGs) do not have to be repaid. Loans (Perkins, Direct, PLUS, Stafford, and FFELs) must be repaid. The FWS program provides eligible students with income from part-time jobs.

Each of these programs is described in this chapter. With the exception of the loan programs, a student must demonstrate financial need to receive assistance from a SFAP program.

INDEPENDENT STUDENT DEFINITION
FOR ELIGIBILITY DETERMINATION

In determining financial need for the independent student, the needs analysis has assumed that a certain amount of financial assistance will be forthcoming from the student's parents. Naturally, there are exceptions, such as an older, nontraditional student or those no longer in contact with their parents. The Higher Education Act Amendments of 1986 and 1992 (PL 96–149 and PL 102–325 respectively) redefined the concept of an independent student and provided student aid counselors and administrators with criteria to allow for exceptions for independent students (even though they do not meet the definition of the law).

For the 1998–99 award year, the following is the standard by which independence is determined:[4]

♦ The student was born before January 1, 1975.

♦ The student is a veteran of the U.S. Armed Forces.

♦ The student will be enrolled in a graduate or professional program (beyond a bachelor's degree) in the current academic year.

♦ The student is a ward of the Court (or was a ward of the Court until the age of 18) or both parents are deceased and the student has no adoptive or legal guardian(s).

♦ The student is legally married on the date the student signs the application.

♦ The student has legal dependents other than a spouse.

A student may also be considered independent if the school can document that:

♦ a legal restraining order has been issued against both parents of the student because of abusive behavior;

♦ both parents of the student have been incarcerated;

♦ the student's parents live in another country and the student has been, or is in the process of being, granted refugee status by the U.S. Immigration and Naturalization Service;

♦ both parents of the student live in a country where they cannot easily leave or get money out; and

♦ the student can provide adequate documentation to satisfy the financial aid administer that the student is truly self-supporting for the financial aid administrator (FAA) to override the student's dependency status.[5]

Some financial aid administrators may require proof of annual income of $10,000 or more. Naturally, it is best to check with your school's chief financial aid administrator to ascertain the school's requirements.

Additionally, a student will not qualify for independent status simply because the student's parents have decided not to claim the student as an exemption on their tax returns or refuse to provide the student financial support. In the past, an income of $4,000 or two successive years of not being claimed as a tax exemption sufficed. If you are reviewing several financial aid guidebooks, these old criteria may still be referenced but they are no longer valid.

Terms used in the independent student definition:

♦ CUSTODIAL PARENT: If a student's parents are divorced or separated, the custodial parent is the one whom the student has lived with the most during the past 12 months. The student's need analysis is based primarily on information supplied by the custodial parent.

♦ LEGAL DEPENDENT: Any person who lives with the student, receives more than half-support from the student, and will continue to receive more than half-support from the student during the award year. Also, the natural or adopted child of the student, or a child for whom the student is the legal guardian, if the child receives more than half-support from the student (the child does not have to live with the student).

♦ OVER 23 YEARS OF AGE: A student who was at least 24 years old on December 31, 1975.

♦ PARENT: A natural, adoptive, foster, or step-parent or legal guardian who has been appointed by a court and directed to use his or her financial resources to support the student.

♦ PROFESSIONAL JUDGMENT: For need-based federal aid programs, the financial aid administrator (FAA) can adjust the Expected Family Contribution (EFC), adjust the Cost of Attendance (COA), or change the dependency status (with appropriate documentation) when extenuating circumstances exist.

♦ PROFESSIONAL STUDENT: A student in pursuit of an advanced degree in law or medicine.

♦ RESOURCES: Includes not only traditional sources of income (such as wages, salaries, tips, interest and dividend income, untaxed income and benefits, fellowships, and veterans' cash benefits) but also any student financial aid (except

PLUS loans) and personal long-term cash loans used for education purposes. These resources, of course, do not include any support from the student's parents.

The SFA programs are intended to provide student financial aid to financially challenged students who are in one of the following categories:[6]

- ◆ A U.S. citizen or national. The term *national* includes citizens of American Somoa and Swain's Island.

- ◆ A U.S. permanent resident. A permanent resident's citizenship status should be evidenced by a comment on output documents noting that the Immigration and Naturalization Service (INS) match has been successful. If no such evidence is available, the permanent residence must provide the school with verifying INS documentation.

- ◆ Citizens of certain Pacific Islands. Eligible citizens of the Republic of the Marshall Islands, the Federated States of Micronesia, or the Republic of Palau may received only three types of SFA program aid:

    Federal Pell grants

    Federal Supplemental Education Opportunity Grants

    Federal Work-Study funds

- ◆ Other eligible noncitizens include refugees or persons granted asylum, Cuban-Haitian entrants, and others who can provide his or her school with INS documentation indicating that they are in the United States with the intention of becoming U.S. citizens or permanent residents.

Table 5.1 describes the eligibility requirements for the seven federal student financial aid programs.[7]

Table 5.1. Eligibility Requirements for Federal Student Financial Aid

REQUIREMENTS	PELL	FFELP	FSEOG	FWS	PERKINS	DIRECT	PLUS
Undergraduate	YES	YES	YES	YES	YES	YES	YES
Graduate	NO	YES	NO	YES	YES	YES	NO
At least 1/2 time	NO	YES	YES	YES	YES	YES	YES
Must pay back	NO	YES	NO	NO	YES	YES	YES
U.S. citizen or eligible non-citizen	YES	YES	YES	YES	YES	YES	YES
Registered with Selective Service (if applicable)	YES	YES	YES	YES	YES	YES	YES
Have financial need	YES	YES	YES	YES	YES	YES	NO
Attend participating school	YES	YES	YES	YES	YES	NO*	YES
Working toward a degree or certificate	YES	YES	YES	YES	YES	YES	YES
Making satisfactory academic progress	YES	YES	YES	YES	YES	YES	YES
Not in default or owe a refund on a federal grant or loan	YES	YES	YES	YES	YES	YES	YES
Having a bachelor's degree makes student ineligible	YES	NO	YES	NO	NO	NO	YES
Conviction of drug distribution or possession may make student ineligible	YES	YES	YES	YES	YES	YES	YES

PELL—Pell Grants

FWS—Federal Work-Study Program

FSEOG—Supplemental Educational Opportunity Grants (NDSL) Program

FFELP—Federal Family Education Loans (FFELs) Program
(authorized under Title IV Higher Education Act in conjunction with
Student Loan Reform Act of 1993—PL 103 66, 312, 107 Stat)

*Must be taking coursework for enrollment in an eligible program

Cost of Attendance

By definition, except as noted below, a student's Cost of Attendance (COA) is the sum of the following:

- ◆ tuition and fees normally assessed a student carrying the same academic workload, including costs for rental or purchase of equipment, materials, or supplies required of all students in the same course of study;

- ◆ an allowance for books, supplies, transportation, and miscellaneous personal expenses;

- ◆ for a student without dependents living at home with parents, an allowance for room and board of not less than $1,500; or, for a student without dependents living in institutionally owned or operated housing, a standard allowance for room and board based on the amount normally assessed most residents; or, for all other students, an allowance of not less than $2,500 based on reasonably incurred room and board expenses for such students;

- ◆ for students with dependents, an allowance based on the estimated actual expenses incurred for dependent care (during periods including but not limited to class time, study time, field work, internships, and commuting time for students) based on the number and age of each dependent, not to exceed the reasonable cost in the community in which the student resides;

- ◆ for study abroad programs that are approved by the student's home institution, reasonable costs associated with such study;

- ◆ for a student with a disability, an allowance for expenses related to the student's disability including special services, personal assistance, transportation, equipment, and supplies that are reasonably incurred and not approved for by other agencies;

- ◆ for students placed in work experience under a cooperative education program, an allowance for reasonable costs associated with such employment; and

- ◆ for students receiving SFA loans, the fees required to receive them. The school may also include the fees required for nonfederal student loans as well. In all cases, the school can either use the exact loan fees charged to the student or an average of fees charged to borrowers of the same type of loan at that school.

Exceptions:

♦ Less than half-time students' COA can include only tuition and fees, an allowance for books, supplies, and transportation, and an allowance for dependent care expenses in accordance with the fourth item above.

♦ Incarcerated students may have an allowance for tuition and fees and, if required, books and supplies. No other expenses can be included. An incarcerated student is ineligible to receive an SFA loan. If the student is incarcerated in a federal or state penal institution, he or she may not receive a Pell Grant.

♦ Correspondence study students can include only tuition and fees. However, if the student is fulfilling a required period of residential training, the student's cost of attendance can also include required books, supplies, travel, and room and board costs specifically incurred.

♦ Students receiving instruction by telecommunications receive no distinction regarding the mode of instruction in determining costs, except the cost of rental or the purchase of equipment cannot be included as an element of the COA. However, if the financial aid administrator determines using his or her professional judgment under section 479A of the Higher Education Act of 1965, as amended, that a course of instruction offered via telecommunications results in a substantially reduced COA to the student, the financial aid administrator must reduce the student's eligibility for grants, loans, or work-study assistance.

Expected Family Contribution (EFC)

The Expected Family Contribution (EFC) is the amount of financial assistance that a family can be expected to contribute toward a student's educational costs. By comparing the EFC to the student's actual cost of attendance (COA), the financial aid advisor can determine the student's financial need for federal assistance from the USDE and other available sources. The EFC formula is used to determine need for assistance for the following Student Financial Assistance Programs:

◆ Federal Pell Grant

◆ Subsidized Stafford Loan (under the Direct Loan Program and the Federal Family Education Loan Program)

◆ Campus-based programs

◆ Federal Supplemental Educational Opportunity Grants

◆ Federal Perkins Loans

◆ Federal Work-Study Programs

The methodology for determining the EFC is contained in Part F, Title IV, Higher Education Act of 1965, as amended. Updated tables for each award year are also published in the *Federal Register,* usually at the end of May, with any corrections appearing in late August.

All data used to calculate a student's EFC comes from the information provided on the USDE Free Application for Federal Student Aid (FAFSA). The student can submit the FAFSA through the Internet by using *FAFSA on the Web,* with the FAFSA Express software, by filing an application electronically at schools that participate in the USDE Electronic Data Exchange (EDE), or by mailing a paper copy of the FAFSA to the USDE. A student who applied for federal student aid the previous award year may be eligible to apply by filing a Renewal FAFSA either by using a paper renewal application mailed to the student's permanent home address or by using the Internet (*FAFSA on the Web*). Applying for federal student aid is free of charge. However, if one is to be considered for nonfederal aid such as institutional aid, a student may have to fill out additional forms and pay a processing fee.

The student's FAFSA information form is sent to a federal central processing system where the EFC is computed from the information provided on the form. Upon completion, each student will receive a Student Aid Report (SAR) that reports the information from the student's application, and if the information provided was correct and the form completely filled out, the student's EFC. The student is advised to check the FAFSA completely prior to submission as well as to check the accuracy of the data contained on the SAR. If corrections to the SAR are necessary, a student's school may submit them electronically (only if the school participates in the EDE program). If the corrections are submitted by mail, using the FAFSA Express, or by using *FAFSA on the Web*, the student may make the necessary corrections on Part 2 of the SAR and return it to the address given at the end of Part 2. If the student has applied electronically through school and would like to make corrections to the initial information supplied by mail, he or she must request a copy of the submitted SAR from the Federal Student Aid Information Center (1-800-433-3243).

FINANCIAL AID ADMINISTRATOR

The Financial Aid Administrator (FAA) is a college or university employee who is involved in the administration of financial aid. Sometimes referred to as a Financial Aid Advisor or a Financial Aid Counselor, he or she is responsible for ensuring the consistency of information submitted at the federal level at that institution regarding a student's eligibility. That individual must also be aware of all sources of aid at that institution and must be able to coordinate with all financial aid programs an institution offers to ensure that a student's aid does not exceed his or her need. The FAA can make individual judgments, based on his or her professional judgment, to override a student's dependency status (from dependent to independent), to adjust the components of a student's Cost of Attendance (COA), and to adjust the data elements used to calculate the student's EFC.

FEDERAL PELL GRANTS

The Federal Pell Grants (FPG) Program is a unique type of federal assistance in that a student's eligibility for a FPG is not based on the availability of funds at the student's school. The USDE provides funds to each participating school to pay eligible students and can increase a school's initial authorization when necessary. Because the USDE pays the award, the school has no responsibility in determining or selecting eligible students. However, the school must ensure that each student meet the FPG eligibility requirements.[8] The student must be an undergraduate and the award is based on the student's EFC and cost of attendance. The 1998–99 award maximum is $3,000.

FEDERAL FAMILY EDUCATION LOAN (FFEL) PROGRAM

Part B of Title IV of the Higher Education Act (HEA) of 1965, as amended, established the guaranteed student loan programs. PL 102-325 (HEA Amendments of 1992) brought together the various loan programs and renamed them the Federal Family Education Loan Program. The FFEL is now comprised of:

- ♦ Federal Stafford Loans (formerly the Guaranteed Student Loans Program)

- ♦ Federal Unsubsidized Stafford Loans

- ♦ Federal PLUS Loans

- ♦ Federal Consolidated Loans

The FFEL provides long-term loans to students attending colleges, universities, vocational, technical, business, and trade schools along with some foreign school attendance.

State or private nonprofit lenders provide the loan principle for FFELs. The federal government guarantees these loans and if the loan is defaulted, the guaranty agency is reimbursed by the federal government. The federal guaranty replaces the collateral (security) usually required to secure a loan of this nature.

Schools certify student eligibility, which is then forwarded to the lender for loan approval. Once approved, the lender sends the loan amount to the borrower's school, which distributes the loan in two equal parts. Loans come in the form of *subsidized* or *unsubsidized*. A subsidized loan is one where the federal government pays the accruing interest on the loan while the borrower is in school, or during certain grace or deferment periods. Unsubsidized loans, on the other hand, accrue interest from the date of origination and the repayment of the interest is the borrower's responsibility.

Federal Stafford Loans provide low-interest, variable rate (rate is dependent on the lender institution) loans to borrowers proving a financial need. Federal Unsubsidized Stafford Loans are available to undergraduate or graduate students regardless of financial need. Interest accrues from the date or origination, during in-school, grace, or deferment periods; the borrower is responsible for repayment.

Federal Plus Loans are designed for parents without adverse credit history. These loans enable parents to pay for educational expenses for each child, regardless of financial need. Federal Consolidated Loans enable a borrower with loans from various lenders or loan programs to consolidate their loans into one. The lender repays the existing loans and establishes a new loan that has one interest rate and repayment schedule. Loans eligible for consolidation include all FFELs, Perkins, and Select Public Health loans.

WILLIAM D. FORD FEDERAL DIRECT LOAN PROGRAM

The William D. Ford Federal Direct Loan (DL) Program completes the loan programs funded and administrated by the federal government. Four types of loans are found in the DL Program:

♦ Federal Direct Plus Loan Program

♦ Federal Direct Consolidated Loan Program

♦ Federal Direct Stafford/Ford Loan Program

♦ Federal Direct Unsubsidized Stafford/Ford Loan Program

The DL Programs were authorized under Title IV of the Higher Education Act of 1965 with the enactment of the Student Loan Reform Act of 1993. The DL is a primary source of federal assistance providing loans to eligible borrowers to help defray the expense of postsecondary education. The program uses loan capital that is provided by the federal government, requires only one aid application, and makes loans available directly through participating institutions rather than through private lenders or guaranty agencies (such is the case with the FFELs).

Like the FFEL Program, the DL Program provides eligible borrowers who have an outstanding balance on either DL's or FFEL loans and are unable to obtain an FFEL Consolidation Loan. The individuals must be currently enrolled in school or in a repayment status. Individuals in default may also qualify if they have made satisfactory arrangements to repay existing loans or if they agree to pay or repay loans under the Income Contingent Repayment Plan (ICRP).[9]

The Federal Direct Plus Loan Program (FDPL) is similar to the FDPL administered in the FFEL Program. Parents without an adverse credit history may borrow on behalf of a dependent postsecondary student. The borrower is responsible for the accruing interest and parents may borrow regardless of need. Loans are originated at the participating institution with funds provided by the federal government; in this particular case the sole lender is the USDE. Borrowers repay the USDE directly and the same terms and conditions apply here as they do with loans originating in the FFEL Program.

The Federal Direct Consolidated Loan Program is for individual borrowers who have an outstanding balance on either a DL or FFEL and are unable to obtain a FFEL Consolidated Loan. The individual borrower must be enrolled in school or in a repayment status. Borrowers in default may also qualify if they have made satisfactory arrangements to repay those loans or agree to repay them under the terms described in the ICRP. This loan combines one or more federal education loans into a single loan. Loans eligible for consolidation include those originating with the FFEL Program, the DL Program, the Federal Perkins Loan Program, and Select Public Health Loans.

The Federal Direct Stafford/Ford Loan Program is designed for individuals who are undergraduate, vocational, or graduate students and have been accepted and are enrolled at least part-time at a participating institution. These loans differ from others within the DL Program in that the federal government pays the accruing interest on the loan(s) while the borrower is in school or during a grace or deferment period. Borrowers must demonstrate a financial need. The loans originate from the participating institution with funds appropriated by the federal government. The USDE is the sole lender and the borrower repays them directly. Many of the same terms and conditions which exist in the FFEL Program are applicable to this program.

The Federal Direct Unsubsidized Stafford/Ford Loan Program is designed for undergraduate, vocational, or graduate students who have been accepted at a participating institution and are enrolled at least part-time. These loans require the borrower to pay all accruing interest including in-school, grace, and deferment periods. However, these loans are available regardless of the borrower's financial need. Loans originate at the participating institution with funds appropriated by the federal government. The USDE is the sole lender and borrowers repay them directly. Many of the same terms and conditions which exist in the FFEL Program are applicable to this program.

CAMPUS-BASED STUDENT FINANCIAL AID PROGRAMS

Campus-based aid programs include the Federal Supplemental Educational Opportunity Grants (FSEOG) Program, the Federal Work-Study (FWS) Program, and the Perkins Loan Program (a.k.a. the National Direct Student Loan [NDSL] Program). They are considered `campus-based' because each participating school or university is responsible for the administration of these programs on its campus. The FAA ensures that funds are furnished to eligible students in accordance with the provisions of the laws and regulations and in cooperation with the Secretary of Education and the USDE. Unlike the Pell Grants, the FFEL Program, and the DL Programs, student eligibility does depend on the availability of funds at each participating institution.

Participating institutions apply for and receive funds directly from the USDE. Each institution must file a Fiscal Operations Report and Application to Participate form for each award year. Participants receive funding based on statutory formulas established each year by Congress. The institution's FAA is responsible for ensuring that eligible students receive program funds.

FEDERAL SUPPLEMENTAL EDUCATIONAL OPPORTUNITIES GRANT PROGRAM

The Federal Supplemental Educational Opportunities Grant (FSEOG) Program was one of the first major federal student aid programs authorized under Title IV of the Higher Education Act of 1965, as amended. The purpose of the FSEOG Program is to encourage schools to provide grants, not loans, to eligible undergraduate applicants with exceptional financial need. A school must make FSEOG Program funds reasonably available to all eligible students, although those who have the lowest EFC will be given first priority.

Along with the other eligibility requirements outlined earlier in this chapter, FSEOG eligible students:

♦ must be enrolled in an undergraduate or vocational course of study at an institution of higher education;

♦ have not earned a bachelor's or first professional degree;

♦ will be considered eligible for only the first four academic years, regardless of length of program;

♦ must have a demonstrated financial need.

FSEOG allocations are based on the institutional request for program funding first on the basis of the institution's 1985 fiscal year program allocation. Each institution is then awarded additional funds on the basis of the aggregate need of eligible students in attendance.

THE FEDERAL WORK-STUDY (FWS) PROGRAM

One of the most commonly known sources of funding for student employees in academic libraries is the Federal Work-Study (FWS) Program. Although Congress has debated recently about the need to continue to appropriate funds at current levels for this program, academic libraries still rely heavily on FWS eligible students to perform a myriad of duties and tasks essential to the daily operations of an academic library.

The FWS program provides funds to be earned by eligible undergraduate or graduate students through part-time employment that helps assist in financing the costs of a postsecondary education. FAA's at participating institutions have considerable flexibility in determining the amount of work-study awards given to eligible students. The hourly wage rate cannot be less than the established federal minimal wage rate.

Institutional allocations are based on institutional requests for program funding under statutory formula. Like the FSEOG Program, funds are distributed to institutions on the basis of the institution's 1985 fiscal year allocation and then on the basis of the aggregate need of the number of eligible students in attendance. Employers of work-study recipients must match a 25 percent funding formula; the remaining 75 percent is provided though federal funding. The exception to this 3:1 ratio is in the case of private, for-profit organizations, which must provide 50 percent of the funding, and in America Reads positions, for which the matching requirement is waived.

Financial need is determined by a USDE standard formula, which has been established by Congress. Along with the EFC, the fundamental elements in the standard formula are the student's, and in the case of dependent students, the parent's income and assets, the family's household size, and the number of family members attending postsecondary institutions. Different assessment rates and allowances are established for dependent students, independent students without dependents, and independent students with dependents.

A participating institution must make FWS jobs reasonably available to all eligible participants. Also, to the extent possible, the institution must also make "equivalent employment"[10] available to all students at the institution who wish to work. To the extent possible and practical, each participating institution must provide FWS jobs that will complement and reinforce each recipient's education or career goals.

FWS jobs may be on or off campus. Off-campus jobs must be in the public interest if the work involved is for a federal, state, or local public agency or for a private, nonprofit organization. An institution may wish to allocate part of its FWS award to provide jobs in private for-profit organizations. Also, FWS employment may be used for community service programs. Some of these programs include:

- ◆ fields such as health care, child care, literacy training, education (including tutorial services), welfare, social services, transportation, housing and neighborhood improvement, public safety, crime prevention and control, recreation, rural development, and community improvement;

- ◆ work in service opportunities or youth corps as defined in Section 101 of the National and Community Service Act of 1990, and service in the agencies, institutions, and activities designated in Section 124(a) of that act;

- ◆ support for students (other than for an institution's own students) with disabilities; and

- ◆ activities in which an FWS student serves as mentor for such purposes as tutoring, supporting educational and recreational activities, and counseling, including career counseling.

In assigning FWS jobs, each institution must consider the student's financial need, the number of hours per week the student can work, the period of employment, the anticipated wage rate, and the amount of other assistance available to each eligible participant. Although no minimum or maximum award limits are established, the amount for each student is determined based on the above mentioned factors.

Each FWS position should have a job description that includes the following:

- the name and address of the student's employer (department, public agency, nonprofit organization);

- the purpose of the student's job;

- the student's duties and responsibilities;

- the job qualifications;

- the job's wage rate or range;

- the length of the student's employment (beginning and ending dates); and

- the name of the student's supervisor.

The job description should:

- clearly define whether the job qualifies under the FWS Program;

- provide the information needed to explain the position to a student and to help him or her select the type of employment most closely related to his or her educational or career objectives;

- help the financial aid administrator (FAA), the student, and the supervisor determine the number of hours of work required at the specified wage rate to meet a student's financial need; and

- establish a written record, for both student and employer, of the job's duties and responsibilities so that there will be no misunderstanding.

Employment Conditions and Limitations

The provisions discussed below apply to all work under FWS, whether on or off campus.

- FWS employment must be governed by employment conditions, including pay, that are reasonable according to the type of work performed, the geographic region, the employee's proficiency, and any applicable federal, state, or local law.

♦ FWS employers must pay students at least the current federal minimum wage.

♦ FWS employment must not displace employees (including those on strike) or impair existing service contracts. If the school has an employment agreement with an organization in the private sector, the organization's employees must not be replaced with FWS students. Replacement is interpreted as displacement.

♦ FWS positions must not involve constructing, operating, or maintaining any part of a building used for religious worship or sectarian instruction.

♦ Neither a school nor an outside employer that has an agreement with the school to hire FWS students may solicit, accept, or permit soliciting any fee, commission, contribution, or gift as a condition for student's FWS employment. A student may pay union dues to an employer if they are a condition of employment and the employer's non FWS employees also pay dues.

♦ The Fair Labor Standards Act of 1938, as amended, prohibits employers (including schools) from accepting voluntary services from any paid employee; any FWS student must be paid for all hours worked.

♦ A FWS student may not be paid for receiving instruction in a classroom, laboratory, or other academic setting. However, the fact that a FWS student may receive academic credit from the work performed does not disqualify the job under FWS.

♦ A FWS student's wages may be garnished only to pay any costs of attendance that the student owes the school or that will become due and payable during the period of the award.

Undergraduate students are paid FWS wages on an hourly basis only. Graduate students may be paid by the hour or may be paid a salary. Regardless of who employs the student, the school is responsible for making sure the student is paid for the work performed.

The school should determine the number of hours a student works based on the student's financial need and on how the combination of work and study hours will impact the student's health and academic progress. There are no statutory or regulatory limits on the number of hours per week or pay period a FWS student may work. The only factor one needs to keep in mind is that a FWS may not work more hours than the award for which he or she has been given.

A FWS student must be paid at least the current federal minimum wage. While there is no maximum wage rate, it is not permissible to pay a lower subminimum or training wage to FWS students. A school may not include fringe benefits as part of the compensation package and may not pay a FWS student commissions or fees. In determining an appropriate rate, the school must consider:

♦ the skills needed to perform the job;

♦ how much persons with those skills are paid in the local area for performing similar types of work;

♦ rates the school would normally pay similar non-FWS employees; and

♦ any applicable federal, state, or local laws that require a specific wage rate.

A FWS student's need places a ceiling on the total earnings allowable but has no bearing on his or her wage rate. It is not permissible to base the wage rate on need or on any other factor not related to the student's skills or job description. If a FWS student's skill level depends on his or her academic advancement, the school may pay a student on that basis. However, students who perform jobs that are comparable to those of other employees should be paid comparable wages, whether the other employees are students at different class levels or are regular employees.

FWS students may be employed during summer, or equivalent vacation periods, if the student is planning to enroll for the next regular session. Some universities require that FWS students enroll for at least a minimum number of hours in the summer to maintain their eligibility. Additionally, some schools may require that, to maintain summer eligibility, a student pre-enroll for a minimum number of hours in the fall semester. During the regular academic year, FWS students must be at least half-time students in order to qualify for FWS jobs.

WORK-COLLEGES PROGRAM

The Higher Education Act Amendments of 1992 authorized the Work-Colleges Program. Schools that satisfy the definition of *work college* may apply with the USDA to participate in the program. An eligible institution may transfer funds from its allocation for the FWS Program and/or the Federal Perkins Loan Program to provide funding for the Work-Colleges Program.

The Work-Colleges Program views and values the use of comprehensive work-learning programs as a valuable educational approach. When used as a part of a school's educational program or as a financial plan that decreases the institutions reliance on grants and loans, the institution may also qualify for this program. This program also encourages student participation in community service activities.

Work College is defined as an eligible institution that:

♦ is a public or private nonprofit school with a commitment to community service;

♦ has operated a comprehensive work-learning program for at least two years;

♦ provides students participating in the comprehensive work-learning program with the opportunity to contribute to their education as well as to the welfare of the community;

♦ requires all students who reside on campus to participate in a comprehensive work-learning program; and

♦ requires providing services as a integral part of the school's education program and as part of the school's educational philosophy.

A comprehensive student work-learning program is defined as a student work/service program that:

♦ is an integral and stated part of the institution's educational philosophy and program;

♦ requires participation of all resident students for enrollment, participation, and graduation;

♦ includes learning objectives, evaluation, and a record of work performance as part of the student's college record;

♦ provides programmatic leadership by college personnel at levels comparable to traditional academic programs;

♦ recognizes the educational role of work-learning supervisors; and

♦ includes consequences for nonperformance or failure in the work-learning program similar to the consequences for failure in the regular academic program.

FEDERAL PERKINS LOAN PROGRAM

The Federal Perkins Loan Program allocations are made to eligible institutions for the purpose of providing low-interest loans to needy undergraduate and graduate students attending that institution. Loans under this program include the Federal Perkins Loan, the National Direct Student Loans, and the National Defense Student Loans. Named to honor the late Carl D. Perkins (D-KY), the former Chairman of the House Education and Labor Committee, the Federal Perkins Loan Program replaces the National Direct Student Loan program in the 1987–88 award year.

To be eligible, undergraduate or graduate students must demonstrate exceptional financial need. The loan is provided from government funds plus a shared contribution by the institution. The institution must also take into consideration evidence related to the student's willingness to repay the loan. A default on previous loans or a history of unpaid debt may render a student ineligible. The fundamental difference between a Federal Perkins Loan and other federal loan programs is that the institution acts as the lender and the loan must be repaid directly to the institution.

STATE STUDENT INCENTIVE GRANTS PROGRAM

The State Student Incentive Grants (SSIG) Program provides grants to states to assist them in providing need-based grant and work-study assistance to eligible postsecondary students. States must administer the SSIG Program under a single state agency and adhere to maintenance of effort criteria. Undergraduate and graduate students demonstrating substantial financial need may apply to the states in which they are permanent residents. The SSIG Program provides funds to the 50 states, the District of Columbia, Puerto Rico, the Virgin Islands, American Samoa, Guam, the Northern Mariana Islands, and the Republic of Palau.

Each state's allocation is based on its relative share of the total national population of "students eligible to participate" in the SSIG Program. If an SSIG appropriation falls below 1979 established levels, each state impacted is allocated an amount proportional to the amount of funds it received in 1979. States must match SSIG grants on a 50/50 ratio with the state funds coming directly from state appropriated money. If a state does not use its entire allotment, the excess funds are distributed to other states in a similar proportion as the original distribution.

The SSIG Program in various states is known by a variety of names and may not even contain the words "student incentive grants" in their program titles. A student who wishes to apply for SSIG Program funding or has questions regarding eligibility or award procedures should contact the appropriate education assistance agency in his or her state.[11]

NATIONAL EARLY INTERVENTION SCHOLARSHIP AND PARTNERSHIP PROGRAM

The Higher Education Amendments of 1992 authorized funds for the establishment of the National Early Intervention Scholarship and Partnership (NEISP) Program. Under this program, states carry out activities of both an early intervention component and a scholarship component.

Under the NEISP Program, the Secretary of Education provides states with grants that encourage them to provide or to maintain guaranteed amounts of financial assistance necessary to provide eligible low-income students who have obtained a high school diploma or its equivalent to attend a postsecondary institution. The NEISP Program also provides financial incentives to enable states, in cooperation with local educational agencies, institutions of higher education, community organizations, and businesses, to provide a variety of early intervention services.

Those services can include providing additional counseling, mentoring, academic support, outreach, and support services to pre-school, elementary, middle, and secondary school students who are at risk of dropping out of school. Other services may also include providing students and their parents with information on the advantages of post-secondary education and on their postsecondary financial options.

When NEISP Program funding falls below the $50 million mark (as anticipated in the 1998–99 award year), states must apply for funding though a discretionary grant competition. Because the nine states currently receiving awards (California, Indiana, Maryland, Minnesota, New Mexico, Rhode Island, Vermont, Washington, and Wisconsin) are expected to use all available funds, no new state applications are currently being considered. Should sufficient federal funds become available in the future, the program will be run as a discretionary grant program and funds will be allocated to states on a competitive basis. The Secretary of Education will review each application as to how well each state has fulfilled its stated mission.

THE ROBERT C. BYRD HONORS SCHOLARSHIP PROGRAM

The Robert C. Byrd Honors Scholarship Program is authorized until Title IV of the Higher Education Act of 1965, as amended. Under this program, the Secretary of Education makes available, through grants to states, scholarships to exceptionally gifted students for study at postsecondary schools. This program recognizes and promotes student excellence and achievement.

Eligible students follow the application procedures established by the State Education Agency (SEA) in the state in which he or she legally resides. The SEA is a state board of education (or the equivalent state agency); it is primarily responsible for the supervision of public elementary and secondary schools. The SEA establishes procedures for selecting scholars after consultations with school administrators, school boards, teachers, counselors, and parents. Before those procedures are set in motion, the state's selection criteria and application procedures are reviewed and approved by the USDE.

Eligible students receive a scholarship for one academic year. Awards can be renewed for up to three additional years, provided that funds are appropriated and the awardee remains eligible. Students are selected on the basis of demonstrated outstanding academic achievement and promise of continued achievement and in a way that each state, the District of Columbia, and Puerto Rico are fairly represented. An awardee may attend any public or private nonprofit postsecondary institution, proprietary institution of higher education, or postsecondary vocational institution.

COUNSELING THE STUDENT ON FINANCIAL AID

By periodically reviewing pertinent information found in this chapter as well as sources cited in the notes and bibliography, you should gain a valuable understanding of how each Student Financial Aid Program operates. For example, if one of your student employees receives a grant, any work-study award they also qualify for will most likely be reduced, thus changing the number of hours that student can work and requiring you to seek, perhaps, additional student employees.

Student employee supervisors are often surprised or caught off guard by the circumstances of individuals and their interconnected financial aid packages. A supervisor who has a basic knowledge and understanding of each program can avoid many unpleasant experiences and work-related situations. Supervisors are strongly urged to contact their FAA should questions arise. Supervisors should also:

+ explore all sources of aid;

+ stress constraints on aid;

+ urge each student employee to read and save all loan and grant documents and related materials;

+ review requirements for satisfactory academic progress;

+ remind students to keep their lenders, private and public, informed;

+ review loan terms and conditions;

+ describe consequences of multiple borrowing;

+ review student rights and responsibilities;

+ review deferment and forbearance conditions;

+ review loan repayment obligations;

+ provide general information on average indebtedness of students;

+ provide data on average, anticipated monthly repayment;

- provide information on debt management strategies; and

- counsel on personal financial planning.

As the supervisor of student employees in an academic library, you have the most frequent contact with students who are receiving some type of federal financial assistance. Understanding the procedures, rules, and regulations of, for example, the Federal Work-Study Program, helps you deal with and understand awards and allotments and also helps you abide by the program's regulations and requirements. As supervisors, we often forget that many of our student employees may also be paying off loans. In recognition of their financial obligations, we as supervisors should do what we can to allow student employees to make up missed work time and attempt to provide long-term employment. If the workload eases, we may think we are helping our student employees by giving them time off, forgetting that those students may have financial obligations that cannot be met without a regular paycheck.

Again, before you advise any of your student employees on federal financial aid programs, check with your Financial Aid Administrator to be certain you know each program's rules and regulations as well as those applicable to your university or college.

INTERNET SITES OF INTEREST

Note that the Internet is fast becoming a primary resource tool, not only to find the latest information regarding student financial aid programs but also for submission to the USDE of financial aid information. The use of the electronic FAFSA form enhances and expedites the chances of a successful award for an eligible student. As always, when using any type of Internet form to submit confidential information, be sure that you and the receiver are using the latest in encryption software to guard against the transmission of sensitive data to those who might use it for illegal means or purposes. (The USDE uses the best software possible.)

Numerous sites currently exist on the Internet. The listings below are by no means comprehensive or inclusive but they should be a good starting point for information residing in an electronic format. One can search the Internet through an appropriate search engine (e.g., Lycos, Webcrawler, etc.) to find additional or new sites.

Compilation of Student Financial Aid Regulations: 34 CFR
http://sfa.ed.gov/

A link to the *Code of Federal Regulations (CFR), Chapter 34*, which contains the latest rules and regulations as promulgated by the federal government on student financial aid.

FinAid: The Financial Aid Information Page
http://www.finaid.org/

This site, compiled by Mark Kantrowitz, author of *The Prentice Hall Guide to Scholarships and Fellowships for Math and Science Students*, provides a comprehensive, independent, and objective guide to student financial aid. Links to all federal sites as well as to private, special interest, newsgroups, and other pertinent sites. Updated regularly. Also contains a link to information on financial aid scams being run on the Internet.

Financial Aid for College—A Guide to Financial Aid Information on the World Wide Web
http://web.lwc.edu/administrative/library/finaid.htm

An Internet guide produced by the Longwood College Library. Provides many links which will take one to additional Internet sites which contain financial aid information.

Funding Your Education, 1999–2000: Student Financial Assistance from the U.S. Department of Education
http://www.ed.gov/prog_info/SFA/FYE/index.html

Another very useful guide produced by the Student Financial Assistance Program of the USDE. Detailed information on various financial aid packages. Also includes forms for applying for financial aid.

Grant Information
http://www.vcu.edu/mdcweb/new/resource/resources/resourc.htm

The Virginia Commonwealth University (VCU) has gathered and compiled a unique page in that it provides links to a variety of financial aid resources from federal, state, business, foundations, and other pertinent resources.

Updated regularly, this site is one that should be reviewed for nonfederal sources of financial aid.

National Association of Student Financial Aid Administrators
http://www.nasfaa.org

Provides a link to the National Association of Student Financial Aid Administrators, a national organization which helps to coordinate information exchange between FAAs.

Other Financial Aid Information
http://www.consortium.org/otheraid.htm

Compiled by the Consortium of Universities, provides links to a variety of sources that provide information on student financial aid. Included is information about the Consortium, which members participate in which federal student aid programs (pending federal legislation on financial aid programs) and the *Chronicle of Higher Education*.

The Student Guide—Financial Need
http://www.ed/gov/prog_info/SFA/StudentGuide/

The most comprehensive guide on student financial aid available from the USDE. Provides a wealth of information on grants, loans, and work-study programs available from the USDE. Updated each award year, this guide provides excellent information and includes a link to the FAFSA electronic application form.

Federal School Code Search Page
http://www.ed.gov/offices/OSFAP/Students/apply/search.html

Provides a link to search for Title IV School Code information, a necessary component of the FAFSA. The Title IV School Code will provide information on the school(s) the applicant wishes to apply for financial aid and whether or not that school(s) participates in a particular federal financial aid program.

USA Group Financial Aid Information & Tips
http://www.usagroup.com/

Provides general information on frequently asked questions regarding student financial aid. Contains a calendar of when one should begin the process for application for financial assistance and links to their own private sources of funding or loans.

Welcome to AFSA's Education Financing Overview
http://www.afsa.com/

A compilation of information, mostly on the various federal loans available, produced by a private enterprise. AFSA, founded in 1967 to provide student loan billing and collections to higher education institutions, is part of the Fleet Financial Group. The information contained is useful to help both eligible students and parents determine which federal loan program is best for them plus provides answers on obtaining and repayment of federal loans.

NOTES

1. Department of Education, Office of Educational Research and Improvement, *Digest of Educational Statistics, 1997* (Washington, D.C.: GPO, 1997), 385.

2. Department of Education, Office of Educational Research and Improvement, *1997 Directory of Post Secondary Institutions, Volume 1, Degree Granting Institutions* (Washington, D.C.: GPO, 1998), XXI.

3. The Higher Education Act of 1965, as amended, includes the following:

Higher Education Act of 1965 (PL 89–329, 79 STAT 1219); Higher Education Act Amendments of 1966 (PL 89–752, 80 STAT 1240); Higher Education Act Amendments of 1968 (PL 90–575, 82 STAT 1014); Higher Education Act Amendments of 1986 (PL 99–498, 100 STAT 1268); Higher Education Act Amendments of 1992 (PL 102–325, 106 STAT 448); Higher Education Act Amendments of 1995 (PL 104–19, 109 STAT 219, Title 1, Ch.4); Higher Education Act Amendments of 1995 (PL 104–66, 109 STAT 715, title 1, Subtitle D); Higher Education Review Act (Cost of) (PL 105–17, 111 STAT 211, Title 4, Sections 40001 to 40007); Higher Education Technical Amendments Act of 1979 (PL 96–149, 93 STAT 351); Higher Education Technical Amendments Act of 1991 (PL 100–150, 101 STAT 335); Higher Education Technical Amendments of 1991 (PL 102–26, 105 STAT 123); Higher Education Technical Amendments of 1993 (PL 103–208, 107 STAT 2457).

4. Department of Education, *The Federal Student Financial Aid Handbook, 1998–1999* (Washington, D.C.: GPO, 1998), 55–56.

5. *Fin-Aid: The Financial Aid Information Page.* http//www.finaid.org/finaid.html/.

6. Department of Education. *The Federal Student Financial Aid Handbook, 1998–1999* (Washington, D.C.: GPO, 1998) 3–4.

7. Ibid.

8. Ibid., 3–6.

9. Under an income contingent repayment schedule, the size of the monthly payments depends on the income earned by the borrower. As the borrower's income increases, so do the payments. The income contingent repayment plan is not available for PLUS Loans.

10. Equivalent Employment jobs are similar nonfederal work-study jobs offered or arranged by a school or university.

11. Department of Education, *The Federal Student Financial Aid Handbook, 1998–1999* (Washington, D.C.: GPO, 1998) 35–36.

BIBLIOGRAPHY

Blum, Laurie. *Free Money for College from the Government*. New York: Henry Holt, 1993.

Choy, Susan P., and Mark D. Premo. *How Low Income Undergraduates Financed Postsecondary Education, 1992–93*. Washington, D.C.: U.S. Department of Education, Office of Educational Research and Improvement, National Center for Education Statistics, 1996.

College Student's Guide to Merit and Other No-need Funding. San Carlos, CA: Reference Service Press, 1996.

Cronin, Joseph Marr, and Sylvia Quarles Simmons, eds. *Student Loans: Risks and Realities*. Dover, MA: Auburn House, 1987.

Cuccaro-Alamin, Stephanie, and Susan P. Choy. *Postsecondary Financing Strategies: How Undergraduates Combine Work, Borrowing, and Attendance*. Washington, D.C.: U.S. Department of Education, Office of Educational Research and Improvement, National Center for Education Statistics, 1998.

Dennis, Marguerite J. *Mortgaged Futures: How to Graduate from School Without Going Broke*. Washington, D.C.: Hope Press, 1986.

Directory of Financial Aids for Minorities. San Carlos, CA: ABC-Clio Information Services, Reference Service Press, 1997.

Financial Aid for Minorities: Awards to Students with Any Major. Garrett Park, MD: Garrett Park Press, 1994.

Fossey, Richard, and Mark Bateman, eds. *Condemning Students to Debt: College Loans and Public Policy*. New York: Teachers College Press, 1998.

Gladieux, Lawrence E., and Arthur M. Hauptman. *The College Aid Quandary: Access, Quality, and the Federal Role*. Washington, D.C.: Brookings Institution, 1995.

McPherson, Michael S., and Morton Owen Schapiro. *The Student Aid Game: Meeting Need and Rewarding Talent in American Higher Education*. Princeton, NJ: Princeton University Press, 1998.

Merrill, Edward, and Michael McCanna. *Financial Aid Resource Guide*. 5th ed. Corvallis, OR: Oregon State University, Indian Education Office, 1996.

O'Sullivan, Marie, and Sara J. Steen. *Financial Resources for International Study: A Guide for U.S. Nationals*. New York: Institute of International Education, 1996.

St. John, Edward P., ed. *Rethinking Tuition and Student Aid Strategies*. San Francisco: Jossey-Bass, 1995.

Sutterlin, Rebecca, and Robert A. Kominski. *Dollars for Scholars: Postsecondary Costs and Financing, 1990–1991*. Washington, D.C.: U.S. Department of Commerce, GPO, 1994.

U.S. Department of Education. *The Counselor's Handbook for Postsecondary Schools*. Washington, D.C.: GPO, 1998.

U.S. Department of Education. *Direct Loans: A Better Way to Borrow*. Washington, D.C.: GPO, 1997.

U.S. Department of Education. *Direct Loans: William D. Ford Federal Direct Loan Program: PLUS Loan Basics*. Washington, D.C.: GPO, 1997.

U.S. Department of Education. Office of Student Financial Assistance Programs. *The EFC Formula Book: The Expected Family Contribution for Federal Student Aid*. Washington, D.C.: GPO, 1997.

U.S. Department of Education. *FAFSA on the Web: the Wave of the Future*. Washington, D.C.: GPO, 1997.

U.S. Department of Education. *The Federal Student Aid Information Center*. Washington, D.C.: GPO, 1997.

U.S. Department of Education. National Center for Educational Statistics. *Federal Support for Education, Fiscal Years 1980 to 1997*. Washington, D.C.: GPO, 1998.

U.S. Department of Education. Office of Educational Research and Improvement, Educational Resources Information Center. *Financing Postsecondary Education: The Federal Role: Proceedings of the National Conference on the Best Ways for the Federal Government to Help Students and Families Finance Postsecondary Education: College of Charleston, Charleston, South Carolina, October 8–9, 1995*. Washington, D.C.: GPO, 1996.

U.S. Department of Education. Office of Student Financial Assistance. *1992–93 Congressional Methodology*. Washington, D.C.: GPO, 1992.

U.S. Department of Education. Office of Student Financial Assistance. *The Federal Student Financial Aid Handbook, 1998–99.* Washington, D.C.: GPO, 1997.

U.S. Department of Education. Student Financial Assistance Programs. *Compilation of Student Aid Regulations: Through 12/31/97: 34 CFR.* Washington, D.C.: GPO, 1998.

U.S. Department of Education. Student Financial Assistance Programs. *The Student Guide: Financial Aid from the U.S. Department of Education, 1995–96.* Washington, D.C.: GPO, 1995.

U.S. Department of Education. *The Student Guide: Five Federal Financial Aid Programs.* Washington, D.C.: GPO, 1995.

U.S. General Accounting Office. *Supplemental Student Loans: Legislative Changes Have Sharply Reduced Loan Volume: Fact Sheet for the Chairman, Committee on Labor and Human Resources, U.S. Senate.* Washington, D.C.: U.S. General Accounting Office, 1990.

U.S. General Accounting Office. *Supplemental Student Loans: Who are the Largest Lenders?: Fact Sheet for Congressional Requesters.* Washington, D.C.: U.S. General Accounting Office, 1990.

U.S. General Accounting Office. *Supplemental Student Loans: Who Borrows and Who Defaults: Fact Sheet for Congressional Requesters.* Washington, D.C.: U.S. General Accounting Office, 1989.

U.S. General Services Administration. *Catalog of Federal Domestic Assistance.* Washington, D.C.: 1997.

HIRING STUDENT EMPLOYEES

> *The advantage of a classical education is that it enables you to despise the wealth that it prevents you from achieving.*
>
> —Russell Green

HIRING AND FIRING

Probably the single most important part of your job as supervisor is to hire the right persons. Any supervisor who has fired student employees realizes how important it is to hire the right people and to train them well, thus reducing their risks of being discharged. In this chapter, we will discuss how to recruit, screen, and interview student employees effectively. For suggestions on handling corrective discipline and termination, see chapter 12.

REFERRAL OF STUDENT WORKERS

The referral of student workers to the library has been improved in recent years. Thankfully, gone are the days when the following exchange was common in university financial aid offices:

Student Employment Counselor: "Do you have any preference as to where you'd like to work?"

Student: "No."

Counselor: "Do you have any special skills?"

Student: "No, but I am carrying 17 hours."

Counselor: "Oh, okay, go to the library. They don't need special skills, and they let you study."

Student: "Where's the library?"

Today, in the student financial aid office, you are more likely to hear a conversation like this:

Student Employment Counselor: "Do you have any preference as to where you'd like to work?"

Student: "Not really."

Counselor: "Do you know any languages?"

Student: "Besides English?"

Counselor: "Spanish, German, French?"

Student: "Yes, I am fluent in German and can read Spanish."

Counselor: "How about computer keyboard skills?"

Student: "Yes, I'm pretty good at that."

Counselor: "Good, I have a request from the acquisitions department in the library for someone who can read German and can learn their automated system. It pays $6.25 to start. Interested?"

Student: "Yes, where's the library?"

Well, even though a slight improvement in the college-wide orientation program is still needed, the student can now be interviewed by a hiring supervisor in the library.

RECRUITING STUDENT WORKERS

The recruitment and screening of student employees for library employment varies greatly from one university to another. Recruitment depends on the available pool of student workers, on their funding sources, and on how prospective employees find their way to the library's hiring supervisors for interviews. On some campuses, the library has a part-time budget that does not depend on work-study students and may not require that part-time employees be current students. Most campuses rely heavily on work-study funding or have a combination of work-study and other part-time employee budgets.

One aspect of recruitment for the library involves keeping the student employment office up-to-date on the skills needed by prospective student employees. Work in the library can be made quite attractive to students looking for employment. Night and weekend hours are a selling point, as are the opportunities for students to set their own schedules in some jobs. Some students are attracted by the prospect of learning more about the library, which they hope will help them in their course work. Capitalize on that interest if you can.

Recruitment for library work can be quite extensive. Some libraries take part in job fairs on campus, advertise in the student newspaper, post job openings around campus, post "help wanted" signs on bulletin boards, and ask present student employees to recruit their friends. The hope is that, because libraries are such attractive places to work, you will have many more applications for jobs than you have openings.

The initial screening process begins when a student completes an application. In some universities, the student employment office screens students for jobs throughout campus. Depending on the system, students who seem to have no usable skills may all be ticketed for the library, making the library's hiring process more difficult. At other universities, the student employment office carefully reviews the library's needs and refers highly skilled students to the library. Many libraries have their own personnel offices to screen student employee applicants for departments of the library.

To screen applicants effectively, the hiring supervisors must provide those who screen applications with job descriptions that not only describe the work but also the skills required to do that work. The screening process is nothing more than a comparison of applications to the skills required for the jobs available. Effective screening will greatly improve the hiring supervisor's ability to hire qualified people.

It is desirable for students who have gone through the screening process and who have met the qualifications for the job to be asked to report to a central location in the library to meet the hiring supervisor. The best place for students to meet the interviewer is the dean/director's office area, the branch library office, or the personnel office.

The supervisor as well as the applicant must prepare for the interview. The following are suggestions for preparing for the interview:

1. One of the best ways for the supervisor to prepare is to review the job description for the position as well as the job application.

2. Set the stage for the interview by planning to conduct the interview in a comfortable private office or conference room. Keep in mind that the interview is a two-way street: you want to give the interviewee a good first impression of the library just as much as the interviewee wants to make a good impression on you.

3. Be sure to set aside enough time for the interview and make certain that there will not be interruptions.

4. Review the application. Is it filled out completely, with no blanks? Is it legible? Does it present a sequential outline of the applicant's work history and education? Does it tell why the applicant left each job?

5. When preparing questions for the interview, don't include questions that are answered on the application.

6. Do prepare most of the questions that will be asked in the interview. The questions asked in the interview should focus on the applicant's employment history, education, schedule, outside activities and interests, and strengths and weaknesses. A list of possible questions as well as questions that are inappropriate are presented later in this chapter.

7. Make certain that you are prepared to answer any questions the interviewee has about the job, the department, and the library. Know ahead of time how soon you will make a decision about hiring for the position.

Interviewing Techniques

Three different techniques are used in employment interviewing. Those techniques are the directed interview, the nondirected interview, and the stress interview.

The directed interview usually involves use of a predetermined set of questions that are asked of the interviewee. The primary advantage is that of thoroughness and consistency. All interviewees are asked the same questions, usually in the same order. The disadvantages or directed interviews are that interviewers sometimes get caught up in asking questions without listening to the answers, and structured interviews tend to cause anxiety in applicants.

The nondirected interview is usually unstructured. The purpose is to allow the interviewees to talk about what is on their minds. The interviewer knows what information to obtain and how to obtain it through skilled questioning. The use of the nondirected approach by skilled interviewers can be very effective but much less so by unskilled interviewers.

The stress interview technique is seldom used. It relies on a series of tough, unexpected, anxiety-producing questions designed to place the interviewee in an uncomfortable situation and to force instinctive reactions. Its purpose is to determine how an individual reacts under pressure. It is a technique sometimes used to screen people for higher-level management positions.

Probably the best approach is a combination of the directed and nondirected interview techniques. With this approach, the interviewer uses a broad list of prepared questions, asking them in no particular sequence. The interviewee is given latitude in responding to questions, some of which are not scripted. The interviewee feels more at ease and the interviewer has some structure. It is necessary to ask essentially the same questions for all applicants for a position.

The following are suggestions on how to conduct the interview meeting:

1. Begin the interview by putting the interviewee at ease. Spend a few moments in small talk but be careful to avoid asking questions that might be considered discriminatory.

2. Let the applicant know the purpose of the interview, which is to try to determine whether there is a fit between the applicant and the position opening in the department.

3. Keep in mind that the interview should privide you with information about the applicant that may not be completely covered in the application and that the interview meeting should provide the applicant with more complete information about the job.

4. Listen to the interviewee's answers. One of the most common mistakes made by interviewers is to concentrate so much on the questions they ask that they forget to listen to the answers.

5. You should maintain control of the interview by establishing the direction of the questions and not allowing the interviewee to wander off in other directions.

6. Never help an interviewee by suggesting the answer to a question; but don't use Gestapo interrogation techniques, either.

7. Keep the interview friendly and comfortable.

8. Take notes during the interview to refresh your memory when making a decision. Another school of thought believes that taking notes disrupts the interview and that the interviewer should develop the ability to remember responses and then take a few minutes after the interview to make notes.

9. The interview is complete when you are sure that you have obtained the information you need to make a decision and when the interviewee's questions have been answered.

10. Close the interview by thanking the interviewee and telling him or her when a decision will be made. If you are able to hire on the spot, discuss schedules, pay rates, starting date, etc.

11. Check references. This step is sometimes left out when hiring student employees, but it is good practice nonetheless.

Sample Questions That May Be Asked

The following are suggested questions that may be asked in the interview. Job-specific questions should be prepared for specific positions in the library.

WORK EXPERIENCE

Describe your work experience at your last job.

What was the most fulfilling aspect of the job?

What was the least fulfilling?

Why did you leave?

What skills did you develop in your previous job?

EDUCATION

What is your major? (This will probably be on the application.)

Why did you select that major?

What is your minor?

What courses do you prefer? Why?

What courses do you dislike? Why?

What courses do you find most and least valuable? Why?

What extra curricular activities are you involved in?

What are your short-term goals?

What are your long-term goals?

LEADERSHIP/INITIATIVE/PERSISITENCE

How do you feel about making decisions? Why?

How do you feel about supervising others? Why?

What is your idea of challenging work?

How do you feel about working in an unstructured environment?

How do you feel about increasing your job responsibilities?

How do you feel about working in a high-pressure area?

How would you react if given an unpleasant task?

LIBRARY JOB SPECIFIC

Tell me about experience you have had with computers.

Tell me about experience you have had in working with customers or patrons.

Describe your experience in using libraries.

What times during the day and week are you available to work?

Types of Questions to Be Avoided

To gain the type of information you need in an interview, avoid the following types of questions:

1. Questions that can be answered with a "Yes" or "No." These should be changed to open-ended questions, which allow the interviewer to see and hear the interviewee use communication skills.

2. Leading questions. Questions that telegraph the expected answers are of little use. For example, "Would you say that you have good interpersonal skills?" definitely calls for a positive response.

3. Obvious questions. "So you graduated from Midvale High School?" is a question that is answered on the application and is a waste of time. Ask questions for which the application does not supply the answers.

4. Questions that are not related to the job. "Do you think the Chicago Cubs will win the pennant?" has nothing to do with the job, even if you are a Cubs fan.

5. Questions that may be considered discriminatory. It is not only advisable but *mandatory* that you avoid these types of questions; examples are given later on in this chapter.

LEGAL IMPLICATIONS OF EMPLOYMENT DECISIONS

All employment decisions, including hiring, promotion, transfer, and terminations, must be made on the qualifications of the individual, not on race, creed, sex, age, sexual preference, national origin, or handicap. To avoid charges of discrimination in employment, supervisors must be aware of laws that protect certain groups from discriminatory practices. At the federal level, there are laws governing equal employment opportunity and protection of employees:

1. Title VII of the 1964 Civil Rights Act, as amended, protects against discrimination in employment decisions based on race, color, religion, sex, and national origin.

2. The Equal Pay Act of 1963 makes it unlawful to pay females less than males who do similar work.

3. The Age Discrimination in Employment Act of 1967, as amended, protects against discrimination on the basis of age. It protects all persons over the age of 40.

4. The Vocational Rehabilitation Act of 1973 prohibits discrimination in employment on the basis of a mental or physical handicap.

5. The Americans with Disabilities Act (ADA), which took effect in 1992, prohibits discrimination against qualified disabled persons by requiring that the employer make reasonable accommodation for those who can perform the job unless that accommodation would create an undue hardship for the employer. Reasonable accommodation requires that the employer modify the job application process so that disabled persons can apply in the first place and adjust the work environment in such a way that the disabled individual can perform the job.

6. The Vietnam Era Veterans' Readjustment Assistance Act of 1974 requires that federal contractors and subcontractors take affirmative action to employ, and advance in employment, qualified disabled veterans and veterans of the Vietnam era.

7. The Pregnancy Discrimination Act of 1978 protects against discrimination in employment because of pregnancy. Pregnancy should be treated as any other temporary disability and an employer may not refuse to hire a qualified female because she is pregnant.

8. The Immigration Reform and Control Act of 1986 (IRCA) makes it illegal to recruit, hire, or refer for hire any unauthorized alien; requires documentation of identity and eligibility of the worker to work in the United States; and prohibits discrimination on the basis of national origin or citizenship status.

9. The Employee Polygraph Protection Act of 1988 protects employees from wrongfully being subjected to polygraphs in prehiring or employment.

The Supervisor's Responsibility

As a supervisor, you are responsible for assuring that discrimination does not occur in hiring or employment. You are also responsible for reporting any instances of discrimination to the appropriate person. Even the perception of discrimination based on race, creed, sex, age, sexual preference, national origin, or handicap in the library must be avoided at all costs. Although it is not expected that supervisors will become experts in employment law, it is the responsibility of supervisors to be familiar with applicable laws.

Student employees who believe that they are victims of employment discrimination have the right to avail themselves of the library's grievance process. The student may also file a complaint with the local or regional office of the Equal Employment Opportunity Commission. If you are named in a discrimination grievance, be prepared to present documentary evidence that will clearly show nondiscriminatory intent or action. The grievance procedure is described in chapter 11.

Nondiscriminatory Interviewing

Nondiscriminatory interviewing simply means asking questions that are job-related. To avoid charges of discrimination in hiring, supervisors must be aware of the types of questions that cannot be asked in the interview. The following are some guidelines:

1. Do not discuss age.

2. Do not ask about child care arrangements.

3. Do not discuss religious preferences.

4. Do not ask about the employment of a spouse.

5. Do not discuss matters relating to the applicant's race, ancestry, or national origin.

6. Do not attempt jokes related to race, national origin, religion, or sex.

7. Do not ask about military discharge or rank at time of discharge.

8. Do not ask a handicapped applicant about the severity of the handicap.

9. Do not ask questions about civil rights litigation with former employers.

10. Do not ask questions about arrests because a person is not judged guilty by an arrest.

11. Do not discuss political affiliation or membership.

REFERENCE CHECKS

You have a right to collect information about prospective student employees regarding past employment, including duration, absences, punctuality, skills, and reasons for leaving previous positions. In most instances, the references provided by the employee will confirm your impressions of the applicant. However, there are times when contacting those references will help you make a final decision between two applicants or even avoid a hiring mistake. When you contact references supplied by the applicants, you must ask the same questions about all applicants for a particular position and you must have a good business reason for seeking the information. The following are suggested areas for reference check questions:

1. Relationship to the applicant

2. Length of time the reference has known the applicant

3. Length of time the reference has supervised the applicant

4. Applicant's employment dates

5. First and last position held

6. Starting and leaving salary

7. Duties and responsibilities

8. Quality of work

9. Quantity of work

10. Attendance and punctuality

11. Cooperation with other employees and supervisors

12. General work habits

13. Amount of time required to learn new jobs

14. Willingness to accept responsibility

15. Reason for leaving position

16. Eligibility for rehire

COMMUNICATING THE HIRING DECISION

The final step in hiring is the offer. Communication of your decision to applicants is important and should not be unnecessarily delayed. Your choice for the position may well find another job if you do not act within a reasonable time; it is also unfair to all applicants to keep them waiting.

Care should be exercised in communicating either acceptance or rejection; it is always easier to give someone good news than bad news. Whether you communicate the bad news in person, by phone, or in writing, you may consider beginning with, "We have a very strong pool of applicants for this position." Continue by mentioning the strengths of this individual's application; it is possible to reject people in a kind way, without adding to the disappointment unsuccessful applicants already feel. Too often, hiring supervisors forget to consider the feelings of the persons being rejected. Consider how *you* would like to be informed that you were not the successful applicant.

The hiring interview is only one of the many face-to-face situations a supervisor experiences. Interviewing isn't just talking with someone; the process has a purpose and structure. Interviews are also used in performance appraisal, termination, and some problem solving situations. Interviewing, if done well, is a very important skill to possess. The resources provided in the bibliography will help you develop hiring skills.

BIBLIOGRAPHY

Adler, Lou. *Hire with Your Head: A Rational Way to Make a Gut Decision*. New York: Wiley, 1998.

American Library Association, Office for Library Personnel Resources. *Hiring Library Staff*. Chicago: American Library Association, 1986.

Arthur, Diane. *Recruiting, Interviewing, Selecting & Orienting New Employees*. 3d ed. New York: AMACOM, 1998.

Biggs, Debra R., and Cheryl T. Naslund. "Proactive Interviewing." *College and Research Libraries News* 48, no. 1 (January 1987): 13–17.

Bowes, Lee. *No One Need Apply: Getting and Keeping the Best Workers*. Boston: Harvard Business School Press, 1987.

Caldwell, Hardy. *The Agile Manager's Guide to Hiring Excellence*. Bristol, VT: Velocity Business Publications, 1998.

Creth, Sheila. *Interviewing Skills: Finding the Right Person for the Job*. Chicago: ACRL, 1984.

Dewey, Barbara I. *Library Jobs: How to Fill Them, How to Find Them*. Phoenix, AZ: Oryx, 1987.

Hodgson, Philip. *A Practical Guide to Successful Interviewing*. New York: McGraw-Hill, 1988.

Mattia, Jan Bailey. *Hiring Made Easy*. Lincolnwood, IL: VGM Career Horizons, 1998.

Medley, H. A. *Sweaty Palms: The Neglected Art of Being Interviewed*. Berkeley, CA: Ten Speed Press, 1984.

Outlaw, Wayne. *Smart Staffing: How to Hire, Reward and Keep the Best People for Your Growing Company*. Chicago: Upstart, 1998.

Rae, Leslie. *The Skills of Interviewing*. New York: Nichols, 1988.

Sanders, Nancy, comp. *Guidelines for Interviewing for the Entry Level Position.* Chicago: Library Administration and Management Association, 1981.

Smalley, Larry R. *Interviewing and Selecting High Performers: A Practical Guide to Effective Hiring.* Irvine, CA: Richard Chang Associates, 1997.

Uris, Auren. *88 Mistakes Interviewers Make . . . and How to Avoid Them.* New York: AMACOM, 1988.

Wood, Robert. *Competency-Based Recruitment and Selection.* Chichester: Wiley, 1998.

Chapter Seven

STUDENT EMPLOYEE COMPENSATION

*I am opposed to millionaires,
but it would be dangerous to
offer me the position.*

—Mark Twain

DIFFERENTIATED PAY

The compensation system for student employees is well established at most academic institutions. The guidelines that have been set will allow only so much flexibility in setting student employee pay rates. It is advisable, however, to examine the library's internal compensation for student workers to assure that it is fair. A fair compensation system should be logical, consistent, equitable, and competitive.

A compensation system that pays beginning searchers in acquisitions the same wage is fair. A system that pays the same wage to student employees who reshelve books as it does to those students who supervise circulation operations during late evening and weekend hours is illogical, inequitable, and inconsistent. There are good reasons to compensate different students for different work if the level of work differs. To be fair to all student employees, it is necessary to pay at different rates for different work. The job descriptions in chapter 4 provide for several levels of positions based on responsibility and difficulty.

Table 7.1. Pay Rate Structures for Student Employees

GROUP	STEP I (START RATE)	STEP II	STEP III	STEP IV
I	Base	Base + $.15	Base + $.30	Base + $.45
II	Base + $.15	Base + $.30	Base + $.45	Base + $.60
III				
Level 1	Base + $.30	Base + $.45	Base + $.60	Base + $.75
Level 2	Base + $.65	Base + $.80	Base + $.95	Base + $1.10
Level 3	Base + $.90	Base + $1.20	Base + $1.35	Base + $1.50

Example:

If the Base is a minimum wage of $5.15, the following schedule would apply:

GROUP	STEP I (START RATE)	STEP II	STEP III	STEP IV
I	$5.15	$5.30	$5.45	$5.60
II	$5.30	$5.45	$5.60	$5.75
III				
Level 1	$5.45	$5.60	$5.75	$5.90
Level 2	$5.80	$5.95	$6.10	$6.25
Level 3	$6.05	$6.35	$6.50	$6.65

The steps in this schedule can be used for longevity increases to student employees. All Group II students, for example, would start work at $5.30 per hour and after 500 hours or two semesters' experience be given an increase to $5.45 per hour. Longevity increases permit the library to reward students for staying in their positions. Of course, they could also be promoted to higher-level positions. Group III positions would be used for advanced positions requiring specialized knowledge, skills, and experience.

STUDENT EMPLOYEE ALLOTMENTS

Allocation of student work-study funds differ widely among academic libraries. The two primary means of setting allocations are to have those allocations of hours or dollars set by student employment offices for libraries or for the libraries to have their own budgets for students, which are then coordinated with students' work-study awards.

The student with a work-study award typically receives notification of the amount of the award and the period in which that amount can be earned, e.g., academic year, summer session, etc. The number of hours a work-study student can work depends on the pay rate for the position. It is important for the student employee supervisor to know the total number of hours a student may work based on the award and pay rate. If there are 20 pay periods (biweekly payroll) in the fall and spring semesters, does the work—study student you are hiring have an award large enough to get through the entire academic year before exhausting the award? Will you be faced with having the student terminated because the award has run out, leaving desks unattended and hours not covered in your department's schedule? Constructing a table like the following is useful in determining how many hours per pay period may be worked so that a work-study student is able to work all year and earn the total award.

Table 7.2. Number of Hours That Can Be Worked in 20 Pay Periods (Divide hours by two to determine hours per week.)

	HOURLY PAY RATE										
AWARD	$5.15	$5.30	$5.45	$5.60	$5.75	$5.90	$6.05	$6.20	$6.35	$6.50	$6.65
$1,000	9.7	9.4	9.2	8.9	8.7	8.5	8.3	8.1	7.9	7.7	7.5
$1,200	11.7	11.3	11.0	10.7	10.4	10.2	9.9	9.7	9.4	9.2	9.0
$1,400	13.6	13.2	12.8	12.5	12.2	11.9	11.6	11.3	11.0	10.8	10.5
$1,600	15.5	15.1	14.7	14.3	13.9	13.6	13.2	12.9	12.6	12.3	12.0
$1,800	17.5	17.0	16.5	16.1	15.7	15.3	14.9	14.5	14.2	13.8	13.5
$2,000	19.4	18.9	18.3	17.9	17.4	16.9	16.5	16.1	15.7	15.4	15.0
$2,200	21.4	20.8	20.2	19.6	19.1	18.6	18.2	17.7	17.3	16.9	16.5
$2,400	23.3	22.6	22.0	21.4	20.9	20.3	19.8	19.4	18.9	18.5	18.0
$2,600	25.2	24.5	23.9	23.2	22.6	22.0	21.5	21.0	20.5	20.0	19.5
$2,800	27.2	26.4	25.7	25.0	24.3	23.7	23.1	22.6	22.0	21.5	21.1
$3,000	29.1	28.3	27.5	26.8	26.1	25.4	24.8	24.2	23.6	23.1	22.6
$3,200	31.1	30.2	29.4	28.6	27.8	27.1	26.4	25.8	25.2	24.6	24.1
$3,400	33.0	32.1	31.2	30.4	29.6	28.8	28.1	27.4	26.8	26.2	25.6
$3,600	35.0	34.0	33.0	32.1	31.3	30.5	29.8	29.0	28.3	27.7	27.1
$3,800	36.9	35.8	34.9	33.9	33.0	32.2	31.4	30.6	29.9	29.2	28.6
$4,000	83.8	37.7	36.7	35.7	34.8	33.9	33.1	32.3	31.5	30.8	30.1
$4,200	40.8	39.6	38.5	37.5	36.5	35.6	34.7	33.9	33.1	32.3	31.6
$4,400	42.7	41.5	40.4	39.3	38.3	37.3	36.4	35.5	34.6	33.8	33.1
$4,600	44.7	43.4	42.2	41.1	40.0	39.0	38.0	37.1	36.2	35.4	34.6
$4,800	46.6	45.3	44.0	42.9	41.7	40.7	39.7	38.7	37.8	36.9	36.1
$5,000	48.5	47.2	45.9	44.6	43.5	42.4	41.3	40.3	39.4	38.5	37.6
$5,200	50.5	49.1	47.7	46.4	45.2	44.1	43.0	41.9	40.9	40.0	39.1
$5,400	52.4	50.9	49.5	48.2	47.0	45.8	44.6	43.5	42.5	41.5	40.6
$5,600	54.4	52.8	51.4	50.0	48.7	47.5	46.3	45.2	44.1	43.1	42.1

WAGES AND SALARIES

It is hard to imagine that there was a time when a worker needed to receive his pay at the end of each day because there were no real guarantees that the laborer would be paid at all. During the Depression era, the federal government stepped in to establish when workers were to be paid, where they had to be paid, how much extra they had to be paid for working especially long hours, how long individuals could be required to work, and under what circumstances children could be employed. The Fair Labor Standards Act of 1938, which has been amended numerous times, controls minimum wages, overtime, equal pay, and the employment of minors.

Wages and salaries are simply the payment received for performing work and are probably the single most important incentive and motivation for coming to work. Although individual library employees may differ on how much importance they place on pay, it is critical. Library managers need to understand how wages and salaries are determined and managed.

Although wages and salaries are often used as synonyms, they are slightly different in meaning. A *wage*, or hourly pay, is an hourly rate of pay and is the basis for pay used most often for production and maintenance employees or blue-collar workers. A salary is a weekly, monthly, or yearly rate of pay. Professional and management employees as well as faculty are usually salaried, or earn a set salary for the week, month, or year.

Hourly (wage earning) employees normally are paid only for the hours they work whereas salaried employees earn a set salary even though the number of hours they work may vary from pay period to pay period. Salaried employees are normally classed as exempt employees—exempt from the provisions of the Fair Labor Standards Act (FLSA).

Before we describe FLSA, you should understand that student employees are nonexempt employees. Not only are they nonexempt, they usually are part-time temporary employees who work without benefits. The FLSA does provide protections to student employees but often not in a manner identical to the full-time, regular staff employees of a library.

FAIR LABOR STANDARDS ACT (FLSA)

The FLSA was enacted in 1938 and has had numerous amendments through the years revising and updating the law. Before describing the provisions of the law, let's examine which employees are exempt from its provisions. Exempt workers may include executive, administrative, and professional employees (as well as outside salespeople) and computer professionals. Two tests decide whether you can be considered an executive, administrative, or professional employee and thus exempt from the minimum wage and overtime laws. Long and short tests are used to determine if employees qualify for exempt status. The long form is used primarily to determine whether or not lower paid (between $155 and $250 per week) employees qualify; the short test is useful to determine whether or not higher-paid (at least $250 per week) employees qualify.

THE LONG TEST:

You are an executive if you

> spend at least 80 percent of your time managing a department or subdivision and/or directing the work of two or more subordinates;
>
> have the authority to hire and fire or to give recommendations regarding hiring, firing, and promotion of employees;
>
> routinely rely on your own discretion; and
>
> are paid at least $155 a week.

You are an administrative employee if you

> spend at least 80% of your time doing office work; or
>
> are on the administration of an educational institution; or
>
> perform tasks requiring special training or experience with only general supervision or exercise general supervision over others; or
>
> regularly help your employer or an executive or another administrative employee;

routinely rely on your own discretion; and

are paid at least $155 a week.

You are a professional employee if you

> spend at least 80 percent of your time doing work that requires an advanced degree or recognized artistic talent; or

> are a certified teacher in an educational institution; or

> do work that is primarily intellectual;

> routinely rely on your own discretion; and

> are paid at least $170 a week.

THE SHORT TEST:

Executive, administrative, and professional employees are considered highly paid employees, and you are highly paid if you

> are paid at least $250 a week; and

> spend at least 50% of your time performing the duties of an executive, administrative, and professional employee described in the long test above.

Computer professionals: To qualify as a computer professional who is exempt, you must be paid at least six-and-a-half times the current minimum wage and your primary duty has to be one or more of the following:

> applying systems analysis techniques and procedures, including consulting with users, to determine hardware and softwarefunctional specifications;

> designing computer systems based on and related to user specifications;

> creating or modifying computer programs based on and related tosystem design specifications; or

creating or modifying computer programs related to machine operating systems.

Exempt Versus Nonexempt

After examining how an exempt employee is defined for the purposes of classification under the Fair Labor Standards Act, note how the exempt and nonexempt differ from one another:

Nonexempt employees earn an hourly wage.

Exempt employees earn a salary.

Nonexempt employee hours are tracked by time clock or recorded on time sheets. Employees report hours worked and hours taken as sick or annual leave on the timesheet.

Exempt employees do not use time clocks or time sheets. Normally, exempt employees report the hours not worked, to be deducted from hours earned for sick days, annual leave, etc.

Nonexempt employees are paid only for the hours reported as worked.

Exempt employees are paid a salary for the month.

Nonexempt employees are eligible for daily overtime, call-in pay, and guaranteed overtime.

Exempt employees are not eligible.

Nonexempt employees have a set maximum number of paid sick days, sometimes cumbersome work rules, and a formal discipline program for lateness and absences.

Exempt employees, except in government, do not have a limit on paid sick days, they have few work rules, and no formal discipline program.

Generally, exempt employees have certain benefits or privileges that nonexempt employees do not, such as fewer work rules, but exempt employees are not eligible for overtime.

Minimum Wage

Under recent amendments to the FLSA, employees must be paid a minimum wage of $5.15 per hour (as of 1999). Some states have set minimum wages higher than the federal rate. Employers must pay the higher of the two rates to its minimum wage employees. This wage is important to libraries in that student employees are directly affected by changes in the minimum wage. As of this writing, there are further discussions at the federal level about raising the minimum wage rate.

Overtime

The FLSA requires employers to pay time and a half (one and one-half times the regular rate of pay) for every hour employees work over 40 in one week, or in some states, for more than eight hours worked in a day. All exempt employees are exempt from the overtime pay requirement. In addition, other groups such as agricultural workers, car salespeople, taxi drivers, people who work on a commission basis, merchant mariners, drivers who work for employers who are subject to the authority of the Interstate Commerce Commission, anyone whose employer is subject to the Railway Labor Act, and radio and television personnel are specifically exempted from the overtime pay requirement of FLSA. State and local government agencies may be allowed to give compensatory time off instead of paying overtime. Unless the nonexempt employee is a public employee, he or she cannot agree to waive payment of overtime, but must accept compensatory time instead of overtime. FLSA requires that employers pay nonexempt employees overtime.

Jury Duty, Witness Duty, and Voting Time

Under the federal Jury System Improvement Act of 1978, the employer cannot discharge an employee for serving on a federal jury. State laws also prohibit employers from disciplining an employee in any way for responding to a summons to serve on a jury in state court. Normally, state employees have the option of either taking their regular pay or the pay offered to jurors, but not both. Federal law prohibits employers from making any deductions from an exempt employee's salary for being absent for less than a week, which would include time spent on a jury. The same rule of thumb applies when an employee is summoned as a witness for a trial. There is no federal law requiring the employer to give employees time off to vote but some states do make employers give time off if there is not enough time outside of regular working hours to get to the polls.

Child Labor Laws

When the FLSA was passed into law in 1938, child labor was a serious social problem in the United States. Today, although this is less of a problem, children are protected nonetheless. Under federal law, minors under the age of 18 may not work in any job that is considered hazardous by the Secretary of Labor. Included in those jobs specifically designated are coal mining, logging, slaughtering and meat packing, wrecking and demolition, and roofing and excavation. Also included are working in explosives plants and any job involving radioactive substances.

Minors under the age of 16 may not work in mining, manufacturing and processing, the operation of motor vehicles, or in public messenger service or hazardous occupations. Exceptions include delivering newspapers and agricultural jobs. Minors under the age of 16 may also be employed as actor or performers. Minors under the age of 12 can only be employed on a family farm.

Federal law does not restrict the number of hours children between the ages of 16 and 18 may work. However, when school is in session, minors between the ages of 14 and 16 may not work during school hours and may not work more than 3 hours a day and 18 hours a week. Also, they may not work anytime between the hours of 7 P.M. and 7 A.M. When school is not in session, 14 to 16 year-olds may not work more than 8 hours a day and 40 hours a week.

Payment of Wages

It is not illegal to pay employees less than they feel they are worth. It *is* illegal to underpay employees in violation of the FSLA or state wage and hour laws. For example, it is illegal to pay an employee for 30 hours of work when the individual has worked 40 hours. One potential area of abuse is in the misclassification of hourly employees as exempt to avoid paying overtime. On the positive side, classifying employees as exempt sometimes gives them additional benefits, such as more annual leave.

EQUAL PAY ACT

An important federal law that specifically addresses equality of the sexes in the workplace is the Equal Pay Act of 1963, which requires equal pay for equal work. Equal work requires essentially the same skill, effort, and responsibility, done under similar circumstances. Fringe benefits are also considered as pay under the act, and therefore equal benefits must be provided to both men and women even if the cost of providing those benefits to both are not the same. Employers cannot lower the pay of one sex to remedy an unequal situation; the pay of the lower group must be raised. The Equal Pay Act does not require the employer to equalize pay in cases where different wages are paid according to a merit or seniority system, a system based on quality or quantity of production, or any other system not based on sex.

"Comparable worth" is a concept related to the Equal Pay Act. The act requires that people performing essentially the same job be given the same pay regardless of sex; comparable worth states that people performing different jobs having essentially the same value to the employer should be paid the same regardless of sex. The justification is that historically female-dominated job classifications with lower wages should be compared with jobs of substantially the same levels of responsibility or requiring the same skill level or effort under similar working conditions.

OVERVIEW OF LAWS GOVERNING THE WORKPLACE

THE LAW: Fair Labor Standards Act (FLSA)

SUMMARY: This act, as amended since 1938, regulates minimum wage, overtime pay, equal pay, child labor, and recordkeeping requirements. *Exempt* and *nonexempt* originate with FLSA—certain groups of employees are exempt from provisions of the law.

ENACTED: 1938; Amended numerous times, notably 1966 and 1972.

COVERAGE: The provisions of the law, originally limited to employees of industrial and commercial concerns engaged in interstate commerce, were extended by the 1966 amendments to schools and hospitals, and by the 1974 amendments to agencies of federal, state, and local governments. Virtually all employers are covered by the act as a result of amendments.

EXCEPTIONS: FLSA provisions on wage and overtime do not apply to executive, administrative, and professional employees.

ENFORCEMENT: Administered and enforced by the U.S. Department of Labor, Wage and Hour Division.

CLAIMS: Claims for unpaid wages must be filed with the Department of Labor within two years of the violation.

LAWSUITS: A private lawsuit may be filed if a claim is not made with the Department of Labor. Employers can be fined up to $10,000 for violations of the child labor provisions of FLSA.

STATE LAW: Some states have laws that prohibit discrimination against workers less than 40 years of age and more than 70 years of age.[1]

THE LAW: Labor-Management Relations Act (LMRA)

SUMMARY: An amendment to the Wagner Act, this landmark legislation, together with the National Labor Relations Act (Wagner Act) and the Labor Management Reporting and Disclosure Act of 1959 (Landrum-Griffin Act), is commonly known as the Taft-Hartley Act. This act gives employees the right to organize and bargain collectively and prohibits employers from engaging in unfair labor practices. It established the concept of neutral arbiter.

ENACTED: 1947.

COVERAGE: Applies to all employers.

EXCEPTIONS: Does not apply to agricultural workers, housekeepers, employees of airlines and railroads, independent contractors, supervisors and other managerial employees.

ENFORCEMENT: Administered and enforced by the National Labor Relations Board

CLAIMS: Unfair labor practice claims must be filed with the National Labor Relations Board within six months of violation.[2]

THE LAW: National Labor Relations Act of 1935

SUMMARY: Commonly known as the Wagner Act, this legislation was intended to control and lessen the disruption to interstate commerce caused by strikes. It provides employees with the right to self-organize, to bargain collectively through representatives of their choosing, to engage in concerted activities for the purpose of collective bargaining or other mutual aid or protection, and to refrain from interfering with any and all of these activities. Amended by the Labor Management Relations (Taft-Hartley) Act (1947) and the Labor-Management Reporting and Disclosure (Landrum-Griffin) Act (1959).

ENACTED: 1935.

COVERAGE: Applies to all employers.

EXCEPTIONS: Does not apply in cases where age is a bona fide occupational qualification of the job.

ENFORCEMENT: Administered and enforced by the Equal Employment Opportunity Commission (EEOC).

CLAIMS: Must be filed with the EEOC within 180 days of the violation.

LAWSUITS: Private lawsuits may be filed within 90 days of receipt of a right-to-sue notice from the EEOC or within 60 days of notification from EEOC that they will not sue on the employee's behalf.

STATE LAW: Some states have laws which prohibit discrimination against workers less than age 40 and more than age 70.[3]

THE LAW: Equal Pay Act

SUMMARY: An amendment to the Fair Labor Standards Act, it prohibits discrimination in the establishment of pay rates on the basis of sex. It requires equal pay for equal work for men and women. Equal work is defined as work which requires equal skill, effort, and responsibility under similar working conditions.

ENACTED: 1963.

COVERAGE: Applies to employers of two or more workers.

EXCEPTIONS: Does not apply in cases where different wages are paid according to a merit or seniority system, a system based on quality or quantity of production, or any other system not based on sex.

ENFORCEMENT: Administered and enforced by the Equal Employment Opportunity Commission (EEOC).

CLAIMS: Must be filed with the EEOC, which must bring a lawsuit within two years of violation.

LAWSUITS: A private lawsuit may be filed if a claim is not made with the EEOC.[4]

NOTES

1. Title 29, U.S. Code, Section 201 et seq.
2. Title 29, U.S. Code, Section 141 et seq.
3. Title 29, U.S. Code, Section 621.
4. Title 29, U.S. Code, Section 206(d).

BIBLIOGRAPHY

Aitchison, Will. *The FLSA, a User's Manual.* 2d ed. Portland, OR: Labor Relations Information System, 1997.

Emerging Issues in Public Sector Labor/Employment Law. Minneapolis, MN: Minnesota Institute of Legal Education, 1997.

Employment Law Handbook Volume 1. St. Paul, MN: Minnesota Continuing Legal Education, 1998.

Employment Law: The Cutting Edge. Columbus, OH: Ohio CLE Institute, 1998.

The Fair Labor Standards Act of 1938, As Amended. Rev. July 1997. Washington, D.C.: U.S. Department of Labor, Employment Standards Administration, Wage and Hour Division, 1997.

Henderson, Richard I. *Compensation Management in a Knowledge-Based World.* Upper Saddle River, NJ: Prentice Hall, 1997.

Jorgensen, Karen. *Pay for Results: A Practical Guide to Effective Employee Compensation.* Santa Monica, CA: Merritt, 1996.

Liebert, John. *The Fair Labor Standards Act: A Public Sector Compliance Guide.* Washington, D.C.: National Public Employer Labor Relations Association, 1998.

Olson, Stephen. "FLSA Compensation Provisions: Avoiding the Pitfalls." *The Bottom Line* 8, no. 1 (February 1, 1993): 10.

Perman, Lauri. *The Other Side of the Coin: The Nonmonetary Characteristics of Jobs.* New York: Garland, 1991.

Reichenberg, Neil E. *The FLSA Salary Basis Test.* Alexandria, VA: International Personnel Management Association, 1996.

Schechter, Susan. *Fair Labor Standards Act Explained: A Wage and Hour Guidebook.* Chicago: CCH, 1997.

Smith, Matthew M., and Steven H. Winterbauer. "Overtime Compensation Under the FLSA: Pay Them Now or Pay Them Later." *Employee Relations Law Journal.* 19, no. 1 (summer 1993): 23.

Smith, Matthew M. "Overtime Pay Liability: The Unexpected Peril of Disciplinary Suspension Policies." *Employee Relations Law Journal.* 20, no. 4 (spring 1995): 503.

Tremper, Charles, and Pam Rypkema. "Who Punches the Clock? Wage and Hour Laws Determine If Person Is Volunteer or Employee." *Business Law Today* 4, no. 2 (November 1, 1994): 38.

ORIENTATION AND TRAINING OF STUDENT EMPLOYEES

> When I was a boy of fourteen, my father was so ignorant I could hardly stand to have the old man around. But when I got to be twenty-one, I was astonished at how much the old man had learned in seven years.
>
> —Mark Twain

TRAINING IS EVERYTHING

Why is good training necessary? Won't employees learn without being trained? Yes, they will, but that's the danger. Whether you train them or not, employees will learn, but not the right way. Some people cringe at the word *training*: "Training is what you do to monkeys; *development* is what you do to people." In fact, training is a specialized and practical form of education that prepares employees to do their jobs well. In academic libraries, supervisors have an obligation both to train student employees to do their jobs and to develop them. A development program is needed to provide students with a broadening experience designed to build on their strengths and give them positive work experiences. In this chapter we will discuss training and orientation as well as training and development programs.

WHY PROVIDE ORIENTATION?

The major reason for providing an orientation for new student employees is that oriented workers do a better job and stay with the library longer than do those who are not given an orientation. Orientation serves to reduce the anxiety associated with a new job and saves time for supervisors and coworkers. The better the orientation, the less time the new employee will take in asking questions of others. An effective orientation helps the new employee develop a positive attitude toward the library and the job. The result is higher job satisfaction and better performance.

Orientation training, or induction training in industry, actually begins the minute an applicant enters the library to fill out an application or appears for an interview. First impressions determine the student's initial feelings about the library. As discussed earlier, it is important to establish a central point to which student employee applicants report. The best place for employee applicants to report is the office of the dean/director, branch library office, or the library's personnel office. The hiring supervisors should be summoned to meet the students and escort them to the department office or work area. New employees, if handled properly, have more positive attitudes toward the library as well as toward their jobs.

Orientation and the New Student Employee

It is essential that you recognize how the student feels when reporting for work on the first day. Think about *your* first day on a new job. Did you feel anxious, confused, out of place, concerned about how others would accept you, and worried about how you would perform? Almost everyone has those feelings. Your new student employees will undoubtedly feel that way too. It is important to follow an employee orientation system that eases new student employees' anxiety and makes them feel welcome.

Effective orientation of new student employees paves the way for future good relations between the employees and the library. The time and personal attention given by the supervisor during the first few days on the job go a long way toward making student employees feel wanted and important. Your personal attention to orientation gives new employees a sense of security and demonstrates that the library is interested in the employees as individuals.

Orientation begins with introductions and a tour of the department. Explain what other employees do and how they work together in the department or unit. You should explain how the job will be learned and who will provide the training. Orienting new employees includes discussing library rules, procedures, and policies, usually included in a student handbook. It is not advisable simply to hand the book to new employees and tell them to read it. Even if you do have a handbook, you should sit down with new student employees and review it with them.

A student employee handbook should include the following information:

1. *Eligibility for student employment.* Included are definitions of the number of credit hours required to qualify for employment. Students must be made aware that if the number of credit hours falls below the required number, they will be terminated. Different libraries have different policies.

2. *Hours of work allowed.* Many libraries limit the number of hours a student may work each week, normally to 20 hours.

3. *Timesheets/timeclock.* Describe how time worked is to be reported.

4. *Pay periods.* Describe how, when, and where student employees receive their paychecks. Provide a schedule of paydays.

5. *Absences.* Describe the library's policy for reporting absences and what they should do when they will be or are late.

6. *Transfer policy.* Some libraries require that students work a certain number of months before they may request a transfer to another department or campus job.

7. *Personnel records.* Inform student employees about employment records and clarify how they are used.

8. *Telephones.* Describe the library's policy on personal use of telephones.

9. *Socializing and studying.* Describe the library's policy on socializing and studying on the job or in the work area.

10. *Library equipment.* Describe the library's policy on the use of university equipment for personal use.

11. *Security/emergencies.* Describe the library's policies on reporting emergencies.

12. *Termination.* Describe what length of notice is required or desired when terminating employment. Describe the process used when termination is for disciplinary reasons.

13. *Grievance procedures.* Describe the library/university grievance procedures and employee rights.

14. *Training.* Note that the new student employee's supervisor will provide further orientation and training.

If your library does not presently have a handbook for student employees, you should consider developing one. A handbook guarantees that all employees are given the same information, regardless of how thorough the supervisors are in providing new employee orientation. Of course, there is no guarantee that the handbook will be read, but if you review the handbook with new student employees, later claims of ignorance about these policies and procedures will have no foundation.

Orientation Checklist

Does your new student orientation provide answers to the following questions?

♦ What does the organization do?

♦ How does the student's work group or job fit into the overall library organization?

♦ How important is the work to the library?

♦ What do the other departments do?

♦ What do the other libraries on campus do?

♦ What is the chain of command?

♦ What exactly will the student do?

♦ What equipment will the student employee be using?

♦ What other employees will the student be working with daily?

♦ What are the work hours?

- Are there scheduled breaks?

- How long is the employee's probationary period?

- When and how will the student employee be evaluated?

- How and how much will the student be paid?

- When is payday?

- Will the employee be paid after the first pay period or is there a delay of one pay period?

- What will be deducted from paychecks?

- How will time worked be reported?

- If a time clock is used, where is it and how is it used?

- If timesheets are used, how are they filled out, and when?

- How are pay increases determined?

- When the student employee has questions, who should he or she ask?

If your new student employees have the answers to these questions, whether provided by a library—wide orientation program or by you, your employees will be ready for job training.

TRAINING AND DEVELOPMENT ARE NOT THE SAME

We have all heard the terms *training* and *development* used interchangeably. The terms do not mean the same thing and it is important to know the difference. Training for the job emphasizes the skills and knowledge necessary to achieve and maintain an acceptable level of performance. Development goes beyond training. It focuses on the growth and improvement of employees as members of the organization and as human beings. The payoffs for training tend to be for the short run, while the benefits of development programs are felt over the long run.

Role of the Student Employee
Supervisor in Training

Your job description may simply say, "supervises student employees," or "hires, trains, supervises, and evaluates student workers." Training is, in fact, an important part of your supervisory role. The role of the supervisor in training varies with different organizations. In industry, the personnel department is often charged with the responsibility for training new employees or there may be a separate training division. In libraries, the student employee supervisor is usually directly responsible for teaching new employees all the skills and information necessary to become full contributing members of the department. Typically, the supervisor is given latitude in developing a training program as long as the training has the desired results. Frequently, the student employee supervisor inherits a training program from a previous supervisor who may no longer be in the department.

There are two types of training which you may use in preparing student employees for their jobs: off-the-job or vestibule training and on-the-job training.

Vestibule training takes place away from the site where the actual work will be done. It may take place in a classroom or at a desk away from the work station. The advantage is that the new employee is given "hands-on" experience without interfering with the flow of work in the department.

On-the-job training is conducted in the department at the actual assigned work station. Most library training is done on the job.

Should Supervisors Do All the Training?

Supervisors approach training in one of two ways. The supervisor may elect to do all the training or place the new student with an experienced employee. By doing all the training, the supervisor can be assured that all employees are trained the same way; but training is time-consuming, taking time from other responsibilities. Having another experienced employee handle the training can be effective, depending on how well the training is done. The best approach is probably a combination of the two.

WHAT DO YOU TRAIN FOR?

It is obvious that you cannot train immediately for everything there is to do on the job. The basic rule is to train for those things that are vital to the job and that will protect the employee and the equipment from harm. You should divide the job into "have to know now," "have to know soon," and "have to know one of these days." The "have to know now" are those things that a person has to know because nothing can be done until they are learned. If they are not learned now, employees could damage a piece of equipment, hurt themselves, or turn away a patron with an incorrect or improper response. You can avoid some training by determining what a student employee already knows.

FOUR-STEP METHOD FOR TRAINING

For supervisors, training can be very simple or very difficult. If you can remember just four fundamental steps, you can be a good trainer. If you do not use this approach, training will always be difficult and may not be effective. The foundation of systematic, structured job training has four steps:

1. PREPARATION. Get the workers ready to learn.

2. PRESENTATION. Demonstrate how the job should be done.

3. PERFORMANCE TRYOUT. Try the workers out by letting them do the job.

4. FOLLOW-UP. Gradually leave the workers on their own.

Step 1. Preparation of the Learner

Until individuals are psychologically and emotionally ready to learn, it is difficult to teach them. It is the supervisor's responsibility to help the trainee prepare for what you will teach. The following will help get the trainee ready to learn the job:

1. Put the student employee at ease—relieve the tension.

2. Explain why the trainee is being taught.

3. Create interest, encourage questions, and find out what the student employee already knows about the job.

4. Explain the why of the whole job, and relate it to some job the trainee already knows.

5. Place the student employee as close to the normal working position as possible.

6. Familiarize the trainee with the work area and equipment and the materials that will be used.

Step 2. Presentation of the Operation

After preparing the student employee to learn, you are ready to begin demonstrating how the job should be done. In this step you will describe and demonstrate one step at a time; stress each key point of the job; and patiently, without giving the trainee more than can be mastered, teach the steps of the job in sequence. These steps are followed in presentation:

1. Explain requirements for quantity and quality.

2. Go through the job at the normal work pace.

3. Go through the job at a slow pace several times, explaining each step. Between operations, explain the difficult parts, or those in which errors are likely to be made. Repeat several times.

4. Go through the job at a slow pace several times, explaining the key points.

5. Have the trainee explain the steps as you go through the job at a slow pace.

6. Have the trainee explain the key points as you go through the job at a slow pace.

Step 3. Performance Tryout

In this step of training, you will give the trainee the opportunity to perform the job while you observe. Performance try-out includes the following:

1. Have the student employees go through the job several times, slowly, explaining to you each step. Correct trainee mistakes, and, if necessary, do some of the complicated steps for them the first few times.

2. You, the trainer, run the job at the normal pace.

3. Have the trainees do the job, gradually building up skill and speed.

4. As soon as the trainees demonstrate proficiency, put the trainees on their own, but don't abandon them.

Step 4. Follow-up

Sometimes, the most difficult step is the last, because of the tendency to think that once the employee is trained, you're done. To guarantee long-term performance, you need to be sure the employee knows where to go for help and to check back frequently to see if all is going well. During this step, you will taper off coaching so the employees don't feel you're watching over their shoulders. Follow-up entails these activities:

1. Designate to whom the trainees should go for help or to ask questions.

2. Gradually decrease supervision, checking student employees' work occasionally against quantity and quality standards.

3. Correct faulty work patterns before they develop into habits. Demonstrate why the method taught is superior.

4. Compliment good work and provide encouragement until the trainees are able to meet quantity and quality standards.

EXTENDING THE TRAINING

Some libraries use the mentor or buddy system to extend the training of student employees after the initial training. Experienced student employees are assigned to new employees to serve as role models and as sources of help after new employees are put on their own in their jobs. If the mentor or buddy is a willing participant in the training process, the relationship can be a positive training support system. It goes without saying that care must be taken to assure that the assigned mentor or buddy will be a positive influence on the new student employee.

Experience, like practice, makes us perfect only if we're doing the right thing. Many of us do things wrong day in and day out, simply because we learned incorrectly in the first place. If you follow the four-step training method but discover that your training is not effective, the cause may be one of the following common training errors:

1. Failure to devote enough time to teaching. A common error for supervisors is to let other responsibilities hurry their training. Remember that the time devoted to training new employees properly is time well spent if the workers are productive.

2. Failure to follow the system step by step. The four-step system takes time but it works if followed correctly. If you skip a step, the system will break down and you will fail. Don't cut corners.

3. Failure to show enough patience with the slow learner. Some new employees will learn more slowly than others. When you teach someone who learns more slowly, you must slow your own pace or you will surely be disappointed in the results. Cover each of the four steps, even if it takes you twice as long. Keep in mind that many slow learners make excellent workers once they master a job, so your time will not be wasted.

JOB INSTRUCTION TRAINING (JIT)

Although the theory and practice of management is constantly evolving and changing, one constant over many years is training. The structured four-step on-the-job training method has been in use ever since it was developed during World War II to improve production; this method is called Job Instruction Training. During and after World War II, special trainers first trained the supervisors in the four-step instruction method. The process was printed on a "trainer card" for quick reference by supervisors. To demonstrate that the method has changed little in 50 years, the text of the "trainer card" is reproduced in figure 8.1.[1]

JOB INSTRUCTION TRAINING (JIT)

First, here's what you must do to get ready to teach a job:

1. Decide what the learner must be taught in order to do the job efficiently, safely, economically, and intelligently.

2. Have the right tools, equipment, supplies, and material ready.

3. Have the workplace properly arranged, just as the worker will be expected to keep it.

Then, you should instruct the learner by the following four basic steps:

Step I—Preparation (of the learner)

1. Put the learner at ease.

2. Find out what he or she already knows about the job.

3. Get the learners interested in and desirous of learning the job.

Step II—Presentation (of the operations and knowledge)

1. Tell, show, illustrate, and question in order to put over the new knowledge.

2. Instruct slowly, clearly, completely, and patiently, one point at a time.

3. Check, question, and repeat.

4. Make sure the learner really knows.

Fig. 8.1 continues on page 186.

Step III—Performance tryout

    1. Test learner by having him or her perform the job.

    2. Ask questions beginning with why, how, when, or where.

    3. Observe performance, correct errors, and repeat instructions if necessary.

    4. Continue until you know learner knows.

Step IV—Follow-up

    1. Put the employee "on his own."

    2. Check frequently to be sure learner follows instructions.

    3. Taper off extra supervision and close follow-up until person is qualified to work with normal supervision.

Remember—If the learner hasn't learned, the teacher hasn't taught.

Fig. 8.1. Job Instruction Training from the 1945 Bureau of Training.

TIPS FOR IMPROVING TRAINING

DON'Ts:

♦ Don't assume that everyone you train will learn at the same pace. We all learn at different rates. Be patient.

♦ Don't assume a task is easy because *you* found it easy. We all find different tasks easy to learn.

♦ Don't assume that because employees are trained, they will continue to do things the way they were taught. Skills slip, and you will have to retrain some people.

♦ Don't assume that because employees have experience they know how to perform some tasks. They may have experience performing tasks incorrectly.

♦ Don't forget that it takes time for good habits to develop.

♦ Don't act as if you are interested in your student employees' learning; *be* interested in their learning.

♦ Don't make fun of employees who make mistakes. We all learn from our mistakes.

DOs:

♦ Do follow the four-step training method.

♦ Do let your student employees know that you expect them to continue doing things correctly.

♦ Do let them know you are always willing to help them learn.

♦ Do give encouragement and recognition for work done well.

♦ Do keep student employees informed on how well they are doing and where they need improvement.

♦ Do ask your student employees what you can do to help them do a better job. Ask them often.

ACTIVE VERSUS PASSIVE LEARNING

We assume our student employees are adults and need to be treated as such. In planning training programs, it is important to understand the adult learning process. Your training program is aimed at adults who learn differently from children. Children are passive learners who are taught to sit quietly, absorb what they are told, and repeat it on command. Adults, on the other hand, demand active learning that is relevant and participative.

Your student employees have learned how to learn, and are in fact engaged in learning daily as part of their undergraduate or graduate experience. Unless student employees see the relevance, your training will not accomplish much. You can establish the relevancy of training by explaining why it is given, how it will benefit them, and why it is important to the work group's productivity.

Adults learn by doing so there should be as much activity as possible throughout the learning process. Because student employees are subjected to being lectured to all day, they will respond better to doing than to hearing about doing. Student employees will absorb an enormous amount of learning by actively participating, far more than from studying manuals. Don't use the same teaching methods you use with children to teach your student employees. Remember, your student employees are adults.

IMPLEMENTING YOUR TRAINING PROGRAM

The following are suggestions on how to prepare and implement your training program:

1. Be sure that you have done your homework. Do some reading in the psychology of learning and motivation.

2. Make notes to yourself about the four step training process and resolve to follow the system.

3. Develop a plan for training and write it down.

4. A checklist of tasks to be taught and how proficiency will be measured is extremely useful.

5. When training, use your checklist to be sure everything is taught.

6. Recognize that training takes time and that retraining is an integral part of your job. At times you will feel that all you accomplish is training but remember, don't cut corners.

7. Identify experienced student employees in the department who can help you and possibly act as mentors to new student employees.

8. Discuss your training plan with your supervisor, ask for suggestions, and get support.

9. Discuss training plans with other student employee supervisors and consider using their ideas.

DEVELOPMENTAL TRAINING

A part of your training responsibility as supervisor is developmental training. Developmental training usually refers to long-term growth: training to improve performance and preparation of employees for higher-level positions. In libraries, the emphasis is normally on preparing regular staff for managerial positions or for other advancement. For student employees, developmental training usually is limited to preparing them for supervisory duties within the department, night supervisor, for example, or for higher-level positions in other departments of the library.

The first step is to determine what kinds of training your student employees need. Because new employees must concentrate on learning the basics of the job, developmental training is designed primarily for experienced employees. For experienced employees, training must meet one of two needs: training to improve performance on the present job and training to prepare them for higher-level jobs. Both types of training are needed for all employees.

Training to improve performance hinges on the difference between "can do" and "will do." If the student employee "can't do" a task, ask yourself these questions: Has this employee ever done the task correctly? Has this employee been taught to do it correctly? If offered a reward to do the task correctly, could the employee do it? If the answer to any of the questions is "no," you have a training problem—the employee "can't do" the task.

If you can answer "yes" to the previous questions, you must determine whether you have a "won't do" problem on your hands. If the employee can do the task but won't do it, this becomes a management, not a training, problem. The way the employee is supervised, the way the job is organized, or the employee's attitude must be examined. No amount of training will solve the "won't do" problem.

To attack the "can't do" problem, the trainer must isolate the task that cannot be performed. Have the employee demonstrate how he or she performs the task. Physically demonstrated skills under your observation are the best way to separate the employee's abilities from inabilities. Once identified, the task that is not performed properly can be taught using the four-step training procedure described earlier.

Training to prepare student employees for higher-level jobs depends greatly on what those jobs are. In general, providing opportunities for student employees to learn a wide range of jobs and develop skills that will help them in future work situations is useful. Such things as computer and keyboard skills, telephone skills, interpersonal relations skills, and the development of good work habits are all useful in future employment. This may also be an opportunity to mentor student employees who express interest in librarianship as a career.

Opportunities for student employees to take advantage of staff development programs in the library or development programs offered by the university should be investigated. Find out whether or not student employees can avail themselves of programs offered to library staff. If so, make every effort to communicate those opportunities to your student employees.

Developmental Training Methods

Libraries with active staff development programs often invite student employees to participate. You, as their supervisor, should encourage participation in those programs that will provide enrichment to their jobs and help them prepare for future careers. At least a dozen developmental training methods are used in industry and education. The most common methods used by libraries are:

1. *Conference.* This training normally involves verbal interaction between an instructor and participants.

2. *Lecture.* Presentation by a knowledgeable person given to a group of employees.

3. *Programmed/computer assisted instruction.* Instruction in which the learner must respond correctly to each part before proceeding.

4. *Case study.* This method involves the use of a written description of a situation that the trainee must read and analyze.

5. *Role playing.* Learners assume the role of other people and interact with other learners in acting out a situation.

Talk to your supervisor and to other student supervisors to learn how they provide developmental training for staff and student employees. Ask questions about programs offered and find out how your student employees can participate. Remember that one of your responsibilities as a supervisor of student employees is to help them grow and develop. Through counseling and coaching, you can provide the ongoing informal training intended to refine skills and give assistance for personal growth.

SUPERVISOR TRAINING CHECKLIST

If you can honestly answer "yes" to all of the following questions, you are well on your way to becoming an effective trainer of student employees:

1. Do you accept full responsibility for training your student employees?

2. Do you consider training to be a continuous, ongoing activity?

3. Do you have an orientation checklist and religiously cover each item on the list?

4. Do you have a training checklist and use it every time you train a new student employee?

5. Do you use the four step training process without skipping any steps?

6. Do you recognize that individuals learn at different rates and are you patient with those who learn slower than others?

7. Do you stay in touch with new employees to be sure they know they can ask questions?

8. Do you have a way to identify present employee performance deficiencies and can you differentiate between "can't do" and "won't do" problems?

9. Do you have a developmental training program for your student employees?

The supervisor's responsibility for preparing workers, training them to perform their jobs, and developing employees cannot be understated. How well these are accomplished may well determine whether the supervisor succeeds or fails.

NOTES

1. Training Within Industry Report, War Manpower Commission, Bureau of Training, 1945.

BIBLIOGRAPHY

Aubrey, Robert, and Paul M. Cohen. *Working Wisdom: Timeless Skills and Vanguard Strategies for Learning Organizations.* San Francisco: Jossey-Bass, 1995.

Baldwin, David A. *Supervising Student Employees in Academic Libraries.* Englewood, CO: Libraries Unlimited, 1991.

Bell, Chip R. *Managers as Mentors: Building Partnerships for Learning.* San Francisco: Berrett-Koehler, 1998.

Bessler, Joanne M. *Putting Service into Library Staff Training: A Patron-Centered Guide.* Chicago: American Library Association, 1994.

Caldwell, Brian J., and Earl M. A. Carter, eds. *The Return of the Mentor: Strategies for Workplace Learning.* Washington, D.C.: Falmer Press, 1993.

Casner-Lotto, Jill. *Successful Training Strategies.* San Francisco: Jossey-Bass, 1988.

Chawla, Sarita, and John Renesch, eds. *Learning Organizations: Developing Cultures for Tomorrow's Workplace.* Portland, OR: Productivity Press, 1995.

Collins, Eliza G. V., and Patricia Scott. "Everyone Who Makes It Has a Mentor." *Harvard Business Review* 56, no. 4 (July–August 1978): 89–100.

Conroy, B. "Human Element: Staff Development in the Electronic Library." *Drexel Library Quarterly* 17 (fall 1981): 91–106.

Craig, Robert L., ed. *The ASTD Training and Development Handbook: A Guide to Human Resource Development.* New York: McGraw-Hill, 1996.

Creth, Sheila. *Effective On-the-Job Training: Developing Library Human Resources.* Chicago: American Library Association, 1986.

Daughtrey, Anne Scott, and Betty Roper Ricks. *Contemporary Supervision: Managing People and Technology.* New York: McGraw-Hill, 1988.

Goldstein, Irwin L. *Training in Organizations: Needs Assessment, Development, and Evaluation.* Pacific Grove, CA: Brooks/Cole, 1993.

Hendricks, William, and others, eds. *Coaching, Mentoring, and Managing.* Franklin Lakes, NJ: Career Press, 1996.

Hunt, Suellyn. "Staff Development: Your Number One Investment in the Future." *Library Personnel News* 1, no.1 (1987): 5–6.

Jacobs, Ronald L., and Michael J. Jones. *Structured On-the-Job Training: Unleashing Employee Expertise in the Workplace*. San Francisco: Berrett-Koehler, 1995.

Kathman, Michael D., and Jane McGurn Kathman. *Managing Student Employees in College Libraries*. Chicago: Association of College and Research Libraries, 1994.

Krissoff, Alan, and Lee Konrad. "Computer Training for Staff and Patrons: A Comprehensive Academic Model." *Computers in Libraries* 18, no. 1 (January 1998): 28.

Library Administration and Management Association and American Library Association. *Staff Development: A Practical Guide*. Personnel Administration Section. Chicago: LAMA and ALA, 1992.

Lipow, Ann Grodzins. *Staff Development: A Practical Guide*. Chicago: Library Administration and Management Association, 1988.

Lucas, Robert W. *Training Skills for Supervisors*. Burr Ridge, IL: Irwin Professional Publishing, 1994.

Marczely, Bernadette. *Personalizing Professional Growth: Staff Development That Works*. Thousand Oaks, CA: Corwin Press, 1996.

Mink, Oscar G., and others. *Developing High-Performance People: The Art of Coaching*. Reading, MA: Addison-Wesley, 1993.

Powers, Bob. *Instructor Excellence: Mastering the Delivery of Training*. San Francisco: Jossey-Bass, 1992.

Rader, Hannelore. "Library Orientation and Instruction, 1987." *Reference Services Review* 16, no. 3 (1988): 57–68.

Richey, Rita. *Designing Instruction for the Adult Learner: Systemic Training: Theory and Practice*. London: Kogan Page, 1992.

Robinson, Dana Gaines, and James C. Robinson. *Training for Impact: How to Link Training to Business Needs and Measure the Results*. San Francisco: Jossey-Bass, 1989.

Rosow, Jerome M., and Robert Zager. *Training, the Competitive Edge*. San Francisco: Jossey-Bass, 1988.

Rothwell, William J., and Peter S. Cookson. *Beyond Instruction: Comprehensive Program Planning for Business and Education*. San Francisco: Jossey-Bass, 1997.

Schneider, Benjamin, and David E. Bowen. *Winning the Service Game*. Boston: Harvard Business School Press, 1995.

Schuyler, Michael. "CATTs, Computer Assistants, and Other Training Tactics." *Computers in Libraries* 18, no. 1, (January 1998): 33.

Shaughnessy, Thomas W. "Staff Development in Libraries: Why it Frequently Doesn't Take." *Journal of Library Administration* 9, no. 2 (1988): 5–12.

Skitt, John. "Setting Up a Staff Development Scheme; Staff Appraisal and Training Needs." In *Management Issues in Academic Libraries*, edited by Tim Lomas, 67–77. London: Rossendale, 1986.

Sparhawk, Sally. *Identifying Targeted Training Needs: A Practical Guide to Beginning an Effective Training Strategy*. Irvine, CA: Richard Chang Associates, 1994.

Theory and Practice. London: Kogan Page, 1992.

Trotta, Marcia. *Successful Staff Development: A How-To-Do-It Manual*. New York: Neal-Schuman, 1995.

Chapter Nine

SUPERVISION TECHNIQUES FOR STUDENT EMPLOYEE SUPERVISORS

*Everything should be made
as simple as possible, but
not simpler.*

—Albert Einstein

MANAGING AND BEING MANAGED

Every person and every organization manages, is managed, or is affected by management. The largest of all of the groups of managers in organizations are the first-line managers, or supervisors. As the term implies, first-line managers are the first line of contact with workers. In the case of libraries, there may be two groups of first-line managers: supervisors of student employees and supervisors of permanent staff. First-line managers direct those they supervise and serve as a conduit for communication with library administration. They must also work with their peers and supervisors. Normally, supervisors of student employees do not supervise other supervisors.

The organization of the academic library determines, to a large degree, how the supervisor of student employees manages and is managed.

HIERARCHICAL LIBRARY ORGANIZATION

Most academic libraries are organized in hierarchies with a dean or director, associate/assistant deans or directors for public and technical services, department heads within each division, and unit heads within departments. There are formal lines of communication and specialization of worker function within each department. Normally an administrative group composed of the dean/director and the assistant deans/directors with selected others are the decision-making body of the organization. Department heads are consulted by the assistant deans/directors and the department heads in turn consult their staff. Control, authority, communication, and interactions between employees are vertical in the traditional hierarchic structure. Decisions are made by the administration and communicated down the hierarchy.

Some academic libraries are transforming their organizations in an attempt to address more effectively today's problems of shrinking budgets, increased materials costs, new technologies, and increased demands for services. One of the approaches being used is team management.

TEAM MANAGEMENT

A hierarchy stresses control; team management stresses facilitation. Responsibility for the performance of work groups falls to the group in a team management situation rather than to the administration in a traditional hierarchy. Team members are involved in problem solving and do not rely solely on decisions from the administration. Another major difference is that team members must communicate with their peers within and outside the organization rather than relying on management as the sole source of information. Katherine W. Hawkins has described how a library can implement a team management approach, emphasizing that commitment must exist for both workers and management in order for it to succeed.[1]

Participative Management

Participative management encourages participation of employees in decision making on matters relating to how the library should be operated. True participative management encourages the involvement of the employees' minds in their thinking and opinions of the work and how it should be performed. Participative management as practiced in the library:

1. Gives people the right to be creative members of a cooperating group. Library faculty and staff serve together on numerous committees.

2. Leads to new relationships being formed between employee and supervisor, and between an employee and other employees. Encourages horizontal communication among departments of the library.

3. Can spur less skilled employees to greater effort, and it encourages them to accept responsibility.

4. Raises human dignity and interest in what other people are doing.

5. Enables change to be accepted much more easily, particularly when those affected by it have participated in deciding its extent and how it should be implemented.

Whether team management or participative management, the library that adopts this approach will involve its staff in the operation of the library. Student employees working in this environment are expected to contribute not only their time and best effort on the job but will be called upon to participate fully as members of their teams.

Regardless of the library's organizational structure, the supervisor performs five basic management functions.

FIVE FUNCTIONS OF MANAGEMENT

The traditional functions of management are the basis of every supervisor's job. The activities carried out by managers are planning, organizing, staffing, leading and motivating, and controlling.

- ♦ The planning function includes determining the mission, goals and objectives, and direction of a unit and developing strategies for achieving them.

- ♦ Organizing involves the creation of a structure for accomplishing tasks, including assigning work.

♦ Staffing is the process of selecting, training, evaluating, disciplining, and rewarding staff.

♦ By creating a climate in which employees accomplish work, supervisors provide leadership and motivation for employees.

♦ Controlling is the process by which supervisors determine if and how well the unit is accomplishing its goals.

Seldom will you find a supervisor who can name the five functions of management, let alone describe the activities or techniques used to perform each of the five functions, but good supervisors do just that. For the supervisor of student employees to be successful, he or she must bear in mind that supervision is more than scheduling and assigning work to students. Supervisors perform all five functions of management, often without realizing it. A review of the principles and techniques of management will help you assess your own abilities. The following section expands on the discussion of authority in chapter 3.

ABOUT AUTHORITY

Authority is given to student employee supervisors by the library by virtue of having assigned them student employees to supervise. Authority is usually handed down to student employee supervisors from their immediate supervisors who in turn receive their authority from those above them.

Authority is handed down from the top, beginning with the highest levels. Those who appoint the governing body of the institution give them authority. Authority for the operation of the institution is delegated to the university president, who delegates authority to the vice president(s), who delegate authority to the dean/director of the library and so on, to the supervisors of student employees. As authority is passed down the line to the student employee supervisor, the delegated authority becomes more specific. The dean/director has the authority to manage the personnel budget and a large staff, but you have the authority needed to supervise a group of student employees with specific jobs and work to perform.

Authority is the power you need to carry out your responsibilities as student employee supervisor. A student employee supervisor who, in the opinion of employees, exceeds supervisory authority will find that employees question or even resist that authority. Student employee supervisors must remember that their authority is retained only so long as its use is approved by the organization and accepted by the majority of employees supervised.

According to Webster's New World Dictionary of the American Language, the definition of authority is 1) the power or right to give commands, enforce obedience, take action, or make final decisions; jurisdiction; 2) this power as delegated to another; authorization: as, he has my authority to do it; 3) power or influence resulting from knowledge, prestige, etc.[2]

Authority is one of those things that is much misused and misunderstood in business and industry. Supervisors often fail to use their authority when it should be used. Other supervisors try to use authority when it does not belong to them, and some even use it to dominate other people. It is extremely important to understand that authority carries with it the responsibility to use it correctly. Supervisors of student employees must respect the problems and needs of their employees and student employees must respect the authority of their supervisors.

The most common misuse of authority can be attributed to new supervisors and to experienced ones who have been assigned special projects. Persons unaccustomed to directing or coordinating the efforts of others must be careful not to let the newly acquired authority affect how they treat people. Overuse of authority almost always causes employees to become less cooperative.

Every supervisor wants to know how to exercise authority well and feel comfortable doing it. It is important to realize that it is not easy for those who are given authority for the first time but who are only used to following orders. Some advice may be in order from supervisors who have experience:

1. Be certain that you know what authority you have and don't have. Clarify this beforehand with your supervisor.

2. Be careful that authority does not go to your head.

3. Realize that good supervisors do not flaunt their positions.

4. Always delegate authority to get the job done, not to show who is boss.

5. When exercising authority, be considerate of others.

6. When exerting authority, try to promote team spirit.

7. Always use persuasion when you can instead of exerting your authority.

In addition to the authority given you by the organization, you will find that you can be more successful and may reinforce your authority or power with one or more of the following:

1. Your job knowledge (What do you know?)

2. Your personal influence in the organization (Who do you know?)

3. Your personal charm (Do you have it?)

4. Your abilities (How good are you at your job?)

5. Your ability to persuade (How well can you communicate?)

6. Your physical strength (How strong are you? Usually not a factor in library work.)

Generally, organizations have three classifications of authority with which supervisors can make decisions:

1. Complete authority. You may take action without consulting your supervisor.

2. Limited authority. You may take action but your supervisor must informed of your actions.

3. No authority. You may not take action without checking with your supervisor.

To accomplish your department's objectives, it will be necessary to delegate responsibility and authority to subordinates; remember that the two go together. In delegating, you must make it clear what authority is being delegated and at what level. Of course, there are responsibilities and authorities that cannot be delegated to student employees—discipline, for example.

Authority is an essential part of a supervisor's job. Always be sure to find out what authority you have and set about exerting it wisely and carefully. Your success as a supervisor may well depend on it. The following section expands on the discussion of responsibility in chapter 3.

RESPONSIBILITY

There is an important difference between the positions of worker and supervisor. A large part of that change is that by accepting a supervisory position, there is an agreement that you will accept the attendant responsibilities of the position.

According to Webster's New World Dictionary of the American Language, the definition of responsibility is 1) condition, quality, fact, or instance of being responsible; obligation; 2) a thing or person for whom one is responsible.[3]

Responsibility and authority go hand in hand but are quite different. Responsibilities are those things for which you are held accountable by your supervisor and library management. Authority is the power you need to carry out your responsibilities as student employee supervisor.

It is important for you, as a student supervisor, to determine with your supervisor what your responsibilities are. If asked, your supervisor may simply reply, "You are responsible for the students in this department." Your next question should be, "Do I also have the authority to take necessary actions without consulting you or do you want me to check with you first?" Your supervisor replies, "Just do what you think is right but keep me informed." In this brief conversation, you have determined that you are entirely responsible for planning, organizing, staffing, leading and motivating, and controlling all aspects of student employment in your department and that your supervisor has given you limited authority: you may take action but your supervisor must be informed.

In addition, obvious legal responsibilities apply to supervisor and employee alike:

1. The responsibility to perform the work for which hired.

2. The responsibility to follow organizational policies, procedures, and rules.

ABOUT MAKING DECISIONS

Without question, being decisive is a valuable attribute for a supervisor. When making decisions, the supervisor exhibits leadership skills while providing assurance to employees that everything is under control. The skill of making decisions under pressure must be developed to be effective.

To be decisive you must want to solve problems and have the confidence to do so. A good decision maker must know how and when to make decisions and be aware of the factors that influence decisions. Most important, you must have information with which to make good decisions. Successful decision makers don't make decisions without the facts. Find out what you need to know. Who is involved? What has been the past practice? When must the decision be made?

The good supervisor is not reluctant to make decisions. You can and should learn to be decisive. The following suggestions will help you develop a pattern of decision making that works.

1. Dispose of minor decisions quickly. By making these decisions promptly, you will have more time to devote to important matters.

2. Be firm in making a decision. Don't leave any doubt about what you have decided.

3. Don't waste time thinking about what you *could* have done.

4. Dispel any thoughts that you might make a mistake.

5. Carry out your decisions promptly.

You can make good decisions if you do not act hastily, get the facts, and take time to think. It is not necessary to have experience with similar problems to make good decisions. There are four basic steps:

First, be sure you understand the problem. If you are able to clearly state the problem, you are well on the way to resolving it. Writing it down often helps you define it.

Second, get information. Look for alternative answers.

Third, examine the good and bad points of each alternative. Will each alternative actually solve the problem? What are the risks of each? What is wrong with what appears to be the first choice?

Fourth, select the best alternative as your decision. Take action and monitor the results.

How can a supervisor determine when a decision must be made or when to leave a condition well enough alone? Even though it is your responsibility to make decisions, occasions arise when the best decision is take no action at all. Experienced supervisors have learned to distinguish real problems from conditions or situations that are merely irritating.

Supervisors are usually required to make a number of decisions each day. At times you may question whether a specific decision is really yours to make or whether it should be made at a higher level. Common sense dictates that decisions should be made at the lowest level of the organization, consistent with the functions of each supervisory position. If the problem requiring a decision fits into the normal duties and responsibilities of your position, the decision should rightly be made by you. If the decision will affect more than your unit's staff, procedures, or services, or if it is in conflict with existing policy, the decision should be made at a higher level.

Much more goes into making a decision than just deciding. You have to consider the feelings of the people affected by your decision. By having others participate in the decision making, you will have much greater acceptance. Timing must be considered. Pick the time and place for announcing a decision. Be certain that you feel good about it before making an important decision.

You will eventually make a bad decision. Probably more than one. The most experienced and successful supervisors make mistakes. When a bad decision is made, you must do what you can to correct it. Be sure to make the extra effort and devote the time needed to making a good decision. When considering reversing a decision, be sure to seek advice to avoid making another bad decision when correcting the first one.

One approach to developing decision-making skills is to examine the causes of poor decisions:

1. *Insufficient or inaccurate information.* Lack of information can lead to false conclusions, and therefore poor decisions.

2. *Insufficient time to decide.* By taking the time to gather information, you increase your chance of making a good decision.

3. *Fear of making a bad decision.* If you lack confidence in your abilities, the quality of your decisions may be affected.

4. *Overcautious.* If you are overly concerned about the risks involved, you may be too cautious.

5. *Not enough authority.* If you have responsibility without the authority, your decisions will be unenforceable.

6. *Underestimate the importance.* If you misjudge the seriousness or importance of the situation, you may not give it enough attention or ignore it all together.

7. *Emotion.* Poor decisions result when emotion rather than reason is used in making decisions.

Finally, not all your decisions will be readily accepted. People have their own opinions, may think differently from you, or have more information than you have. In most cases, a decision is challenged because people do not understand it or why you made it. If you have made a good decision, you should have no trouble explaining it. Persons who have valid and logical arguments may still disagree. When questioned, calmly say that you would be glad to discuss their opinions. Listen to their points of view and if you discover that you have made a bad decision, be willing to admit it and correct it. Listening is, without question, one of the most important skills in communication.

ABOUT COMMUNICATION

The term *communication* is defined as the process in human relations of passing information and understanding from one person to another. Communication between supervisor and employees is extremely important as are communication between supervisors and between supervisor and boss. Human communications suffer the same problems as mechanical or electronic communications: poor reception, interference, or being tuned to the wrong channel.

For a supervisor, nothing is better than face-to-face communication with employees. A real advantage is that you can see how your words are affecting the person to whom you are talking. Your haste, tone, mood, gestures, or facial expression may affect how the individual reacts. The opportunity for two-way communication is extremely important. A disadvantage is that it takes time. At the end of the day you may feel that you have done nothing but talk.

Communication with individuals may take the form of informal talks, planned appointments, or telephone calls. Face-to-face communication should always be used when the subject is of personal importance to either person. Written communication may take the form of memos, letters, or reports. The advantage of written communication is that all recipients are given exactly the same information. It is needed for messages that are intended to be formal, official, or long term. The use of memos should not be overdone. They should be used as seldom as possible. Face-to-face communication is much preferred.

Effective communication with groups requires special skills. The best way of developing group cohesiveness is the use of regular, informal staff meetings, supplemented with individual face-to-face communication. Scheduling a time when all student employees in your unit can meet is always a problem. It is important, however, to recognize the need to schedule such meetings if at all possible. Written communication for groups normally takes the form of bulletin board notices or a "must read" notebook. The notebook is an effective way to make certain that all written information is seen by all student employees in your unit.

In the long run, people will not listen to you if you will not listen to them. Employees will learn to talk to you if you will demonstrate that you will listen. How can you improve your listening skills?

1. Don't assume anything. Allow the employee to tell you what is wanted. Don't anticipate. If the student employee feels you already know what will be said, why bother?

2. Don't interrupt. Wait for the employee to finish speaking. Don't give anyone the impression that you do not have the time to listen.

3. Try to understand the need. Look for the reason the employee wants your attention. Often what the employee says is wanted is not the real thing. Student employees are typically more straightforward and able to express themselves better than many employee groups.

4. Don't react too quickly. Try to understand the other person's viewpoint. Be patient and do not jump to conclusions.

Listening cannot be overemphasized. When employees come to you with a problem and the solution is very clear, offer it. If it is possible, help student employees develop their own solutions.

What is the best form of communication? For a supervisor, nothing can beat face-to-face communication. In a participative management environment, student employees are involved in the discussions and decisions on procedure and policy. Good communication is critical to your success as a supervisor.

GROUP EFFORT

Organizations depend on the effectiveness of group effort. The success of any supervisor is dependent on how well the employees in the group perform their work. The individuals assembled to perform work comprise the work group. In the library, student employees work varied schedules, often with their hours spread throughout a work week of 80 to 100 hours. In a situation where the supervisor needs a minimum of three students workers on duty all the hours the library is open, it is not unusual for two students in the same department never to work at the same time. Turnover in the student work force also contributes to changes in the group. At any given time the supervisor is supervising different combinations of student workers in an ever-changing work group.

What groups do best is solve problems. One important technique in getting group support for problem solving is participation. To get individuals to work together to attain common goals, it is necessary to get individuals in groups to work with you. By sharing knowledge and information, sharing decision making, and sharing credit with the group, you can assure that the group will work most effectively.

GIVING DIRECTION

The successful supervisor is able to be the boss without being obvious about it. It used to be assumed that all a supervisor had to do was order an employee to do something and the employee would do it. This attitude will get you nowhere. Today's employees deserve more consideration. If employees feel they are offered some say in decisions that affect them, they will work harder when they have had the opportunity to participate. Student employees do not need to be ordered. In general, a request carries the same weight as an order but it implies that the employee has some choice in the matter.

Guidelines for Giving Direction

1. Avoid an "I'll show you who's boss" attitude when giving direction. You should project the idea that there is a situation that requires the employee's attention, and that it is based on more than your whim.

2. Be firm when giving direction. If delivered in an offhand manner, the request may not be taken seriously.

3. Watch what you say when giving direction. Be specific so there is no misunderstanding about what you want done.

4. Don't assume the employee understands. Give the student employees a chance to ask questions or to complain about the assignment if they wish. It is better to clear up any questions or concerns right away.

5. Don't overdo it. Be selective in issuing instructions and avoid giving too many orders. Don't give complex instructions when brief ones will do. Think about what information the person you are talking to really needs.

6. Avoid conflicting instructions. Make certain that you are telling your student employees the same thing as supervisors in similar departments are telling theirs.

7. Don't overwork the cooperative employee. Some people are more cooperative than others. Be sure you do not give directions only to those you know will cooperate without complaint.

8. Distribute the unpleasant tasks fairly. Resist the temptation to punish certain employees by assigning the difficult or unpleasant jobs to them only.

9. Don't flaunt your authority. You don't have to crack the whip to gain student employees' cooperation and respect.

Getting Cooperation

Good supervision is the art of getting others to do what you want, when you want it, and how you want it. To succeed as a supervisor, you must get others to cooperate with you. You must be able to develop good relations with those you supervise and earn their cooperation. Here are eight ways to promote cooperation:

1. Stress team effort whenever possible. Use the word *we* when talking with employees.

2. Reward people who do more than you ask of them.

3. Set realistic goals with the help of your employees.

4. Praise your employees. Never criticize an employee in front of others.

5. Supervise with persuasion, not force or pressure.

6. Help your employees when they need and request it.

7. Be honest about problems and issues with your employees.

8. Involve your employees with solving problems and making decisions.

MOTIVATION

All supervisors want motivated employees. There will always be highly motivated individuals and self-starters who wish to work in the library and some of them will work for you. However, many employees are unmotivated, resulting often in low morale, absenteeism, and high turnover. Employee motivation can be defined as those techniques used that influence the action of an individual to help the employee integrate personal needs and goals with those of the organization.

The individual's motivational drives and societal attitudes toward work affect employee motivation. The supervisor can inhibit or contribute to an individual's motivation but it is primarily self-directed. Employee motivation is an important aspect of any supervisor's job and one which seems quite difficult on the surface.

Job satisfaction and motivation are closely tied. To help you understand how your employees can become motivated from the job itself, think about the worst and best jobs you've ever had. When you consider the worst jobs, more than likely what will come to mind are things that made them unbearable: long hours, bad weather, dirty, boring, bad boss, and no chance for advancement. The things that made the job bad were mainly bad environment, rather than the job itself.

When you consider the best job you've had, you may think about how hard you worked, how long the hours were, how you couldn't wait to get to work, and how you couldn't believe how fast the time went. The best job probably provided challenge, responsibility, variety, recognition, and meaning. The good job has some of the same characteristics as the bad—long hours, poor working conditions, not enough money. In addition, however, the good job carries with it responsibility, challenge, recognition, and meaning. If your student employees' jobs carry some responsibility and provide challenge, recognition, and meaning, does it not make sense that the job itself can be a motivator to employees? Examine your students' jobs and determine how you can add some of these elements. Motivation can also be accomplished through coaching.

Coaching

Coaching can be considered as continuous training. Just as an athletic coach provides the knowledge and skill training for athletic competition, the manager is charged with the responsibility of not only training but keeping up the skills and knowledge of employees required on the job.

As employees begin to slip away from the basic skills that made them productive, coaching is needed. There are many possible reasons for slippage in a person's skills. Boredom with routine tasks causes many employees to look for shortcuts which, taken over time, diminish the employees' ability to remember exactly what the tasks were originally. The shortcuts or changes in the job are attempts to add variety to the job. This deterioration of skills is called "professional degeneration." Another reason for skills deterioration is that employees want independence and will want to try things their way. Although employees often bring fresh ideas on how the job should be done, they need to be kept on the right track so that the job is done correctly and accomplished efficiently. Regular coaching is one of the best ways of getting employees back on the right track.

Although certain employee behaviors can be changed by holding group meetings, individual coaching is usually the most effective means of coaching. It is not uncommon for supervisors to hold group training sessions to correct the behavior of one individual. It should be remembered that individual performance causes group performance and for the group to succeed, each individual must succeed. Coaching one-on-one is the most effective means for changing individual behavior.

First, you must be able to identify the behavior that needs changing and know what behavior you want. How do you change it? Saying to the employee, "Look, Mary, I've shown you twice how to do that. If you don't do it properly, your replacement will do it right," will prove counterproductive. Coaching is teaching, not scolding. Here is a logical step-by-step process:

1. Observe the present behavior, compare it to the ideal behavior, and identify what must be changed.

2. Discuss the needed changes with the employee. Does the student employee know the present behavior is wrong? Does the employee know the correct behavior?

3. Get the employee to talk about ideas for improving the task.

4. Demonstrate the desired behavior until the employee can do it correctly and can explain the reason for doing it that way.

5. Praise the employee for correct behavior.

A good supervisor coaches student employees in much the same manner as a football coach coaches a team. Corrective measures are taken when a change is needed in an observable behavior. Coaching is an excellent way to alter behavior, making a good employee an excellent employee. It is both a continuous process and an extension of training.

ABOUT COUNSELING

Counseling has a more personal aspect to it than coaching. Coaching is intended to improve a person's skills, but counseling is a private discussion of problems that have a bearing on job performance. When something is worrying the employee, the supervisor must discover it and correct it if possible.

You will encounter two types of counseling sessions: those you initiate and those initiated by the student employee. Neither is more important than the other and you must be available whether the purpose is to discuss a personal problem or to allow the employee to "blow off steam."

You may need to call a student employee in if you have heard or observed that things are not going well for the student. The employee has exhibited behavior that tells you something is wrong and you feel that a counseling session is needed.

The following is a step-by-step procedure will help you improve the counseling sessions you call:

1. Determine why the student employee is exhibiting the wrong behavior. Talking privately with other employees and observing the employee may turn up the reasons. Try to determine the cause before you talk to the affected employee.

2. Plan ahead for the counseling session. Carefully think through what you want to discuss.

3. Notify the employee that you want to meet a day or two in advance of the meeting. Never call a counseling session on the spur of the moment unless it is an emergency.

4. Meet privately. If you can't stop the phone calls and interruptions, hold the meeting away from your office.

5. Put the employee at ease. Discuss anything but the topic at hand for a few minutes. If the purpose is to discuss poor performance, first stress the positive aspects of the job.

6. Get to the point of the session. Encourage the employee to talk while you listen.

7. Help the student employee save face by letting the employee know that you or others have faced similar situations.

8. Come to an agreement about what needs to be done.

9. Offer your assistance if possible and set a time to discuss what has been done.

10. Make a written note of the discussion for the file which includes date, time, location, subject, and outcome. File the note for future reference if needed.

When *you* call the meeting, you have the advantage of being able to plan for it. The situation is quite different when the employee asks to talk to you. It often starts when the employee appears at your office door and says, "Do you have a minute, Steve? I need to talk to you," or "Mary, when could I see you for thirty minutes?" A good practice is not to jump into a counseling session unless it is an emergency. If you can, ascertain what the subject of the meeting is beforehand and then set a time for later in the day or the next day if possible. It is entirely possible that you will not know the subject of the meeting until it takes place. The procedure for an employee-initiated meeting is similar to the supervisor-initiated meeting with a few differences:

1. You may only be needed as a sounding board for the employee, someone to talk to about a personal problem.

2. Know your limitations. Psychologists and psychiatrists have the proper training to counsel students with emotional problems. Your advice or answers may do more to complicate the problem than solve it for the student employee.

3. Be careful to avoid becoming involved in a student's emotional problems.

4. After the student employee has vented the problem, ask the employee to offer possible solutions.

5. After possible solutions have been discussed, offer encouragement and ask if the employee would like to schedule a future meeting to discuss the situation.

6. What the two of you have discussed is confidential. Keep it that way.

You, as the supervisor of student employees, should be familiar with all the counseling services available on campus and be prepared to describe them to your student employees. Remember that you are not alone. Seek the advice of your supervisor or fellow student employee supervisors, making sure to maintain confidentiality. Be aware that no one may have had precisely the same problem with the same circumstances.

It must be noted that not all counseling sessions are negative. The student employee may be interested in discussing prospects for advancement on the job or in seeking your advice. A good supervisor makes it a habit to counsel employees regularly. Most of us do not consider this to be counseling, but it is good practice to give student employees the opportunity to discuss the job or anything they wish to talk about.

Counseling can be used to resolve employee problems or to give them opportunities to discuss anything on their minds. It lets them know you are interested in them as employees and individuals.

SUPERVISORY PRINCIPLES

The quotation from Benjamin Spock's *Baby and Child Care* seems quite appropriate here: "Trust yourself. You know more than you think you do." Many of the principles that make up the basis of supervision are plain old-fashioned common sense. It is important that you develop a foundation of knowledge in supervision; but when in doubt, use your common sense.

The next chapter describes how to resolve problems common to student employee supervision.

NOTES

1. Katherine W. Hawkins, "Implementing Team Management in the Modern Library," *Library Administration & Management* (winter 1989): 11–15.

2. *Webster's New World Dictionary of American English*, 3d College edition (Cleveland, OH: Webster's New World, 1988), 92.

3. Ibid.

BIBLIOGRAPHY

Baldwin, David A., and Robert L. Migneault. *Humanistic Management by Teamwork: An Organizational and Administrative Alternative for Academic Libraries.* Englewood, CO: Libraries Unlimited, 1996.

Bittel, Lester R. *Practical Management for Supervisors.* 2d ed. Westerville, OH: Glencoe Division, Macmillan/McGraw-Hill, 1993.

Brown, Nancy A. "Managing the Coexistence of Hierarchical and Collegial Governance Structures." *College and Research Libraries* 46 (November 1985): 478–82.

Burckel, Nicholas C. "Participatory Management in Academic Libraries: A Review." *College and Research Libraries* 45 (January 1984): 25–34.

Chapman, Elwood N. *Supervisor's Survival Kit: Your First Step into Management.* 6th ed. New York: Macmillan, 1993.

Gardenswartz, Lee, and Anita Rowe. *Managing Diversity: A Complete Desk Reference and Planning Guide.* Burr Ridge, IL: Irwin Professional Publishing, 1993.

Giesecke, Joan, ed. *Practical Help for New Supervisors.* 3d ed. Chicago: American Library Association, 1997.

Good, Sharon. *Managing with a Heart.* Naperville, IL: Sourcebook, 1997.

Hilgert, Raymond L., and Edwin C. Leonard, Jr. *Supervision: Concepts and Practices of Management.* 6th ed. Cincinnati, OH: South-Western College, 1995.

Kaplan, Louis. "On the Road to Participative Management: The American Academic Library, 1934–1970." *Libri* 38, no. 4 (1988): 314–20.

Lee, Dalton S., and others. *Supervision for Success in Government: A Practical Guide for First Line Managers.* San Francisco: Jossey-Bass, 1994.

Marr, John N., and Richard T. Roessler. *Supervision & Management: A Guide to Modifying Work Behavior.* Fayetteville, AR: University of Arkansas Press, 1994.

Maurer, Rick. *Caught in the Middle: A Leadership Guide for Partnership in the Workplace.* Portland, OR: Productivity Press, 1996.

Migneault, Robert LaLiberte. "Humanistic Management by Teamwork in Academic Libraries." *Library Administration & Management* (June 1988): 132–36.

Mosley, Donald C., and others. *Supervisory Management: The Art of Empowering and Developing People.* 3d ed. Cincinnati, OH: College Division, South-Western College, 1993.

Rooks, Dana C. *Motivating Today's Library Staff: A Management Guide.* Phoenix, AZ: Oryx, 1988.

Thompson, Brad Lee. *The New Manager's Handbook.* Burr Ridge, IL: Irwin Professional Publishing, 1995.

Chapter Ten

STUDENT EMPLOYEE PROBLEM RESOLUTION

> *Three things in human life are important.*
> *The first is to be kind. The second is to*
> *be kind. The third is to be kind.*
>
> —Henry James

STUDENT EMPLOYEE PROBLEMS

Included in this chapter are the problems most common to the supervision of student employees in academic libraries. The suggestions offered are certainly not the absolute answers. The situations, circumstances, and the people involved differ from one problem to another. You, the supervisor, will have to evaluate each problem you face individually and decide what course of action would be the most appropriate for the student employee and the library.

After reading through this chapter, you will find that many of the problems can be resolved by talking to or counseling student employees. Be careful to avoid becoming involved in a student's emotional problems. Know your limitations. Psychologists and psychiatrists have the proper training to counsel students with emotional problems. Your advice or answers may do more to complicate the problem than solve it.

Before labeling a student employee a problem, consider the possibility that the cause may be poor management. One study found that about half of the employees labeled problems by supervisors were victims of poor supervision. These employees had not been adequately trained, had not been given counseling when needed, or had not received written warnings when required. Supervisors who do not have the patience or the ability to help employees or change their behavior should resolve to improve or seriously consider getting out of supervision.

Remember that you are not alone. Seek the advice of your supervisor or fellow student employee supervisors. Be aware that no one may have had precisely the same problem with the same circumstances. There are also numerous books on supervision that can be consulted. Mix in all you learn from colleagues and books with a large dose of common sense and humaneness and you will do fine.

The Student Employee Who Complains

Student employees who complain are a constant source of frustration to supervisors. Student employees who are chronic complainers often do a poor job or avoid work. A poor attitude exhibited by complaining manifests itself in poor work performance and unhappiness. Supervisors need to take action when complaining affects the amount of work being accomplished or is unsettling to others in the department.

For the student employee who complains to one and all about seemingly everything, the first step is to talk privately to the student. Remember that a complaint is always justified from the point of view of the complainer and the complaint (or complainer) must be dealt with promptly. Explain that you understand that the employee is unhappy with the work and has complaints about the library. Investigate the nature of the complaint with questions.

Ask, "What's wrong?" or "What happened?" Get the facts by listening carefully. Empathize with the complainer and show your concern.

Poor communications are behind many complaints. Providing a clear explanation may resolve the complaint. Some complaints are the transfer of anger type. Something may have happened to put the employee in a poor frame of mind. A few questions about how things are going in general may reveal the situation.

Handling a complaint or complainer is one of the most difficult parts of a supervisor's job. You have to put yourself in the complainer's position and try to understand how the complainer feels.

The Unmotivated Student Employee

The unmotivated student employee is a constant concern to supervisors. Whether the person does not like the work, appears to be lazy, dawdles on the job, is bored, or feels unappreciated, the reason is usually that the employee is dissatisfied with the job.

Motivation is a severe problem for many student employees. Their primary focus is on their education. Most work in the library because they need the money; they are not interested in working in the library for longer than is necessary.

The unmotivated employee can be a poor influence on fellow workers and the problem must be addressed. The first step is to talk with the employee. Determine the cause.

If the student does not like the work, there may be something else in the department or the library more suited to the employee's interests and abilities. If not, the student employee should be referred to student employment for reassignment.

If the student appears to be lazy or dawdles on the job, calling the student employee's attention to it may help the individual make adjustments, if only temporarily. If the student employee continues to exhibit the same behavior, make it clear in a private conversation that unless there is a change in behavior, the employee and the department would be better off if the student worked somewhere else.

If the student employee is bored, an effort should be made to see if the job can be enriched with other duties. Calling attention to the obvious boredom may help the employee make adjustments. If the student employee continues to exhibit the same behavior, inform the employee that termination may result and that the employee might be more suited to other work.

If the student feels unappreciated, the supervisor must take steps to address the problem. Inform the employee that you and the library depend on the student employee's contribution. Give your full attention and show interest when the employee communicates with you; compliment the employee in the presence of others. It is important that you show the student employee that you are interested.

In dealing with the unmotivated employee, supervisors must be alert to the need to make all employees feel a part of the department's team. It is important to remember that being a member of a group is important for job satisfaction and good productivity and that good compatibility among workers promotes good performance.

Consult chapter 9 for more suggestions on motivating employees.

The Student Employee with Low Morale

Closely related to motivation problems with employees, low morale can disrupt the workplace. Low morale can be caused by a number of things, including low pay, schedules, lack of advancement, and working conditions. Low morale is exhibited most often by student employee complaints about wages and working conditions.

To understand the causes of low morale, supervisors must know that all humans share five basic needs. These needs, which cause behavior, vary in intensity for different people and must be satisfied in order from outer needs to inner needs. These five basic needs are physical needs, security needs, the need to belong, ego needs, and achievement needs.

Physical needs are the basic animal needs for food and shelter. Until these needs are satisfied, the others are unimportant. Once satisfied, other needs emerge. The need to be protected from bodily harm and the need for job and financial security are security needs. Once an individual feels secure, the need to belong must be satisfied. This is the human herd instinct: to be accepted by others, to have friends, and to identify with others. After the need to belong is satisfied, ego needs become important. Ego needs include the need to be recognized and well thought of, to be independent and avoid embarrassment, to have a good self image, and to be in control of situations. Once ego needs have been essentially met, the last set of needs becomes important: achievement needs. Achievement or self fulfillment needs result in the drive to be the best and to advance on the job.

The physical and security needs and the need to belong are for the most part satisfied in most student employees as are the ego and achievement needs. Those student employees with low morale most often complain about wages (security need) and lack of advancement (achievement need).

Efforts must be made to be certain that student employees are paid for work performed. First, find out whether the student is being paid fairly in relation to other student employees performing duties at the same level. If you find that the student is paid fairly, explain explicitly how wages are determined. If the student is in a position of needing more pay to meet financial obligations, refer the employee to the employment office to see if placement in another position in the library or on campus is possible. If there are other duties that can be assigned and that would result in a higher wage and if it is within the supervisor's authority to assign them, the student's security and achievement needs may be satisfied and the problem of low morale resolved. It is also very important that the student be made to feel that the student and the student's work is essential to the successful operation of the department.

The Disloyal Student Employee

Unfortunately, not all employees are loyal to the organization they work for. Therefore, some student employees are disloyal to the library. So what? The student employees are paid to work, nothing else. Of what possible harm could there be in having student employees who are not loyal? They show their disloyalty to the library in one or more ways, both on and off the job. Their actions or inactions hurt the library and themselves. Disloyalty is shown by employees who speak badly of the library, fail to keep promises, take advantage of the library in work procedures, or threaten to leave. Loyal student employees, on the other hand, are concerned about the library, its success, and its future, yet disloyal student employees seem determined to oppose those things. Supervisors must be alert to signs of disloyalty among student employees and act when they see or hear indications of it.

Employees often withhold loyalty until the supervisor and the library have earned it. As a supervisor, you must know that loyalty cannot be bought or won with favors. It must be built by making employees feel that they belong and are a part of the library. Student employees must be made to feel that the success of the library depends on each of them doing his or her share and cooperating with coworkers and supervisors.

Student employees' value to the library depends not only on their talents and abilities but also on a willingness to use those abilities and talents to help the library. By not using those talents and abilities for the good of the library, employees are hurting themselves as well as their employer and coworkers.

Supervisors may need to examine how much their student employees are involved in planning for the department. When employees are involved in planning, they feel a commitment to helping carry out the plans they helped formulate. The student employee who is involved in planning and is an important member of the team may fail to keep up his or her end of the bargain by not performing as expected or by being absent too often. It is important to talk to the student, making sure the importance of everyone's contribution to the accomplishment of departmental objectives is understood. If the student fails again, inform the employee of the consequences of this action and follow through with disciplinary action at the next offense.

The student employee who criticizes the library can have a negative effect on other employees. Student workers who have contact with library users can seriously harm the library's programs. If you were to ask the student employee how loyal he or she was to the library, your sanity might be questioned. Most employees tend to think about the library's loyalty to their employees rather than employees' loyalty to the library. They think of the benefits, such as job security, etc., extended by the library, which help employees meet personal needs.

The supervisor must determine the cause of the criticism. Has the library in some way mistreated the student? Can the student employee give you examples of how the library has treated the student or other employees unfairly? When you learn the reasons for this attitude you can either prove to the student employee that it is the wrong attitude or correct a problem if one exists.

The Student Employee Who Violates Library Rules

Violation of company rules has always plagued business and industry. To deal with it, companies provide employees with handbooks outlining regulations and procedures. A handbook is a poor substitute for personal training because the handbooks are seldom read or understood. Supervisors should inform new student employees about library rules and regulations as soon as possible after they are hired.

When a rule is broken, the supervisor must first determine whether or not the student worker was aware of the rule and understood the reason for it. You the supervisor are responsible for disciplining chronic rule breakers because by overlooking a violation and saying nothing, you are condoning the action, making that particular rule completely unenforceable. Supervisors must speak and act with authority. Appearing unsure only causes anxiety and worry.

Remember that the purpose of discipline is corrective, not punitive. Avoid using sarcasm or threats and never penalize anyone without an explanation. Spend time discussing the rule and describe what you expect of the employee in the future.

The library's policies should clearly spell out personnel rules and regulations and must be communicated to student workers. A student handbook, although not guaranteed to be read and understood, is needed. Part of the orientation of new employees is stressing the importance of their reading the handbook and accepting responsibility for abiding by the policies described.

The Student Worker with Absenteeism Problems

Probably the most frequent problem with student employees is their inability to work all the hours scheduled. Student workers, whether they are scheduled to work at the circulation desk or to search new book orders, are relied upon to perform their duties on a scheduled basis. The library must maintain a certain level of staffing, especially for night and weekend service hours. Students are required to meet specific requirements for courses, for example, field trips, special lectures, or performances. Students are not immune to illnesses or family crises that require their absence from work. The obvious solution is for the library to maintain sufficient permanent staffing so as not to rely on student workers. In the real world of academic libraries, funds are not available to hire all the new staff members needed; therefore, student employees are and will continue to be critical to the daily operation of libraries. Student employee absences must be accepted and approved and policies must exist to regularize the library's response to absences.

Rules about attendance are critical to the operation of the library. Student employees are expected to establish a schedule for work and stick to it. Because of the commitments students have for their course work and other activities, schedule changes can be expected. Rules must be in effect relating to how much notice of schedule changes must be given, how the work or hours will be covered, and whether or not the hours missed can be made up in advance of or after the absence. Once established, these policies must be communicated to student workers and adhered to by all supervisors.

Questions that should be answered by an absence policy include the following:

1. What constitutes an unexcused absence?

2. How many unexcused absences are allowed before disciplinary action is required?

3.   What disciplinary action is to be taken?

4.   What constitutes an excused absence?

5.   How is an anticipated absence to be reported?

6.   What notice is required?

7.   Will someone have to take the absent student's place during the hours missed?

8.   Whose responsibility is it to find a replacement?

9.   Can students switch hours with one another?

10.   How is a switch to be communicated to supervisors?

11.   Is there a limit to the number of excused absences allowed?

An unexcused absence is normally an instance where the employee does not come to work for the scheduled hours and fails to notify the supervisor. Many libraries require that after one unexcused absence, the student employee be given a warning in writing that a second unexcused absence will result in termination.

An excused absence is normally an instance where the employee makes prior arrangements to be absent during specified scheduled hours or calls in prior to the scheduled hours to report the inability to come to work. Where replacements must be found, the amount of advance notice is critical.

You will have to make a judgement as to whether these absences interfere with the department's ability to meet its objectives. Is the morale of the department affected by this employee's absences? Are you being fair in your treatment of all employees? When talking with a student worker about excessive absences, make it clear that presence on the job is important and describe how absences affect the department. If the student employee cannot assure you that the number of absences will be reduced, you should consider reassigning the student to other duties or asking that the employee be reassigned to another department or on-campus job.

Counseling will probably help those student employees whose pressures off the job affect their commitment to work; those for whom work appears dissatisfying; those student employees who have unpleasant relationships with coworkers; and those for whom a straightforward word to the wise would help. Counseling would probably not be successful for those student employees for whom the pay and the job have no attraction, for whom off-the-job activities have much greater appeal than the job, and for whom the sole purpose of their being absent is to inconvenience, punish, or disrupt the department. For this latter group, termination may be the only recourse.

Time, Telephone, and Dress Policies

Rules regarding arriving and leaving on time should be included in the student employee's handbook. The supervisor must speak to the student to ascertain the reasons for arriving late or leaving early. It is possible that the schedule can be adjusted to allow for a student to arrive early and leave early or arrive late and leave late, as long as the student is present during the number of hours to be worked. Disciplinary actions should include warnings and termination of habitual rule breakers.

Another common library rule relates to the use of telephones for personal calls. Common business practice is to permit employee use of the telephone as long as it is not abused and does not interfere with the work. As to what constitutes abuse, the individual supervisor will have to determine and consistently enforce.

Library rules regarding dress in public universities have become passé. A good rule of thumb can be found at the entrances to many places of business: NO SHIRT, NO SHOES, NO SERVICE. Supervisors are within their rights to require shirt, shoes, and decency but should go no farther. Some private institutions have enforceable dress codes. In matters of personal hygiene, the supervisor may privately suggest to a student that cleanliness is a concern.

The Student Who Is Dishonest

A problem that occurs rarely, but is nonetheless a concern, is cheating on timesheets. It is the supervisor's responsibility to review and verify reports of time worked for the purpose of determining wages. By signing a timesheet, the supervisor verifies that the student worker is entitled to be paid at a predetermined rate for the hours reported as worked. The student who arrives late, leaves early, or does not work scheduled hours and signs a timesheet that certifies that all of the scheduled hours have been worked will have cheated on the timesheet.

Falsifying a timesheet is a serious offense. The supervisor who knows that hours are incorrectly reported (and it is your responsibility to know) should first talk with the student. Point out the errors on the timesheet and allow the employee to correct them. Make certain the employee understands the importance of correctly reporting time worked and the consequences of falsifying time reports. The student employee who purposely falsifies a time sheet should be warned when there is doubt and terminated when there is proof. Timesheets should never be completed by student employees in advance of time worked unless directed by their supervisors to do so.

Procedures should be established that call for auditing cash receipts and balancing the cash box or register on a regular basis. Wherever possible, establish procedures that protect student workers from suspicion should shortages occur. The procedure should require that someone other than the persons taking in or passing out cash perform the count and do the balancing. The location of lost and found can also be a problem. If items are turned in at circulation, they should be claimed in the library office in order that the circulation staff not be placed in the position of being accused of stealing those items.

The student employee suspected of theft (cash, personal items, library materials/supplies) should be warned when there is doubt and terminated when there is proof. Involvement of campus or local police is a local issue that should be addressed by university policy.

The Student Employee Who Violates University Rules

Normally, the student government association governs the behavior of students. University rules relating to academic honesty and classroom behavior are enforced by the student government, the faculty, and the university administration. It is the duty of library employee supervisors to cooperate with those bodies. A student who is expelled for whatever reason is normally ineligible for employment by the library, especially those students who receive college work-study or other university financial awards.

The Student Employee with Personality Problems

First, you cannot label just anyone as having personality problems because you don't like that person. Second, you cannot solve real personality problems, nor does anyone expect you to solve those problems. Third, extreme cases must be left to psychiatrists and psychologists. Fourth, student services on university campuses are available to students and you should know about those services and how to refer students to those services.

The definition of personality problems, for the purposes of this discussion, are those persons whose work habits, attitudes, and outlook on life are difficult to understand, and persons who indulge in public displays of emotion and who tend to affect the morale and productivity of their coworkers. You are probably not a trained psychologist or psychiatrist but you may help some student employees by communicating with them, understanding them, and treating them the same way you treat all student employees. This common sense advice is applicable to all workers.

Types of personality problems include persons who are frequently angry, easily hurt, eccentric and unpredictable, negative and pessimistic, or who are excessive talkers.

Persons who frequently "fly off the handle" or lose their tempers are difficult to work with, and are not to be tolerated. Because talking constructively to an angry person is difficult, avoid doing so. Set up another time to talk; if the student becomes angry, you must listen, not talk. When you are able to talk to the individual, inform the individual that the behavior is unacceptable and that it interferes with the employee's work and the work of others. Disciplinary action may not change these individuals but will let them know that the library will not tolerate the behavior. Give a warning that if the problem is not corrected on the job, the employee will be terminated. If you are going to give a warning, be sure you are prepared to follow through.

Persons who are sensitive to criticism and easily hurt can be a problem. When a student employee who needs constructive criticism reacts by bursting into tears, the first inclination is never to criticize. When criticism must be given, it should be offered with kid gloves. If possible, use the words *we* and *our* when referring to the work and how it is to be done. Avoid anything that will undermine this person's self-confidence. Praise for work well done and an expression of appreciation to these persons will help them gain confidence and improve their ability to accept direction.

The eccentric or unpredictable student employee is not uncommon in university libraries because what is a university if not a place for young people to test their ideas and investigate alternative lifestyles? It is not unusual for a student to change during the college years and during employment in the library. Should you accept this behavior or try to change the person? It is unlikely that you or anybody else can change this individual or the way he or she handles the job. You can, however, expect the eccentric student employee to perform the assigned duties in the same manner as other student employees. This employee is to be held to the same level of accountability as other students. If the creative approach to the job does not result in acceptable performance or interferes with the work of others, this behavior needs to be addressed privately.

The negative or pessimistic student employee can be a disruption in a work group. The common sense advice for dealing with this student is accentuate the positive. Be sure you are always positive when talking with the employee. Assign tasks at which you know the employee can excel. The secret of getting people to think positively is to convince them that positive thinking is good for them. When the supervisor conveys a positive attitude to workers, they feel better and want to do a good job.

The employee who talks excessively is usually not productive and wastes the time of others. Excessive talking on the telephone should be addressed by pointing out the library's policy on telephone use. If the employee persists in wasting time and the time of others, the employee must be talked to privately. Inform the employee that the issue is time, not personality. Point out that excessive talking wastes time and interferes with the work to be done. Tell the employee that you have to guard against talking too much yourself and that many people have the same problem on the job. If the problem persists, inform the employee that if the problem is not corrected, you will need to take disciplinary action.

Remember that you cannot and should not attempt to solve severe personality problems. You should be aware of student services offices on campus, which are set up to assist students. If the student comes to you for help, do not hesitate to suggest an appropriate office. You can help some student employees by communicating with them, understanding them, and treating them the same way you treat all student employees.

The Student Employee with Personal Problems

We all have personal problems of one type or another: family, financial, relationship, etc. In addition, student employees may have academic problems that most of us don't have. To a point, you can help some student employees by communicating with them, understanding them, and treating them the same way you treat all student employees.

Family problems may require that the student be absent for a period of time. The student employee is usually concerned about having a job upon return. Arrangements can usually be made to hold the position for the employee. How do you deal with financial and relationship problems? The inclination is to give students advice you would give your children. Whether or not you give advice depends on your confidence in counseling young people; it is often advisable to not get involved. Academic problems may require that the student reduce the number of hours worked. Whether this can be permitted depends entirely on your staffing situation. Tutoring help for students is available on most campuses.

When a student employee voluntarily brings a problem to you, you can be most helpful by listening without interruptions, advice, prescriptions, solutions, pontifications, or preaching. Then, recognize your own limits in dealing with situations like this.

Dealing with Rumors in the Workplace

Few organizations can claim that their people don't start or spread rumors. Because one of the primary responsibilities of supervisors is to keep staff informed, rumors must not be ignored. The most effective way to dispel them is to determine whether there is any truth to the rumor and to inform your staff about what you learn. If there is no truth to a rumor, tell your staff. If you have no information, tell them that. The best way to dispel rumors is to give your staff the facts. If the supervisor keeps staff informed, there will be no need for rumors.

It is important to let your staff know that they can come to you to check out rumors; they should be encouraged not to repeat them. It is even more important to keep student workers informed because they work different schedules. A library newsletter distributed to all staff and routed to student workers is a good way to keep students informed of library activities.

The Student Employee
Who Procrastinates

People procrastinate most often when faced with unpleasant or difficult jobs to do. Procrastination is one of the biggest barriers to getting work done. Student employees are as susceptible as any other employee. Because everyone procrastinates to some degree, it is important to be able to overcome it in yourself as well as others.

You will not procrastinate nearly as often if you develop a positive attitude about work. Nothing is as difficult as it seems. Once you have completed a job you have dreaded doing, the satisfaction derived is that much greater.

Student employees who procrastinate must learn to overcome the problem. If you want to help someone who is procrastinating, you must learn why that person is putting off doing something that should be done. If the tasks students avoid are either difficult or boring, sharing the load among several student workers will lessen the tendency to procrastinate.

If your boss is procrastinating on something important to you or your staff, you may be able to help. By subtly applying pressure, by persuasion, and by offering to assist with the job, you may provide the incentive that is needed. Of course, you must be diplomatic in what you say or do. You do not want to be judgmental or a nag. If the boss offers an excuse for not doing something, drop it. Your help is not wanted.

The Student Worker Who Resists Change

In academic libraries today, changes occur in procedures, policies, staffing, and job duties at a greater rate than ever before. Major changes brought about in libraries have been made and continue to be made by the automation of technical and public services functions.

Changes that affect the duties of student workers will sometimes require that their jobs be reclassified. Most student employees like change and accept it graciously. They are probably the most adaptable of all library staff. Although change is inevitable on the job, some people do resist it. Supervisors must do all they can to help employees expect, understand, and accept change. If you do this, resistance will be greatly reduced.

One of the most effective ways to overcome resistance is to involve student workers in changes before they are made. Change is more acceptable if it is kept simple and done without a lot of fanfare. You need to give people time to adjust to change and you must recognize that some resistance may never be completely overcome.

Dealing with Stress

Stress can develop on any job and in any employee. It is true, however, that stress usually does not occur in employees who adjust easily to change or to persons in good mental and physical condition and who have a positive attitude. All stress is not bad. Stress that causes fear, anger, or frustration can be harmful. Employees who fear making mistakes or losing their jobs waste energy in combating those fears. Stress that challenges, encourages initiative, and raises competitive feelings can be positive.

In many cases, a heavy work load is the cause of stress. Reducing that work load may not reduce the level of stress because an individual's personality often determines the amount of stress the employee perceives. Student employees are likely to be under greater stress during mid-term or final examinations than at other times of the year. Probably as much as or more than other groups of employees, student workers are likely to bring stress to the job as a result of their course work.

For the student worker who is affected by stress from academics, there is not a lot that can be done. You may receive requests for time off that can be granted. Some libraries do permit students to study at work for limited amounts of time during final examinations. For more information on stress, see chapter nine.

Dealing with Insubordination

Insubordination can take one of two forms: 1) an employee may willfully refuse or refrain from carrying out a direct order or 2) an employee may direct threats, abusive language, or physical violence at a supervisor.

When a worker refuses to carry out a direct order, the supervisor must first mentally reconstruct the conversation to be certain an order was given. Once certain, the supervisor should try to determine the reason for refusal. Was the employee unable to do what was requested? Did the employee feel that the order was irrational? Talk with the employee and ask for an explanation. Explain the consequences of insubordination in the library.

Normally, insubordination is grounds for immediate termination. If it is determined by the supervisor that the order given was reasonable and within the capabilities of the student employee, the supervisor can warn or terminate the employee.

Insubordination that takes the form of physical violence toward the supervisor is not so easily handled. The policy in most libraries is that physical violence or the threat of physical violence in the presence of others is grounds for immediate termination. No counseling or conversation is required or expected when the supervisor's personal safety or that of other workers is threatened.

Dealing with the Older Student Employee

The average age of students enrolled in colleges and universities is becoming steadily higher. Returning students, or nontraditional students, are becoming more and more common on today's campuses. Nontraditional students can be real assets to the library. Supervisors must be careful to treat the older student in the same way as all other students.

PROBLEM RESOLUTION

Please remember that the suggestions offered are not absolute answers. The situations, circumstances, and the people involved differ from one problem to another. You will have to evaluate each instance individually and decide what action would be the most appropriate.

Know your limitations. Your advice or answers may do more to complicate the problem than solve it. Remember that you are not alone; seek the advice of your supervisor or fellow student employee supervisors. Be aware that no one may have had precisely the same problem with the same circumstances. Mix in all you learn with a large dose of common sense.

BIBLIOGRAPHY

Carr, Clay. *The New Manager's Survival Manual*. 2d ed. New York: Wiley, 1995.

Collins, Eliza G. C., ed. *The Executive Dilemma: Handling People Problems at Work*. New York: Wiley, 1984.

Federal Communications Commission. *Dealing with Performance Problems*. Washington, D.C.: Federal Communications Commission, 1987.

Flynn, W. R., and W. E. Stratton. "Managing Problem Employees." *Human Resources Management* 20 (summer 1981): 28–32.

Giesecke, Joan, ed. *Practical Help for New Supervisors*. 3d ed. Chicago: American Library Association, 1997.

Good, Sharon. *Managing with a Heart*. Naperville, IL: Sourcebook, 1997.

Imundo, Louis V. *Employee Discipline: How to Do it Right*. Belmont, CA: Wadsworth, 1985.

Kaiser, Tamara L. *Supervisory Relationships: Exploring the Human Element*. Pacific Grove, CA: Brooks/Cole, 1996.

Kent, Robert H. *25 Steps to Getting Performance Problems Off Your Desk—and Out of Your Life!* New York: Dodd, Mead, 1986.

Library Administration and Management Association. *Problem Employees: Improving Their Performance*. LAMA Program, Dallas ALA Conference, 1984. Chicago: American Library Association, 1984.

Marr, John N. *Supervision & Management: A Guide to Modifying Work Behavior*. Fayetteville: University of Arkansas Press, 1994.

Martin, William T. *Problem Employees and their Personalities: A Guide to Behaviors, Dynamics, and Intervention Strategies for Personnel Specialists*. New York: Quorum Books, 1989.

Maurer, Rick. *Caught in the Middle: A Leadership Guide for Partnership in the Workplace*. Portland, OR: Productivity Press, 1996.

O'Reilly, C. A., and B. A. Weitz. "Managing Marginal Employees: The Use of Warnings and Dismissals." *Administrative Science Quarterly* 25 (September 1980): 467–84.

Thompson, Brad Lee. *The New Manager's Handbook*. Burr Ridge, IL: Irwin Professional Publishing, 1995.

Van Fleet, James K. *The 22 Biggest Mistakes Managers Make and How to Correct Them*. West Nyack, New York: Parker, 1973.

Weaver, Richard G. *Managers as Facilitators: A Practical Guide to Getting Work Done in a Changing Workplace*. San Francisco: Berrett-Koehler, 1997.

Weiss, W. H. *Supervisor's Standard Reference Handbook.* 2d ed. Englewood Cliffs, NJ: Prentice-Hall, 1988.

Wubbolding, Robert E. *Employee Motivation: What to Do . . . When What You Say Isn't Working!* Knoxville, TN: SPC Press, 1995.

Ziegenfuss, James T. *Organizational Troubleshooters: Resolving Problems with Customers and Employees.* San Francisco: Jossey-Bass, 1988.

Chapter Eleven

PERFORMANCE APPRAISAL

> *I always thought there was at least one person in the stands who had never seen me play, and I didn't want to let him down.*
>
> —Joe Dimaggio

HOW AM I DOING?

Everyone wants to know, "How am I doing?" Performance appraisals provide one opportunity to tell student employees how they are doing. It should not be the only time workers are told how they are doing, but a performance evaluation system guarantees that they are given feedback at least one or two times each year, depending on the schedule. Appraising the performance of employees is a basic task of managers. It is impossible to make intelligent managerial decisions about employees without measuring their performances in some manner.

Formal performance appraisal is as old as the concept of management and informal appraisal is as old as human history. All employees want and deserve to know not only how they are doing, but what's being done well, how it can be done better, and how the job itself can be improved.

PRAISES AND RAISES

Student employees, like all employees, want "praises and raises." Performance appraisals offer the opportunity for supervisors to communicate and document formally how their employees are doing and to provide the evidence for "praises" and, if applicable, "raises." Supervisors are cautioned that performance appraisals can be debilitating for student employees if done poorly. Those individuals who have received poor evaluations from supervisors, deserved or not, know that criticism is difficult to accept and that no matter how tough-skinned people are, or think they are, the experience can be devastating. Performance appraisals do not always result in "praises or raises," but they can and should be constructive and positive experiences for you and your student employees.

JOB EVALUATION VERSUS PERFORMANCE APPRAISAL

Job evaluation is an evaluation of the duties and responsibilities of a specific job or group of jobs. Performance appraisal is a measurement of how well an employee is doing that job. Performance appraisal or performance evaluation is sometimes called a merit rating. Essentially, job evaluation is a technique for evaluating a job; the other evaluates an individual.

Performance appraisals have two basic purposes: employee evaluation and employee development. For most companies, evaluation for administrative purposes has been the most common use of the process. Appraisals of employee performance provide the basis for administrative decisions about promotions, demotions, terminations, transfers, and rewards. The development purpose has generally been secondary. Evaluations used to improve performance on the job is becoming more common in industry. The following chart (table 10.1) shows how companies used performance evaluations in 1984 and indicates a shift to a more balanced approach.[1]

Table 10.1. Purpose of the Performance Appraisal Process

PURPOSE OF APPRAISAL	PERCENTAGE OF RESPONDENTS
compensation	85.6
counseling	65.1
training and development	64.3
promotion	45.3
manpower planning	43.1
retention/discharge	30.3
validation of selection technique	17.2

Academic institutions view performance appraisal from a development viewpoint. There are three basic reasons for performance appraisal for library student employees:

1. To encourage good performance and to correct or discourage substandard performance. Good performers expect a reward, even if it is only praise. Those employees who perform below standard should be made aware that continued poor performance will at the very least stand in the way of advancement. At worst, poor performance may lead to termination.

2. To satisfy the student employees' curiosity about how well they are doing. It is a fundamental drive in human nature for individuals to want to know how well they fit into the organizations for which they work. Although a student employee may dislike being judged, the need to know is very strong.

3. To provide a foundation for later judgments concerning employees: pay increases, promotions, transfers, or termination. Supervisors are to be cautioned not to stress pay raises as part of the appraisal process. It is natural for student employees whose performance is rated good to expect a pay raise to follow. If your institution or library's compensation plan doesn't work that way, don't mislead student employees by telling them that their good work will result in a promotion or pay increase. It is important to tell students just how the appraisal will be used.

HOW FORMAL SHOULD THE PERFORMANCE APPRAISAL BE?

The formality or informality of the process varies greatly. Some libraries have detailed evaluation procedures and others leave it up to the supervisors. The relative value of student employees to the library is often reflected in its student employee evaluation process. Many formal programs are dictated by the university's student employment office. Others have been carefully developed by the libraries. If given the choice of evaluating or not evaluating, you should do it. If you don't presently have a formal procedure for providing performance feedback to student employees, you should propose one. Examples from evaluations used by libraries are included in this chapter.

The evaluation of student employees is a managerial/supervisory responsibility that is not easily shared with others and should not be delegated. Peer evaluation, however, is one technique that can be used to gain input for the appraisal. Because coworkers have more continuous contact and opportunities to observe each other's performance, peer ratings can be quite valid measurements. Peers judge performance from a perspective that is different from the supervisor's, and although subject to influence by friendships, peer comments are often perceptive.

Peer evaluation deserves consideration by student employee supervisors in organizations that have developed a climate of interpersonal trust among coworkers and have noncompetitive reward systems. Peer evaluation is an effective tool for libraries using team management. Student employee supervisors are cautioned that unless peer evaluation is an established part of your library's appraisal program, it should be avoided. Improper use of peer evaluation can cause enormous problems. It is often helpful, however, to gather input from persons the employee comes in contact with and to discuss your opinions with your supervisor as you prepare student employee evaluations.

A good performance appraisal includes facts as well as the supervisor's opinion. Included in the information gathered for an appraisal are facts on quantity of work, quality of work, dependability, and records of work incidents, good and bad. These facts comprise the objective factors used in the evaluation. Subjective factors tend to be opinions about attitude, personality, and adaptability, which may or may not be substantiated by data.

QUESTIONS TO BE ANSWERED IN AN APPRAISAL

Although the questions that are answered in student employee evaluations vary from one appraisal plan to another, there are some basics:

1. What has the individual done since the last evaluation?
2. How well has it been done?
3. How much better could it be done?
4. In what ways have strengths and weaknesses in the student employee's approach to the job affected performance?
5. Are the weaknesses ones that could be improved upon?
6. What is the student employee's potential?
7. How well could this person do if given a chance?

HOW OFTEN SHOULD STUDENT EMPLOYEE APPRAISALS BE DONE?

If student employees are evaluated too often, those evaluations are likely to be affected too much by day-to-day occurrences. If done too seldom, the supervisor is likely to forget some of the incidents that need to be included in an appraisal. If annual evaluations are required, it is a good idea to do an informal unwritten appraisal more often. Twice-a-year performance appraisals, one formal and one informal, serve to keep the student employees informed of their performance and not create undue hardships for supervisors.

SEQUENCE OF ACTIVITIES IN PERFORMANCE APPRAISAL

Performance appraisal follows an established sequence of activities. This sequence is 1) to set performance standards; 2) to communicate those standards; 3) to observe employees doing their work; 4) to collect data; 5) to have employees do self-appraisals; 6) to do a supervisor's appraisal; and 7) to provide feedback.

Set Performance Standards

What are the expectations for the student employees? Performance standards are those benchmarks against which the student workers' performance are measured. In some libraries, those standards are based on historical data and the same form is used for all student employees. An example of the standards (rated on a scale of "exceeds objective," "meets objective," or "does not meet objective") found on one library's student employee performance evaluations are the following:[2]

1. *Quantity of Work.* Maintains a pace adequate to accomplish all assigned tasks within work period; is able to accommodate normal work flow.

2. *Quality of Work.* Performs tasks with precision and neatness; meets all responsibilities; all facets of job are executed correctly and in the appropriate sequence.

3. *Reliability.* Punctual; able to work without direct supervision when necessary; conduct is appropriate for work environment.

4. *Initiative.* Commences necessary actions without direction; exercises independent judgment in problem situations; devises and applies appropriate solutions to work-related problems.

5. *Staff Relationships.* Works harmoniously with staff members at all levels.

Communicate Standards

Student employees should know from the beginning what is expected of them and what the basis of their evaluations will be. What constitutes good, acceptable, marginal, and unacceptable performance? The evaluation form in use by the library should be shown to student employees as part of their orientation. Make sure there is no question about what will be evaluated and how it will be done.

Observe Employees Performing Work

Employees should be observed during the appraisal period as they perform their daily tasks and information regarding their performance should be noted. Do not observe them only in the last minutes or days before the evaluation.

Collect Data

Data for the performance evaluation should be collected throughout the appraisal period, not just prior to the evaluation. Supervisors of student employees should record both positive and negative incidents on the job. These reports become part of the file of information referred to when evaluating performance. In addition, records of attendance, etc., should be checked. Accurate, current information is critical in making objective judgments of worker performance. Unfair, inequitable, subjective decisions are often made because of incomplete data.

Have Employees Complete Self-Appraisal

Student employees may be asked to complete an appraisal of their own performances. The following procedure should be followed:

1. Discuss the purpose of self-appraisal with the student employee.

2. Review the format and clarify what the employee should do.

3. Provide the student employee with the form at least a week before it is to be completed and returned.

4. Set a specific time for the self-appraisal to be completed.

5. Stress the importance of the self-appraisal to the total performance appraisal process.

Use the Information Gathered

The information gained from observation, data collection, and the self-appraisal will be useful to the supervisor in completing the student employee performance appraisal. In preparing the performance appraisal, remember that the information may be used in five primary ways:

1. To make administrative decisions, such as promotion, suspension, demotion, transfer, or termination.

2. To make decisions on who should receive merit increases.

3. To identify training needs, such as what kind of training is needed and who can benefit from it.

4. To motivate and provide feedback by letting student employees know how they are doing, what their strengths are, and what improvements are needed.

5. To validate the selection process by comparing worker performance to desired performance. If a significant percentage of the workers are performing below expected levels, the selection criteria should be examined to determine whether the requirements for the job are accurate and what qualities should be sought in students to be hired in the future.

Evaluate the Employee

Plan a time when you can concentrate on writing performance evaluations and when you will not be disturbed. Plan a procedure that you will follow for each student employee. Gather all the performance data and review all the data on each employee before writing that employee's evaluation. Write a draft copy and set it aside for at least an hour. Go back to the draft and try to read it as if someone else had written it. Rewrite the evaluation as necessary. Remember to evaluate the employee on performance, not on personal traits or characteristics.

In writing the evaluation, remember that performance has at least two major elements: motivation and ability. When performance is poor, a common supervisor error is to assume that if the employee doesn't perform, it is a motivation problem. Although it may be true, there are many times when the employee can't do the work because of lack of ability or lack of proper training. Corrective strategies for "won't and can't" are quite different and it is very important to recognize the difference.

Provide Feedback

Performance appraisal feedback should be given to student employees by providing a copy of the written appraisal and by holding a meeting to discuss the evaluation. Policies on conducting a meeting with the student employee vary. Usually an invitation is made for the employee to schedule a meeting with the supervisor to discuss the appraisal. Some institutions require a meeting.

Most supervisors do not like to conduct performance appraisal meetings. Performance appraisal meetings with employees often make supervisors nervous and uncertain. The first ones are always the most difficult but careful planning can make them less stressful. The purposes of the performance appraisal meeting between the supervisor and the student employee are

1. to be sure there are no misunderstandings about the performance appraisal ratings;

2. to allow employees to share their feelings about their performances;

3. to provide an opportunity for a straightforward and honest discussion; and

4. to build a better relationship between supervisors and student employees.

THE APPRAISAL MEETING

The meeting between supervisor and student employee is an opportunity for the supervisor to inform, to encourage, and to give recognition to the employee. The following checklist provides guidelines for preparation by supervisors for this meeting:

1. Schedule the meeting far enough in advance.

2. Ask the employees to come prepared to appraise their own performances.

3. Make it clear that the purpose of the meeting is to discuss performance on the job.

4. Find a comfortable setting for the meeting.

5. Review the employee's job description, performance standards, and the appraisal.

6. List specific good things that you can compliment.

7. List the bad things and plan to discuss them.

8. Note what reactions you think the employee might have and plan to handle them.

9. Keep a detailed list of facts supporting your appraisal.

10. Make a list of corrective actions if needed.

11. Plan how to present and gain acceptance of corrective actions.

12. Note follow-up activities that may be needed.

If you are well prepared for the performance appraisal meetings, and are comfortable with your appraisals of the student employees, the stress of conducting such meetings will disappear. Conducting the meetings also requires planning. Review what you will say to the employees, define the order in which you will discuss the evaluations, and make the performance appraisal meetings productive experiences for the employees and you. Here are suggestions on how to make each experience a positive one:

1. State the purpose and create a positive attitude. Put the employees at ease.

2. Ask how they see their jobs and working conditions.

3. Ask if there are problems that need discussion.

4. Give your view of their performances, avoiding comparisons to other employees.

5. Mention desirable behavior that you would like to continue.

6. Capitalize on their strengths.

7. Identify opportunities for self-improvement.

8. Prepare employee improvement plans that are theirs, not yours.

9. Review future opportunities for advancement, pay increases.

10. Warn poor performers, if necessary.

11. Ask if there are questions.

12. End the meetings with constructive, encouraging comments.

Many supervisors find it easy, and even enjoyable, to give employees good evaluations. Often, however, you must also be prepared to give student employees unfavorable comments on their performance when needed. The following are suggestions for handling the performance appraisal meetings with poor performers:

1. Don't be too harsh.

2. Be firm, be specific, and don't rub it in. Nothing is to be gained by being soft on student employees. If performance has been bad, say that performance has been bad and be specific.

3. You can be firm and direct without being cruel. Leave the student employees with their self respect. One useful technique is the "sandwich" technique, described in the next section.

4. Summarize items that are satisfactory as well as items that are unsatisfactory.

5. Always end your appraisal meetings with positive, encouraging comments.

Supervisors dislike giving "bad news" almost as much as employees dislike getting it. You should remember that by giving negative feedback, you are trying to correct one or two things in an employee's behavior. Yet, when the discussion gets started, the overall objectives can get lost. When a performance discussion starts to get rough, the tendency is for the participants to begin digging out all the ammunition they have. If the employee gets defensive and brings up side issues, don't retaliate even though you may feel backed against the wall. Don't allow additional issues to dilute your original objectives. Explain that those issues will be discussed at a later meeting if desired. The best strategy is to resolve the minor issues and gripes as they arise and don't let them accumulate.

A technique for discussing performance that needs improvement is the "sandwich" technique. This is done by starting the discussion with a compliment, then discussing the performance that must be improved upon, and finishing with something good about the employee's work. For example, "I'm very pleased with your handling of reserve check-outs. Your accuracy, however, must be improved. You must remember to follow all the steps for the transaction to be properly recorded. I'm sure you will be able to do that because your other work is very good." This technique can be used throughout the appraisal meeting. No matter how bad an evaluation, you should be able to stress the good things and to make the discussion a positive one.

When discussing poor performance with student employees, be sure to give them every opportunity to explain why performance is substandard. They will, if given the chance to explain, tell you which obstacles stand in the way of their doing well. Don't interrupt their explanations or say, "That's just an excuse." Be patient and let them talk. If you listen carefully, the employees will tell you the real reasons for their poor performances. Don't get into an argument and don't show your anger, even if the student employee gets angry.

Unfavorable criticism that hurts the employee so much that the person being criticized may well charge you with favoritism. Your denial will likely fall on deaf ears. Instead, try to determine why the employee feels that way.

Supervisor: "Judy, why do you think I might be favoring Sheila?"

Employee: "Because you give Sheila the easy jobs all the time, and you never let me do them."

Supervisor: "That may be true. I just find it easier to ask Sheila to do things. You seem hesitant to accept additional work because you just don't act like you want to be here."

Employee: "Well, I do. I don't think I'm appreciated."

Supervisor: "If you can assure me that you are willing to take on extra tasks, I will ask you more often. If I've been favoring Sheila, I will consciously make an effort to treat you more equally."

Denial is a natural reaction to criticism, but don't let a charge of favoritism divert your attention from the original point. Make sure you cover all the items you originally planned to discuss in the appraisal meeting.

Here are some of the more common errors that must be guarded against when conducting performance appraisals of workers:

1. Personal bias: unfairly judging members of different races, religion, sex, or national origin.

2. The halo effect: letting your appraisal of one factor affect your appraisal of all other factors.

3. Central tendency: judging most workers as average, thus making no distinction between good and poor performers.

4. Harshness: judging everyone at the low end of the scale.

5. Leniency: judging everyone at the high end of the scale.

6. Similarity: judging people who are like you higher than people who are different from you.

7. Timing of events: allowing what happened recently to affect your judgment of the person's performance over the entire evaluation period.

8. Seniority: unfairly judging workers on how long they have been on the job.

9. Acquaintanceship: letting how well you know workers affect your appraisal.

Validity and Reliability

Good performance appraisals measure what they should (validity), and the outcomes are consistent (reliability). When a performance appraisal is valid, it measures the things the supervisor wants it to measure. Performance evaluations are not valid when they fail to measure performance-related behaviors or when the performance measures are inappropriate to the job. When a supervisor allows a worker's hair length, style of clothing, or political beliefs to influence an evaluation, it is invalid. These are not performance-related behaviors and have no value in a performance appraisal.

When a performance appraisal is reliable, it provides a consistent measure of work performance. Supervisors must strive for consistency in evaluating every employee on the same basis. The most common types of reliability problems in appraisal are constant errors and random errors. Constant errors occur when all evaluations are in error to the same degree and in the same direction. For example, a supervisor who rates all employees one point higher than their true ratings is making a constant error. Who hasn't known a supervisor who rates all employees in a department as "excellent" when we know they should be "good"? A random error occurs whenever a rating is unpredictably higher or lower than the individual should receive.

One way to deal with reliability errors is to have multiple observations. If one of the criteria to be evaluated is job speed, then there should be two or more questions on the rating form that relate to job speed. If the rating on one shows that the worker is very slow, then the answers to the other questions relating to speed should match. If they do not, there is an inconsistency. Multiple observations help supervisors correct erroneous evaluation responses and attain consistency.

Making Nondiscriminatory Appraisals

We are living in a litigious society. More and more employers are being sued by employees and former employees; therefore, it is important to be aware of what is legal and permissible in appraising employee performance. The key to making nondiscriminatory appraisals is quite simple—evaluate all employees on the basis of job performance only, be consistent in your application, and apply criteria objectively to all employees. Evaluating employees on the basis of job performance means judging them only on the way they do their jobs without regard to age, race, sex, religion, or national origin. It also means putting aside any personal likes or dislikes.

Confidentiality of Appraisals

The entire appraisal process should be confidential. The appraisal of one student employee should never be discussed with other student employees. You cannot control what student employees discuss with one another, but the supervisor should never be the source of information for those discussions. Avoid comparisons of student employees when conducting your appraisal meetings. Make it clear that each student knows that you treat each rating and each appraisal as confidential.

Good Evaluations Don't Always Result in Advancement or in More Money

The student employee who consistently gets very good appraisals finds it hard to accept that it is not possible to move up in a seniority-based system until the person ahead gets promoted or quits.

Employee: "Every time, you tell me I'm doing a good job but it hasn't gotten me a better job. I know John is not doing as well but he still makes more money—just because he's been here longer. All the appraisal does for me is to rub salt in the wound."

A good way to handle this complaint is to admit that the situation exists. Even though the employee's claim about a coworker may be true, don't discuss relative worth of your student employees with them. Tell the student that one of the purposes of appraisals is to provide feedback on performance and that without them, performance can slip without notice. Make certain the student understands that the seniority system applies to everyone and that the time will come when less senior student employees will probably register similar complaints when the student being evaluated becomes the most senior member.

If your compensation system is not tied directly to your appraisal system, tell your student employees. Make it clear to student employees just what the appraisal process is all about. If merit increases are possible, describe the process to your employees. If longevity is the deciding factor in raises, tell them so. Misconceptions about how the performance appraisals are used must be cleared up so everyone has a common understanding of the process.

What Happens to the Appraisal Forms?

Be sure that student employees know what will happen to the appraisal forms and how they may be used. Who has access to them? A written library policy is needed. Does the library give references for former student employees and are the appraisal forms used? This too, should be covered by library policy.

Follow Up the Appraisal

The appraisal is done, the meeting has been held, and the forms have been filed. Is that all there is? No, appraisal is not something that is done today and forgotten tomorrow. If it is to be of value, you should follow up the appraisal meeting:

1. Keep your promises. If you have agreed to do something during the appraisal meeting, do it. If, for example, you've said that you will show the employee data you've referred to in the meeting, be sure to follow through.

2. Implement an employee development plan. If you said the employee needs training in an area, make arrangements to provide that training. Locate courses, workshops, or seminars that will provide the needed training, or talk to the individual who will train the employee. Communicate those arrangements to the employee.

3. Keep in touch. Continue to show interest in the development of the student employee. Monitor the employee's performance, give credit for improvement, and point out deficiencies if you're not satisfied.

Appraisal Formats

The library probably has an evaluation form developed internally or by the student employment office. The form most commonly used is what is known as an absolute format: a graphic rating scale or a narrative. To understand evaluation forms, it is necessary to look at a number of basic types of forms. There are three basic types of performance appraisal forms: comparative, absolute, and outcome-based.

If a comparative format is used, the supervisor evaluates employees in relation to each other. Comparative methods include ranking, paired comparisons, and forced choice. When absolute formats are used, the supervisor evaluates each employee's performance without comparing employees to each other. Absolute methods include narrative, critical incidents, graphic rating scales, weighted checklists, and behaviorally anchored rating scales (BARS). If an outcome-based format is used, supervisors evaluate employees on the basis of performance outcomes. Common forms of outcome-based formats are standards of performance and management by objectives (MBO).

If you are involved in the development of an evaluation instrument, bear in mind that the form is a device to be used by human beings. Ratings on the forms will be the result of complex human processes including interpersonal perception, memory, evaluation, and decision making. Persons using the form will typically have many other responsibilities besides supervision. Develop a form that is usable.

Employee performances are compared to one another in comparative appraisal forms. The ranking method requires the supervisor to compare employees on an overall basis and then list employees in ascending (lowest to highest) or descending (highest to lowest) order. The ranking is usually done by identifying the best performer, the worst performer, the next best, the next worst, and so on until all employees have been listed. Ranking is the simplest way to do comparative evaluation.

Supervisors using paired comparisons must compare each employee to every other employee being appraised. Employee A is compared to Employee B and given a "1" or "2," and then compared to every other employee in the same manner. The total number of points given to each results in a numerical ranking for all employees being appraised.

Forced choice is a method requiring that a percentage of employees be forced into certain groups, for example:

excellent	10 percent
above average	20 percent
satisfactory	40 percent
below average	20 percent
unsatisfactory	10 percent

Comparative formats are fairly simple to use but do not provide any measure of the differences between the rankings. An employee ranked fourth in a group of eight may be considerably better than the person ranked fifth. The employee receives a ranking that provides little information and the system provides no basis for employee development. Comparative formats are seldom used in academic settings.

Absolute appraisal forms do not require comparison to other employees. The narrative form requires the supervisor to write a description of an employee's performance. The narrative describes the worker's strengths, weaknesses, and potential. Much depends on the supervisor's writing ability. A standardized form may be used to provide some uniformity to the information to be recorded. The narrative form is more commonly used for faculty and/or staff evaluations than for student employees.

Critical incidents is an appraisal form that asks that supervisors list both the good and the bad things that employees do in performing their jobs. As with narrative forms, the critical incidents form may be dependent upon the supervisor's writing skills.

Then graphic rating scale is the oldest absolute appraisal method and the most common type of evaluation used by libraries for student employees. The scale contains a number of items relating to job performance and the evaluator checks where the employee fits on the continuum, for example, DEPENDABILITY on a scale of one to five. The graphic rating scale is criticized because DEPENDABILITY has different meanings to different evaluators. To be used effectively, graphic rating scales should also include a brief description of the behavior and a definition of what is needed to earn a "1," "2," or "5."

Weighted checklists assign a value to each of the traits or job behaviors, according to the importance of the item. For example, "quality of work" may be more important than "quantity of work" and count more (20 points) than quantity (15 points).

Behaviorally Anchored Rating Scales (BARS) concentrate on job behaviors and not on personal characteristics. A committee determines the "behavioral anchors" or statements that describe behaviors to be evaluated.

The best known forms of outcome-based methods are standards of performance and management by objectives (MBO). Standards of performance involves comparing performance to a list of standards established through negotiation between the worker and the supervisor. The list of standards are conditions that must be met if the job is considered to have been done well.

MBO is a method of evaluation that focuses on specific objectives or goals established by negotiation between the employee and the supervisor. The employee is judged on how well those objectives are met. Performance Management provides a foundation for outcome-based appraisal and is being implemented in many organizations.

DON'T WAIT FOR THE ANNUAL REVIEW

Frequently, supervisors and student employees assume too much. Supervisors assume that student employees know exactly what is expected of them and how well they are doing. Student employees assume they are performing their work to their supervisors' satisfaction. The "no news is good news" syndrome operates in many libraries until tempers flare, feelings are hurt, and productivity declines. The annual or semiannual performance appraisals are certainly useful in alleviating the problem but performance appraisal should be an ongoing activity. There should be no surprises at appraisal time if you give your employees feedback on their performances, discuss their work, and talk with them regularly. The performance appraisal itself ceases to be a confrontational or traumatic experience for you or for the employees when you show your interest and concern on a regular basis.

POSITIVE APPROACH TO PERFORMANCE APPRAISAL

Supervisors usually take one of two stands on performance appraisal: 1) they see the value of the process and turn performance appraisal into a positive tool; or 2) they see no purpose in the process and fight it all the way. Supervisors who approach appraisal in a positive manner will discover that their employees will benefit from the evaluation. Those who fight the process will find that their employees mirror their feelings. Here are suggestions on how to make appraisal a positive experience:

1. Accept the fact of performance appraisal. Of course you should make suggestions on how it can be improved, but accept the system and make it work for you.

2. Turn the appraisal meetings into profitable counseling sessions. They may be the only regularly scheduled face-to-face meetings you have with your student employees.

3. Don't take the easy way out. Be honest in your appraisals. Remember that you are evaluating performance, not personality.

4. Discuss the evaluation with the employee—don't just deliver it.

5. Don't hurry the evaluation, either its preparation or the appraisal meeting.

6. Make the appraisal a positive tool. Remember that the appraisal is not a tool used to embarrass, to intimidate, or to harass the employee.

7. Be careful with promises. Don't make promises to the employees you cannot keep.

8. Follow-up. Remember that good follow-up is essential to the success of the system.

The resources provided in the bibliography provide additional information on performance appraisal.

NOTES

1. Evelyn Eichel, and Henry E. Bender, *Performance Appraisal: A Study of Current Techniques* (New York, American Management Association, 1984), 7.

2. University of Rochester River Campus Libraries, "Student Performance Evaluation," *Student Assistants in ARL Libraries*, SPEC Kit 91 (Washington, D.C.: Association of Research Libraries, 1983), 96.

BIBLIOGRAPHY

Alexander Hamilton Institute. "Will Your Next Performance Appraisal Land You in Court?" *Management Studies* 31, no. 7 (July 1986): 5–9.

Allan, Ann, and Kathy J. Reynolds. "Performance Problems: A Model for Analysis and Resolution." *Journal of Academic Librarianship* 9 (May 1983): 83–89.

American Library Association, Office for Personnel Resources. *Managing Employee Performance.* Chicago: American Library Association, 1988.

Association of Research Libraries, Office of Management Studies. *Performance Appraisal in Research Libraries.* Washington, D.C.: Association of Research Libraries, 1988.

Association of Research Libraries, Office of Management Studies. *Performance Appraisal in Reference Services.* Washington, D.C.: Association of Research Libraries, 1987.

Belcastro, Patricia. *Evaluating Library Staff: A Performance Appraisal System.* Chicago: American Library Association, 1998.

Bruns, William J. Jr., ed. *Performance Measurement, Evaluation, and Incentives.* Boston: Harvard Business School Press, 1992.

Creth, Sheila. *Performance Evaluation: A Goals-Based Approach.* Chicago: ACRL, 1984.

Gibbs, Sally E. "Staff Appraisal." In *Handbook of Library Training Practice,* edited by Ray Prytherch, 61–81. Brookfield, VT: Gower, 1986.

Kenney, Donald J., and Frances O. Painter. "Recruiting, Hiring, and Assessing Student Workers in Academic Libraries." *Journal of Library Administration* 21, no. 3–4 (1995): 29–45.

Kroll, H. R. "Beyond Evaluation: Performance Appraisal as a Planning and Motivational Tool in Libraries." *Journal of Academic Librarianship* 9 (March 1983): 27–32.

Lindsey, Jonathan A. *Performance Evaluation: A Management Basic for Librarians.* Phoenix, AZ: Oryx, 1987.

Murphy, Kevin R. *Understanding Performance Appraisal: Social, Organizational, and Goal-Based Perspectives.* Thousand Oaks, CA: Sage Publications, 1995.

Neal, James E., Jr. *Effective Phrases for Performance Appraisals.* 5th ed. Perrysburg, OH: Neal Publications, 1988.

Pinzelik, Barbara P. "A Library Middle Manager Looks at Performance Appraisal." In *Energies for Transition, Proceedings of the Fourth National Conference of the ACRL,* edited by Danuta A. Nitecki, 141–45. Chicago: Association of College and Research Libraries, 1986.

Reneker, Maxine H. "Performance Appraisal in Libraries: Purpose and Techniques." In *Personnel Administration in Libraries,* edited by Sheila Creth and Frederick Duda, 227–89. New York: Neal-Schuman, 1981.

Rice, B. "Performance Appraisal: The Job Nobody Likes." *Psychology Today* 19 (September 1985): 30–36.

Russell, Carrie. "Using Performance Measurement to Evaluate Teams and Organizational Effectiveness." *Library Administration & Management* 12, no. 3 (summer 1998): 159–65.

Vincelette, J. P. "Improving Performance Appraisal in Libraries." *Library and Information Science Research* 6 (April 1984): 191–203.

Waters, Richard Lee. "Peer Review: A Team-Building Way to Evaluate Employees." *Public Library Quarterly* 16, no. 1 (1997): 63–67.

Chapter Twelve

EMPLOYEE/EMPLOYER RIGHTS AND RESPONSIBILITIES

It's noble to be good. It's nobler to teach others to be good, and less trouble.

—Mark Twain

EMPLOYEE/EMPLOYER RIGHTS

It is not uncommon to hear comments by employees like "You can't do that—I know my rights!" It would seem that rights are a one-way proposition. In fact, the employees do have rights, but so do employers. Supervisors of student employees must understand employee rights and clearly communicate them to the employees. By the same token, it is important that the student employee supervisor have a basic understanding of the law as it relates to employment. Employees' rights may be legally guaranteed or granted by the library or university.

LEGAL RIGHTS

Employees are protected by certain inalienable rights. Those rights include the right to a safe work environment and a nondiscriminatory and harassment-free workplace. Employees also have last resort termination rights, privacy rights, and where applicable, the right to participate in unions.

RIGHT TO A SAFE WORK ENVIRONMENT

The Occupational Safety and Health Act of 1970 (OSHA)[1] guarantees employees a safe work environment. Under the terms of the law, all employees have the right to request a Department of Labor inspection of any perceived safety or health problem. The request must identify specific violations and be sent to the Department of Labor with a copy to the employer. The employee requesting an inspection must sign the Department of Labor request but need not sign the employer copy. Employees may refuse to work or perform a task if the work itself or the work environment is felt to be unsafe. The following conditions must be met before an employee can refuse to work:

1. Normal procedures to resolve the problem have not been successful.

2. The employee has notified the appropriate management officials and tried to correct the problem, but the unsafe conditions remain.

3. The worker's fears of unsafe conditions are supported by evidence and the worker believes that conditions are unsafe.

The Occupational Safety and Health Act was enacted to ensure safe and healthful working conditions for every worker in the United States. Provisions of the act: to create public safety and health standards, to conduct inspections and investigations; to issue citations and propose penalties; and to require employers to keep records of job-related injuries and illnesses.

RIGHT TO A NONDISCRIMINATORY WORKPLACE

As a supervisor, it is your responsibility to assure that discrimination does not occur in hiring, promotion, transfer, or termination of student employees. It is also your responsibility to report any instances of discrimination to the appropriate person. Even the perception of discrimination based on race, creed, sex, age, sexual preference, national origin, or handicap in the library must be avoided. Among the laws designed to protect individuals from employment discrimination are the Civil Rights Act of 1991; Title VII of the Civil Rights Act of 1964; Title 42 of the United States Code, Section 1981; the Americans with Disabilities Act (ADA) of 1990; the Age Discrimination in Employment Act; the

Equal Pay Act of 1963; and the First Amendment to the U.S. Constitution. The following are brief descriptions of major U.S. law relating to employment discrimination:

> **Title VII of the Civil Rights Act of 1964 (Title VII).** As amended by the Equal Employment Opportunity Act of 1972. Simply stated, Title VII of the Civil Rights Act of 1964 prohibits an employer from refusing to hire or from discriminating against an employee on the job because of the employee's race, color, religion, sex, or national origin. Enacted in 1964 with major amendments in 1972 and 1991.[2]

> **Civil Rights Act of 1991.** An amendment to Title VII of the Civil Rights Act of 1964, it makes employment discrimination laws applicable to all aspects of the employment relationship and allows women, disabled individuals, and members of religious minorities to sue for damages for intentional discrimination and to choose trial by jury.

> **Executive Order 11246 (E.O. 11246).** Prohibits discrimination by federal contractors and subcontractors and requires that they have written affirmative action plans outlining the action they will take to hire and promote women and minorities. Employers found in violation of E.O. 11246 may have their federal contracts canceled and future contracts denied. Enacted in 1978.[3]

SEX DISCRIMINATION

Discrimination based on sex occurs when an individual is treated differently because of his or her gender. Federal and state laws prohibit discrimination against anyone because of sex. An individual who is refused a job or a promotion, or is fired or discriminated against in any terms or conditions of employment based on sex may have a discrimination claim.

Additional protections are provided by the Equal Pay Act of 1963, which makes it unlawful to pay females less than males who do similar work; the Vietnam Era Veterans' Readjustment Assistance Act of 1974 requires federal contractors and subcontractors to take affirmative action to employ, and advance in employment, qualified disabled veterans and veterans of the Vietnam era; and the Pregnancy Discrimination Act of 1978 protects against discrimination in employment because of pregnancy. Pregnancy should be treated as any other temporary disability and an employer may not refuse to hire a qualified female because she is pregnant.

SEXUAL ORIENTATION

Federal court decisions have served to declare that Title VII of the Civil Rights Act of 1964 protects job applicants and employees from discrimination based on sexual orientation, but there is no federal law specifically addressing the issue. Sexual orientation relates to an individual's preference for heterosexuality, homosexuality, bisexuality, or identification with one of these preferences. Sexual orientation may also be referred to as *lifestyle*.

Eight states have comprehensive nondiscrimination laws and more than 25 cities and 100 counties in the United States now have ordinances and policies banning discrimination based on sexual orientation since the widespread attention given to Anita Bryant's campaign to repeal a Dade County, Florida, gay rights ordinance in 1977. Cities and counties across the United States have either decided to include sexual orientation in their antidiscrimination statutes or have repealed such ordinances. Fully one fifth of the American population is covered by such ordinances or policies as of mid-1994. The ordinances differ greatly from one locale to another, but they typically amend the human rights or antidiscrimination statute by adding "sexual orientation" to the list of protected categories. Most of the ordinances and policies are found in large cities with virtually none in smaller communities. Employee protections on the basis of sexual orientation or individual lifestyle are afforded only to those in communities with ordinances.

As an example of a library organization's stand on the issue, the American Library Association's (ALA) antidiscrimination policy (54.3) states, "ALA is committed to equality of opportunity for all library employees or applicants for employment, regardless of race, color, creed, sex, age, or physical or mental disability, individual life-style or national origin."[4] By advertising through ALA services, libraries and other organizations agree to comply with the policy. Direct or implied biases are edited out of ads placed in ALA publications. Controversies surrounding gays in the military and discrimination against gays in federal hiring demonstrate that the issue of discrimination based on sexual orientation remains largely to be resolved.

DISABLED WORKERS

The Vocational Rehabilitation Act of 1973 was passed by Congress to protect the employment rights of disabled workers. That act applied only to federal contractors and subcontractors. The Americans with Disabilities Act (ADA), which took effect in 1992, extends coverage to all employers of 15 or more workers. A disabled individual, for the purposes of the law, is a person who has a physical or mental impairment that limits one or more major life activities, has a record of such impairment, or is regarded by others as having such an impairment. Impairments that limit major life activities must be substantial as opposed to minor and include impairments that limit seeing, hearing, speaking, walking, breathing, performing manual tasks, learning, caring for oneself, and working. An individual with paralysis, substantial hearing or visual impairment, mental retardation, or learning disability would be covered, but an individual with a minor, nonchronic condition of short duration such as a sprain, broken bone, or infection would normally not be covered. A person with a history of cancer or of mental illness would be covered. The third part of the definition protects individuals who are regarded and treated as though they have a substantially limiting disability, for example, the law would protect an individual who is disfigured from adverse employment decisions because the employer feared negative reactions from coworkers. AIDS victims are included in the latter definition as well.

The basic provision of the ADA prohibits discrimination against qualified disabled persons by requiring that the employer make reasonable accommodation for those who can perform the job unless that accommodation would create an undue hardship for the employer. To be a qualified disabled person, the individual must have an impairment that limits one of the major life activities yet must be able to perform the essential functions of the job. The sole fact that an individual is disabled can't eliminate the individual from consideration. Reasonable accommodation requires that the employer modify the job application process so disabled persons can apply in the first place and adjust the work environment in such a way that the disabled individual can perform the job. It should be noted here that the employer may make pre-employment inquiries into the ability of a job applicant to perform job-related functions. However, an employer cannot ask whether the applicant suffers a disability.

A reasonable accommodation might include altering the structure of the work area to make it accessible, acquiring new equipment, modifying work schedules, or simply putting a desk on blocks to accommodate a wheelchair. An accommodation does not have to be made if it would create an "undue hardship." An undue hardship on an employer depends in large part on the type and cost of the accommodation needed, the size of the organization, and the size of the budget. A large organization would have to go to greater lengths than a small business to make a reasonable accommodation. An accommodation could also be considered an undue hardship if it would unduly disrupt other employees or customers, but not if the disruption is caused simply by fear or prejudice. Even in the case of undue hardship, an employer may be required to provide an alternative accommodation.

The ADA excludes from coverage applicants and employees who are currently illegally using drugs but not those individuals who have been successfully rehabilitated. ADA calls largely for common sense solutions to making accommodations for disabled workers who, with the accommodation, can perform the essential functions of the job. A larger, more difficult problem, revolves around those few individuals who would take advantage of a disability to find a way to sue.

The Vocational Rehabilitation Act of 1973 (Rehab Act) is legislation that extended Title VII antidiscrimination protections to disabled individuals. The act prohibits discrimination in employment on the basis of a mental or physical disability. The act defines a disabled person as one who "has a physical or mental impairment which substantially limits one or more of life's major activities, has a record of such impairment, and is regarded as having such an impairment."[5]

The Americans with Disabilities Act (ADA) prohibits discrimination against qualified disabled workers in hiring, compensation, and other terms and conditions of employment. The act requires employers to make reasonable accommodations for individuals who are otherwise qualified to perform the essential functions of the job as long as those accommodations would not be an undue hardship on the employer. Enacted in 1990.[6]

AGE DISCRIMINATION

The Age Discrimination in Employment Act (ADEA) protects employees from discrimination because of age. Workers over the age of 40 are protected by the ADEA, and state laws have been passed to extend that protection in many cases. The law forbids employers from specifying any age preference in job ads except minimum age requirements, for example, for an individual who will serve alcoholic beverages. Employers can't refuse to hire, pay employees less, or discriminate in any way because of age. Courts recognize four elements necessary for a *prima facie* for age discrimination:

1. The individual is in the protected age group—over 40 under the ADEA or younger for some states.

2. The individual was terminated, not promoted, or was the object of an adverse employment decision.

3. The individual was qualified for the position.

4. The adverse decision was made under circumstances that give rise to an inference of age discrimination.

In 1989, the Supreme Court ruled that the ADEA did not apply to employee benefit plans; however, in 1990, Congress passed the Older Workers Benefit Protection Act, which extended age discrimination prohibitions to benefits. The Act states that if an employer has an employee benefit plan, the employer has to expend the same amount of money for the older worker's benefits as for the younger worker, even though the resulting coverage may be less; for health insurance coverage, premiums and benefits must be equal.

The Age Discrimination in Employment Act (ADEA) was enacted in 1967 and amended by additional law, including the Older Workers Benefit Protection Act (OWBPA) of 1990. Prohibits discrimination against workers between the ages of 40 and 70 on the basis of age.[7]

NATIONAL ORIGIN DISCRIMINATION

The only question relating to citizenship an employer can ask a prospective employee related to country of origin is whether or not the applicant is authorized to work in the United States. Once hired, the individual must comply with the provisions of the Immigration Reform and Control Act (IRCA), under which the employer and employee complete applicable sections of the INS I-9 form. Under federal law, employees cannot be discriminated against because of place of origin or because employees have physical, cultural, or linguistic characteristics of a certain nationality. Simply put, employees are protected from employment discrimination because they "look foreign" or have a "foreign accent."

The prohibitions against harassment on the basis of national origin are the same as for sexual harassment. Title VII of the Civil Rights Act of 1964 protects workers against ethnic slurs or conduct which serve to create a hostile working environment.

The Immigration Reform and Control Act (IRCA), 1986, makes it illegal to recruit, hire, refer for hire any unauthorized alien; requires documentation of identity and eligibility of workers to work in the United States; and prohibits discrimination on the basis of national origin or citizenship status. Employer and employee complete applicable sections of the INS I-9 form.[8]

RELIGIOUS DISCRIMINATION

Individuals are protected from discrimination based on religion by the First Amendment of the U.S. Constitution.

Amendment I (1791) states that "Congress shall make no law respecting an establishment of religion, or prohibiting the free exercise thereof; or abridging the freedom of speech, or of the press; or the right of the people peaceably to assemble, and to petition the government for a redress of grievances.

The overriding concern in employment is that all individuals be treated equally, whether equally good or equally bad. Inasmuch as more than 70 percent of the employees in an organization are likely to fall into one of the protected groups discussed in this chapter, the minority, in effect, are the majority. Thus, it simply makes sense to treat all employees equally.

RIGHT TO A HARASSMENT-FREE WORKPLACE

Harassment can be verbal abuse, subtle pressure for sexual activity, or physical aggressiveness. Verbal abuse may also be discrimination in the form of ethic, racial, or sex-related jokes, slurs, or name-calling. Employees have a right to expect their supervisors to put an end to this form of harassment. Victims of verbal abuse which is discriminatory may file a grievance or a complaint with the Equal Opportunity Employment Commission.

Although sexual harassment most often takes place in a situation of power differential between the persons involved, sexual harassment may occur between persons of the same status: student-student, librarian-librarian, or staff-staff. It may take place between two males or two females and is not restricted to male-female or female-male incidents. Although the vast majority of victims are female and the vast majority of offenders are male, the prohibition of sexual harassment applies regardless of the genders of the parties. Guidelines issued by the Equal Employment Opportunity Commission define sexual harassment as unwelcome sexual advances, requests for sexual favors, and other verbal or physical conduct of a sexual nature occurring under any of the following three conditions:

1. Submission to the conduct is an explicit or implicit condition of an individual's employment.

2. Submission to or rejection of such conduct by an individual is used as the basis for employment decisions affecting the individual.

3. Such conduct has the purpose or effect of interfering with an individual's work performance or creating an intimidating, hostile, or offensive work environment.

As a supervisor, it is important that you know the employer is liable for sexual harassment charges if the supervisor is aware of, or should have known about, such activity taking place. The supervisor must be aware of what is happening in the work area and put an immediate end to any activity that even hints at sexual harassment. It is critical that you, the supervisor, be familiar with your library/university's policy on sexual harassment.

LAST-RESORT TERMINATION RIGHTS

Student employees have certain rights relating to the termination of their employment with the library. Legally, an employee's termination may be declared invalid if any of the following conditions exist:

1. Discharged for a reason specifically prohibited by federal or state standards. Termination which is in direct violation of Title VII of the Civil Rights Act of 1964, or the Occupational Safety and Health Act, for example, is illegal.

2. Discharged for complying with a statutory duty. Termination for performing jury duty, for example, is illegal.

3. Discharged in violation of implied promises made at employment. For example, if your handbook says employees may be terminated only for unsatisfactory performance, what happens if the student employee is caught stealing the overdue fine money?

4. Discharging an employee without providing due process. The employee has the right to certain procedural steps and the right to know the reason for termination. A reason for termination may not be needed during a probationary period.

5. Discharge which is motivated by malice or retaliation may be ruled to be invalid.

Of course, there is a right way and a wrong way to terminate student employees. Your library's policies should be clear on how termination is to be handled. For additional suggestions on how to handle termination of student employees, review chapter 13.

PRIVACY RIGHTS

Employees have the right to keep personal information from those who have no need to know. This privacy includes employment references, personnel files, and protection from unreasonable searches.

The best practice to follow when prospective employers contact you for employment references for current student employees is to provide only the most basic employment information to them. Basic information includes a confirmation of employment, dates of employment, and the specific position held. Many libraries have policies forbidding supervisors from giving employment references for their staff or student employees. One exception is that an employer is ethically bound to pass on negative information about the moral character of a former student employee, if relevant. For example, if a student employee is discharged for stealing and has applied for a position with a financial institution, the prospective employer has a right to know.

Student employees have a right to expect that the information contained in their personnel files is confidential. Employees have a right to see most of the information in their files. Management has the right to withhold some information, for example, a confidential memorandum discussing a promotion which was not given. Information that is irrelevant to the employees' jobs or performance should be purged from all personnel files. Supervisors tend to keep their own personnel files, duplicating the centralized files. If those files contain information not relevant to a student employee's job or performance, remove and destroy it.

Constitutional protection against unreasonable searches is provided by the Fourth Amendment of the U.S. Constitution. Although the focus is on searches by government officials and not by private employers, it appears that private employers can conduct searches without fear of constitutional violation. Employers considering establishing a search policy must make sure that it provides for giving employees adequate advance notice. The best policy is to seek advance consent before any search of employees' lockers, desks, etc. The following guidelines apply:

1. The search policy should be based on legitimate employer interest. The prevention of theft, drinking, or the use or possession of drugs are legitimate employer interests.

2. The policy should include all types of searches, including searches of the person, lockers, and personal possessions.

3. The policy should advise employees that lockers are library property, and that lockers may be routinely searched.

4. The search procedure should be applicable to all employees.

5. A statement should be included that a request to undergo a search does not imply an accusation.

6. The search policy must be communicated to all employees. It should be included in handbooks, and employees should be asked to sign a consent statement at the time of employment.

7. Those responsible for conducting searches should be given explicit instructions regarding search procedure.

8. The search should be conducted in a dignified and reasonable manner. Never conduct a search of an employee's person in the presence of other employees.

Those libraries with access to the services of a campus police department should seek their advice and assistance in all matters regarding employee searches. Remember, employees have a right to expect that unreasonable searches will not be conducted.

UNION PARTICIPATION RIGHTS

Although this does not apply to the majority of libraries, it should be noted that union and nonunion employees have the right to participate in organizing and maintaining membership in a union. This right is guaranteed by the National Labor Relations Act (Wagner Act). The supervisor should note the following:

YOU MAY tell employees about current wages and benefits and how they compare to other jobs.

YOU MAY tell employees you will use all legal means to oppose unionization.

YOU MAY tell employees the disadvantages of having a union (especially the cost of dues, assessments, and requirements of membership).

YOU MAY show employees articles about unions and negative experiences others have had elsewhere.

YOU MAY explain the unionization process to your employees accurately.

YOU MAY forbid distribution of union literature during work hours in work areas.

YOU MAY enforce disciplinary policies and rules in a fair manner.

YOU MAY NOT promise employees pay increases or promotions if they vote against the union.

YOU MAY NOT threaten employees with termination or discriminate when disciplining employees.

YOU MAY NOT spy on or have someone spy on union meetings.

YOU MAY NOT make a speech to employees or groups at work within 24 hours of the election.

YOU MAY NOT ask employees how they plan to vote or if they have signed authorization cards.

YOU MAY NOT urge employees to persuade others to vote against the union (such a vote must be initiated solely by the employee).[9]

UNIVERSITY-GRANTED RIGHTS

In addition to those rights granted to employees by law, some rights are granted by the employing institutions. Rights granted by universities usually include the right to an appeal and grievance process and the right to equitable compensation. These are usually described in detail in the policies of the college or university personnel handbook.

Right to an Appeal and Grievance Process

Universities, and in turn their libraries, grant to all employees the right to a *grievance and appeal process*. Some universities grant the same rights to student employees and permanent staff while other universities provide slightly different processes to the two groups. The difference is commonly in how far a grievance may be taken. Temporary employees and employees during their probationary period are often given access to only the first step of the process. Student employees may be considered as temporary employees in some libraries.

The primary purpose of an appeal and grievance procedure is to provide a means by which employees, without jeopardizing their jobs, can express complaints about their work or working conditions and obtain a fair hearing through progressively higher-levels of management. Complaints charging discrimination based on race, creed, sex, age, sexual preference, national origin, or handicap may be handled by the regular grievance procedure or be dealt with by the university's affirmative action office. The appeal and grievance procedure serves to avoid the high costs of court action, both in terms of dollars and morale.

A *two-step grievance and appeal process* is common in university libraries. The time limits for the process may vary. In step one, a grievance must be filed in writing by the employee within five working days following the act or discovery of the condition that gave rise to the grievance. Normally, the written grievance is submitted to an office in university personnel. A personnel officer will conduct a preliminary investigation of the grievance and attempt to mediate the dispute. If the grievance is resolved to the satisfaction of both parties, the officer prepares a report of the resolution, provides copies to both sides, and the grievance is considered closed. If the grievance is not resolved through mediation, a report to that effect is prepared and provided to both parties. If student employees are given access to the second step, an appeal to step two of the procedure may be made.

An appeal must be filed in writing by the employee within five working days from receipt of the step one report. Failure to file within the specified period constitutes forfeiture of the right to appeal, and the grievance will be considered closed. The appeal is heard by a grievance review committee that is composed of the director of personnel, the dean/director of the library, and one other uninvolved employee selected by the aggrieved employee. The written decision of the review committee, including a discussion of the case and the rationale for the decision, is provided to the employee and employer, usually within 15 working days of the hearing. There is no further right to appeal in the procedure. Any further action by the employee must be taken in civil court.

In the previous two-step grievance procedure, both mediation and arbitration are used. Mediation is provided by the personnel office and arbitration by the review committee.

Mediation is a procedure by which an impartial third party helps the employee and the employer to reach a voluntary agreement on how to settle a grievance. The mediator often makes suggestions or recommendations and attempts to reduce the emotions and tensions that prevent resolution of the complaint. To be successful, the mediator must earn the trust and respect of both parties. If, in step one, the mediator is unable to get the parties to agree, the mediation effort is ended without resolution.

If an appeal is made, arbitration is required. *Arbitration* is a procedure in which a neutral third party, in this case, the grievance review committee, studies the grievance, listens to the arguments on both sides, and makes recommendations that are binding on both.

Common Types of Grievances

The grievance is a formal charge made by a student employee that the employee has been adversely affected by a violation of university or library policy. Grievances always allege that there has been a violation. Often the situation begins as a gripe by the employee, and when it is not handled by the supervisor to the employee's satisfaction, a grievance is filed. Some of the most common types of grievances deal with the following situations:

1. Discipline or termination for absenteeism, insubordination, misconduct, or substandard work.

2. Promotion or transfer of student employees.

3. Complaints charging discrimination based on race, creed, sex, age, sexual preference, national origin, or handicap.

When a Grievance Is Filed Against You

Library management hopes that student employees will never resort to turning in grievances, yet few libraries are able to completely avoid them. That is not to say that libraries that have no grievances have student employees who are all pleased with their jobs and their supervisors. Of course, it is better to have the problems openly discussed than to have a staff who do not express their feelings. It is hoped that complaints and employee concerns are addressed by the supervisor and that grievances will not have to result. When a lot of grievances occur, management must look at its supervisors.

Supervisors must know how to handle a complaint before it becomes a grievance. If a grievance is filed, it is important that the supervisor not consider it an attack on supervisor authority, only that a situation has not been resolved to the employee's satisfaction. Remember that employees have the right to file grievances without jeopardizing their jobs.

If you can determine the nature of the grievance, you have taken the first step to successfully handling it. Determine whether the stated complaint is the problem or if it is only a symptom of the real problem. Investigate the grievance objectively and thoroughly. One of the biggest mistakes supervisors make is to make light of complaints. If the employee files a grievance, it is important and the employee will not be satisfied until the grievance is resolved. The supervisor must be willing to work with the mediator in a grievance, and if you've made a mistake, admit it. When the grievance is resolved one way or the other, do not punish the grievant. The employee is exercising a right given by the university.

Right to Equitable Compensation

In addition to the right to an appeal and grievance process, employees have a right to fair and equitable compensation for the work they perform. Student employees are entitled to pay equity and should be made aware of the pay schedule for different jobs in the library. All student employees should be rewarded fairly in relation to what other student employees are paid for the work they perform. Pay rates for student employees are discussed in chapter 5.

EMPLOYEE RESPONSIBILITIES

Employees must recognize that in addition to their rights, they have responsibilities as well. The legal responsibilities of employees are the responsibility to perform the work for which they were hired and the responsibility to follow the library's policies, procedures and rules.

Employees also have a responsibility to contribute positively to the library's image. In the eyes of many people, student employees *are* the library. A patron's image of the library is often formed by his or her view of the student employees. Loyalty to the library is an ethical responsibility of student employees. Given the opportunity, student employees should speak positively about the library; if employees have gripes, they should be taken to supervisors, not to persons outside.

Other specific moral and ethical actions for which student employees should be held responsible include:

1. Come to work for all scheduled hours, unless excused.

2. Comply with instructions issued by the supervisor.

3. Complete assigned work.

4. Be safety conscious.

5. Take care of library materials and property.

6. Be honest in dealings with the public and the library.

7. Avoid abusive, threatening, coercive, indecent, and dis-courteous language.

8. Be sober and drug free on library time, library property, or while conducting library business.

9. Keep accurate records and avoid any hint of intentional falsification of time reports.

10. Cooperate with coworkers.

ETHICS FOR SUPERVISORS

Student employees and the public make few distinctions between lower-level and upper-level management of the library. To most of the university community, supervisors are part of library management and you can be expected to be tarred with the same brush as that of your supervisor and the dean/director. As a result, you must be concerned with managerial ethics.

Ethics is concerned with what a person does that is right or wrong according to what individual, friends, coworkers, and society think is right or wrong. A fine line exists between acceptable and unacceptable behavior in organizational life. The following questions present problems that have answers society judges as ethically correct. It is a rare individual who would not bend one of these ethical standards.

Answer the following questions as truthfully as you can. Only you can judge their significance or the correct answers.

♦ Would you ask a maintenance person employed by the university to do a small repair job at work on your own kitchen appliance?

♦ If offered a chance, at no cost to you, would you go on a vacation sponsored by the company that sells supplies to the library, if your supervisor has said it is okay?

♦ If you had the opportunity to approve a promotion for a family member who was less qualified than other candidates, would you do it?

♦ Would you take home for your personal use such office supplies as pencils or scratch pads?

♦ If no one said you could not, would you use the library's telephone to conduct a private business of your own?

♦ Would you use the library's telephone to make long-distance personal calls at university expense?

♦ If given the opportunity, would you work on a personal, non-job-related project on library time?

♦ If you discovered a technicality that enabled you to dismiss a particularly troublesome employee, even though in this instance the employee was blameless, would you do it anyway?

Library Ethics

The concern for ethics must be addressed by both the individual and the organization. Supervisors of student employees must adhere to the same ethical standards as their supervisors and the librarians in the organization. The American Library Association has had a Code of Ethics since 1939.[10]

AMERICAN LIBRARY ASSOCIATION STATEMENT ON PROFESSIONAL ETHICS, 1981

Since 1939, the American Library Association has recognized the importance of codifying and making known to the public and the profession the principles which guide librarians in action. This latest revision of the Code of Ethics reflects changes in the nature of the profession and its social and institutional environment. It should be revised and augmented as necessary.

Librarians significantly influence or control the selection, organization, preservation, and dissemination of information. In a political system grounded in an informed citizenry, librarians are members of a profession explicitly committed to intellectual freedom and the freedom of access to information. We have a special obligation to ensure the free flow of information and ideas to present and future generations.

Librarians are dependent upon one another for the bibliographical resources that enable us to provide information services, and have obligations for maintaining the highest level of personal integrity and competence.

CODE OF ETHICS

I. Librarians must provide the highest level of service through appropriate and usefully organized collections, fair and equitable circulation and service policies, and skillful, accurate, unbiased, and courteous responses to all requests for assistance.

II. Librarians must resist all efforts by groups or individuals to censor library materials.

III. Librarians must protect each user's right to privacy with respect to information sought or received, and materials consulted, borrowed, or acquired.

IV. Librarians must adhere to the principles of due process and equality of opportunity in peer relationships and personnel actions.

V. Librarians must distinguish clearly in their actions and statements between their personal philosophies and attitudes and those of an institution or professional body.

VI. Librarians must avoid situations in which personal interests might be served or financial benefits gained at the expense of library users, colleagues, or the employing institution.

Managerial Ethics

Although the American Library Association Code of Ethics may guide you in certain situations, a different code of ethics relates directly to managers and supervisors:[11]

CODE OF ETHICS FOR MEMBERS OF THE INSTITUTE OF CERTIFIED PROFESSIONAL MANAGERS

I will recognize that management is a call to service with responsibilities to my subordinates, associates and supervisors, employer, community, nation, and world.

I will be guided in all my activities by truth, accuracy, fair dealings, and good taste.

I will earn and carefully guard my reputation for good moral character and citizenship.

I will recognize that, as a leader, my own pattern of work and life will exert more influence on my subordinates than what I say or write.

I will give the same consideration to the rights and interests of others that I ask for myself.

I will maintain a broad and balanced outlook and will look for value in the ideas and opinions of others.

I will regard my role as a manager as an obligation to help subordinates and associates achieve personal and professional fulfillment.

I will keep informed on the latest developments in the techniques, equipment, and processes associated with the practice of management and the industry in which I am employed.

I will search for, recommend, and initiate methods to increase productivity and efficiency.

I will respect the professional competence of my colleagues in the ICPM and will work with them to support and promote the goals and programs of the institute.

I will support efforts to strengthen professional management through example, education, training, and a lifelong pursuit of excellence.

Consult the following resources for more information on employee/employer rights and responsibilities.

NOTES

1. Title 29, *U.S. Code*, Sec. 651 et seq.

2. Title 42, *U.S. Code*, Sec. 2000e.

3. Executive Order 11246.

4. "Career Leads: ALA Guidelines," *American Libraries*, 26, no. 8 (September 1995): p. 832. ALA's guidelines appear each month in the classified advertisements section of *American Librairies*.

5. Title 29, *U.S. Code*, Sec. 701 et seq.

6. Title 42, *U.S. Code*, Sec. 12101 et seq.

7. Title 29, *U.S. Code*, Sec. 621.

8. Title 8, *U.S. Code*, Sec. 1324.

9. Adapted from Robert L. Mathis, and John H. Jackson, *Personnel*, 4th ed. (St. Paul, MN: West, 1985), 576.

10. American Library Association, *Statement of Professional Ethics* (Chicago: American Library association, 1981).

11. Institute of Certified Professional Managers, *Code of Ethics* (Dayton, OH: ICPM, 1980).

BIBLIOGRAPHY

Aggarwal, Arjun Prakash. *Sex Discrimination: Employment Law and Practices.* Clearwater, FL: Butterworths, 1994.

Babcock, Michael W. "The Role of the Federal Employers' Liability Act in Railroad Safety." *Workers' Compensation Law Review* 15 (1992): 531.

Bible, Jon D., and Darien A. McWhirter. *Privacy in the Workplace: A Guide for Human Resource Managers.* New York: Quorum Books, 1990.

Bloch, Farrell E. *Antidiscrimination Law and Minority Employment: Recruitment Practices and Regulatory Constraints.* Chicago: University of Chicago Press, 1994.

Button, James W., and others. "Where Local Laws Prohibit Discrimination Based on Sexual Orientation." *Public Management* 77, no. 4 (April 1995): 9–12.

The Civil Rights Act of 1991: Its Impact on Employment Discrimination Litigation. New York: Practicing Law Institute, 1992.

Coleman, Francis T. "Creating a Workplace Free of Sexual Harassment." *Association Management* 45, no. 2 (February 1993): 69.

Crow, Stephen M. "Excessive Absenteeism and the Americans with Disabilities Act." *The Arbitration Journal* 48, no. 1 (March 1993): 65.

Dworkin, Terry Morehead. "Harassment in the 1990s." *Business Horizons* 36, no. 2 (March 1993): 52.

Egler, Theresa Donahue. "Legal Trends: Five Myths About Sexual Harassment." *HR Magazine: On Human Resource Management* 40, no. 1 (January 1995): 27.

Etter, Irvin B. "Ergonomics: Don't Wait for OSHA." *Safety & Health* 151, no. 2 (February 1995): 3.

Foos, Donald D., and Nancy C. Pack, eds. *How Libraries Must Comply with the Americans with Disabilities Act.* Phoenix, AZ: Oryx, 1992.

Gutek, Barbara. "Sexual Harassment: Rights and Responsibilities." *Employee Responsibilities and Rights Journal* 6, no. 4 (December 1993): 325.

Hames, David S. "Disciplining Sexual Harassers: What's Fair?" *Employee Responsibilities and Rights Journal* 7, no. 3 (September 1994): 207.

Hasty, Keith N. "Worker's Compensation: Will College and University Professors Be Compensated for Mental Injuries Caused by Work-Related Stress?" *The Journal of College and University Law* 17, no. 4 (spring 1991): 535.

Larson, Lex K. *Civil Rights Act of 1991.* New York: Matthew Bender, 1992.

Lindemann, Barbara, and David D. Kadue. *Sexual Harassment in Employment Law.* Washington, D.C.: Bureau of National Affairs, 1992.

Mook, Jonathan R., ed. *Americans with Disabilities Act: Employee Rights & Employer Obligations.* New York: Matthew Bender, 1992.

Nager, Glen D., and Edward K. M. Bilich. "The Civil Rights Act of 1991 Going Forward." *Employee Relations Law Journal* 20, no. 2 (fall 1994): 237.

Parliman, Gregory C., and Rosalie J. Shoeman. "National Origin Discrimination or Employer Prerogative? An Analysis of Language Rights in the Workplace." *Employee Relations Law Journal* 19, no. 4 (spring 1994): 551.

Paul, Niall A. "The Civil Rights Act of 1991: What Does It Really Accomplish?" *Employee Relations Law Journal* 17, no. 4 (spring 1992): 567.

Simon, Howard A., and Erin Daly. "Sexual Orientation and Workplace Rights: A Potential Land Mine for Employers?" *Employee Relations Law Journal* 18, no. 1 (summer 1992): 29.

Smith, James Monroe. "The Legal Rights of People with HIV/AIDS." *EAP Digest* 13, no. 5 (July 1993): 30.

Steiner, Alison. "The Americans with Disabilities Act of 1990 and Workers' Compensation: The Employees' Perspective." *Mississippi Law Journal* 62, no. 3 (spring 1993): 631.

Susser, Peter A. "The ADA: Dramatically Expanded Federal Rights for Disabled Americans." *Employee Relations Law Journal* 16, no. 2 (fall 1990): 157.

Warner, Daniel M. "We Do Not Hire Smokers: May Employers Discriminate Against Smokers?" *Employee Responsibilities and Rights Journal* 7, no. 2 (June 1994): 129.

Waxman, Merle. "Constructive Responses to Sexual Harassment in the Workplace." *Employee Responsibilities and Rights Journal* 7, no. 3 (September 1994): 243.

Chapter Thirteen

PROGRESSIVE DISCIPLINE AND TERMINATION PROCEDURES

> *Noise proves nothing. Often a hen who has merely laid an egg cackles as if she has laid an asteroid.*
>
> —Mark Twain

DISCIPLINE AND DISCHARGE

Two of the most unpleasant responsibilities of your job as supervisor are disciplining and terminating student employees. The most emotionally difficult is having to fire an employee. Termination is very difficult for the supervisor, for the person being fired, and for the other people in the department. Any supervisor who has fired a student employee realizes the importance of hiring the right people and training them well in order to reduce the possibility that an employee will have to be involuntarily terminated.

Disciplining and discharging student employees requires that specific procedures be followed. Those procedures should be spelled out in each university's personnel/student handbooks. What follows are suggestions on how to handle discipline and discharge; readers are cautioned, however, to pay close attention to their library/university policies and to seek the advice of their supervisors and campus legal counsel as needed.

TERMINATION OF EMPLOYMENT

As surely as student employees will be hired, they will terminate employment in the library. The very nature of student employment requires turnover in student employee positions. After all, they are students first and it is our hope and theirs that they will graduate. Termination of employment, as used here, is the process by which student employees end their employment in the library, whether voluntary (resigned) or involuntary (fired).

All terminations of employment may be categorized as one of the following:

1. *Resignation.* The vast majority of terminations are resignations at the employee's request (voluntary).

2. *Release.* Some employees are released when temporary jobs are completed (involuntary, but usually known beforehand).

3. *Relieved.* Employees terminated during a probationary period are considered to have been relieved (involuntary).

4. *Layoff.* In the case of a reduction in force or lack of work, employees may be laid off (involuntary).

5. *Discharge.* Terminated for cause (involuntary).

Resignation

Most student employees leave the library through resignation. While not usually specifically required, student employees are asked to give two weeks notice of resignation in order to allow supervisors to plan for replacements. In some organizations, employees are considered to have resigned if they walk off the job, fail to report to work for their scheduled hours without permission to be absent for three consecutive work days, or fail to return to work within a prescribed period of time following a leave of absence.

Release

In some libraries, all student employees are considered temporary employees. As temporary employees, they are automatically terminated at the end of each semester, academic year, or summer session and must be rehired if they are to continue working during the next award period. This process allows the student employment office to clear its files for a new allocation period.

Relieved

A probationary period for all new student employees of three to six months is used by many libraries. The student employees are being trained and it is important for the supervisor to make an assessment of progress during this period. If a student employee appears to be ill-suited for the job, cannot perform the work, or will not work out for whatever reason, this is the time to terminate the employee. In most cases, probationary employees may be terminated any time before the completion of the probationary period without recourse. Employees terminated before the expiration of their probationary periods are usually not allowed to avail themselves of the grievance and appeal process.

Layoff

Student employees may be terminated because of a reduction in force due to lack of funds, lack of work, or other compelling reasons. Selection of student employees for layoff should be made on the basis of qualifications and performance but may be made on the basis of seniority if all are substantially equal.

Discharge

Sometimes referred to as "terminate," "fire," "let go," "dismiss," or even "derecruit," this is the last resort for supervisors who have exhausted all the means available to remedy the situation. Whatever it is called, it is an unpleasant event for both parties—the supervisor and the employee. A student employee should be discharged when the seriousness of the matter is such that the student employee should not be permitted to remain on the library's payroll.

Before resorting to the termination process, the supervisor should provide the student employee with an opportunity to become aware of and correct the misconduct or substandard performance; the supervisor may then restore the employee as a productive member of the work group through corrective discipline.

REASONS FOR TERMINATION

Termination, as used here, is the process by which the student employee ceases working for the library, whether it be voluntary (resigned) or involuntary (fired or discharged). The following list of reasons for terminations are taken from a form which supervisors are required to complete for the Personnel Office at the University of New Mexico:

LACK OF WORK

- Reduction in force
- Job eliminated
- Reorganization
- End of temporary employment
- End of seasonal employment
- Project completed
- Partially unemployed reduced hours
- Temporary

QUIT

- Reason unknown
- Abandoned job
- Walked off job
- Did not return from leave
- Did not return from layoff

- Personal—not job related
- Returned to school
- Marriage
- Relocated
- Family obligations
- Unable to obtain babysitter
- Transportation
- Accepted another job
- Go into business
- Illness
- Maternity
- Enter military
- Dissatisfaction—work hours
- Dissatisfaction—salary
- Dissatisfaction—working conditions
- Dissatisfaction—performance review
- Dissatisfaction—supervisor
- Dissatisfaction—policies

DISCHARGE

- Insubordination
- Violation of rules or policies
- Violation of safety rules
- Reported under influence of alcohol
- Reported under influence of drugs
- Destruction of property—willful
- Destruction of property—carelessness

- Fighting
- Leaving work station
- Falsification of employment application
- Dishonesty—falsified records
- Dishonesty—unauthorized removal of property
- Dishonesty—monetary theft
- Dishonesty—other
- Absenteeism—unreported
- Absenteeism—excessive and/or unauthorized
- Tardiness—frequent
- Excessive garnishments
- Quality of work
- Quantity of work
- Poor performance
- Probationary—not qualified for job
- Poor judgement—no misconduct
- Lack of technical knowledge
- Inability to work—illness

MISCELLANEOUS

- No information whatsoever
- Refusal to work
- Disciplinary suspension
- Death

REDUCING THE NUMBER OF PROBLEM EMPLOYEES

Although it is not possible to avoid entirely having problem employees who must be disciplined and/or discharged, there are ways to reduce their numbers:

1. Don't hire persons who provide clues during the interview that there may be problems.

2 Train new employees thoroughly.

3. Make sure new employees understand organizational rules and policies and the consequences of breaking those rules or violating library or university policies.

4. Take advantage of the probationary period. Don't hesitate to let a student employee go before or at the end of a probationary period if he or she is not performing satisfactorily. Terminating an employee during a probationary period is much easier than doing it later.

5. Review employee performance at regular intervals and deal with problems as they occur.

6. Don't pawn off your problem employees on another student employee supervisor. Deal with your own problems.

7. Before you discharge an employee, be certain that progressive discipline is not called for instead.

For suggestions on how to deal with specific problems, consult chapter 10.

Corrective Discipline

Corrective discipline, also called progressive discipline, is designed to make employees aware of misconduct or poor performance and to give them an opportunity to correct their behavior or improve their performance. The first step in corrective discipline is to give the employee a verbal warning for minor infractions or to correct poor performance. A written warning addressed to the employee is used if the infraction or deficiency is serious or if the employee does not heed the verbal warning. An employee may be suspended without pay for serious offenses, for continued poor performance, or for misconduct after previous attempts to bring about improvement have been unsuccessful. Termination is not necessarily a corrective discipline step but may be the result if previous steps of corrective discipline do not result in the desired behavior.

It is not essential that the steps be followed sequentially. Each situation must be judged independently and appropriate action taken. A specific situation may require, for example, a written warning or a suspension as a first step or, in some instances, immediate discharge. The following are examples of when a particular step is called for:

> *Verbal warning.* Substandard work performance, unexcused absences, or tardiness.

> *Written warning.* Continued substandard work performance, unexcused absences, or tardiness.

> *Suspension.* Continuation of the above behaviors, insubordination, drinking or intoxication, gambling, fighting, or sleeping on the job.

The warnings and suspension are intended to allow an individual to correct a situation. The last step or first and only step in some situations is termination. The following are examples of when discharge is appropriate:

> *Discharge.* Applicable to all previously listed examples if continued after attempts to correct, and all of the actions listed in the earlier section on just cause for termination.

Before taking any corrective discipline steps, supervisors and managers are advised to consult with the appropriate authorities in the library and/or governing body.

Predischarge Rights of Public Employees

One of the most important aspects of public employment is job security. Classified employees are given a "property interest" in their jobs that cannot be taken away without the "due process of law" to put them beyond the reach of partisan political retaliation. The rights of classified employees were established by the Lloyd-LaFollette Act of 1932.[1] The act provided classified public employees the right to postdischarge appeals and established the concept of property interest for nonprobationary public employees. Under the act, the employee must receive a written copy of the charges against him or her and a reasonable period of time in which to respond in writing to the charges.

The Supreme Court ruled in the 1985 case of *Cleveland Board of Education v. Loudermill* that "the tenured public employee is entitled to oral or written notice of the charges against him, an explanation of the employer's evidence, and an opportunity to present his side of the story." It noted that "where the employer perceives a significant hazard in keeping the employee on the job, it can avoid the problem by a suspension with pay."[2] These then are the predischarge rights of public employees. When a public employee is "Loudermilled," the letter of notice has been delivered as specified in the Supreme Court ruling.

Steps to Take Before Terminating an Employee

The first rule in any disciplinary situation is document, document, document. It is doubly true for situations in which the employee is to be discharged. The following steps should be followed in every situation except those instances where an employee should be immediately terminated:

1. Implement the appropriate corrective discipline steps.

2. Gather all of the facts, including any that the employee may add.

3. Determine whether there is a policy that calls for discharge in this situation and be prepared to cite it.

4. Determine whether or not the employee is or should be aware of the policy.

5. Determine whether or not, in similar situations, exceptions have been made to the policy.

6. Be absolutely certain that discrimination is not involved, especially if the individual is a member of a protected class.

7. Be absolutely certain that this action is not retaliation for an earlier, unrelated act.

8. Determine whether or not this termination will make the employee a "martyr," and if so, prepare to deal with that issue with employees who remain.

9. Make certain that the employee's file contains the proper documentation supporting the termination.

10. At the time of actual termination, arrange to have another manager present.

11. Make certain that the procedures used in this termination are the same as those used in previous terminations.

HOW TO TERMINATE AN EMPLOYEE

Before terminating an employee, make certain that the previous 11 steps have been taken. There must be written documentation defining and supporting the termination. The termination of an employee for poor performance should never come as a surprise to him or her. Through proper training, coaching, and corrective discipline steps if necessary, employees should always know where they stand. For those employees who must be terminated, however, consideration must be given to the termination interview itself and to what can and must be communicated to other employees about the termination.

Let's say that, based on all of the above-mentioned information, the decision has been made to terminate an employee. The following questions must be answered before calling in the employee:

1. *Who should terminate the employee?* The employee's supervisor must be the one who gives the message, however, another manager should be present as a witness and for support.

2. *Where should the termination meeting be held?* It must held in a confidential setting, ideally in an empty office or conference room. That way, when you are through with the meeting, you can leave. It is difficult to walk out of your own office, and it may be difficult to get the terminated employee to leave.

3. *When should the termination meeting be held?* When planning the termination meeting, review the individual's file. To lessen the impact, avoid termination on the employee's birthday or anniversary date. Consider the employee's medical and emotional state. Does the employee anticipate termination? Friday or the day before a holiday are the worst days to conduct terminations of employees. The termination meeting should be held early in the week.

4. *What will the employee be told?* You and the employee may want to discuss resignation instead of termination, if that is an option. If resignation is not an option, the termination message should be clear and irrevocable. Avoid debates and rehashes of the past. Do not allow the employee to trap you into "who said what" discussions. Make it clear that the decision has been made and that the decision is final. Be empathetic but uncompromising. Know ahead of time what you plan to say, and don't let the meeting become sidetracked. Make it mercifully brief.

After the termination meeting, you will also have to resolve these questions:

1. What will the individual's coworkers be told?

2. What will persons who inquire for references be told?

The Impacts of Termination

Although announcement of resignations, retirements, and other voluntary terminations are often followed by departmental get-togethers, well wishes, and friendly farewells, involuntary terminations are seldom occasions for celebration. In nearly every involuntary termination, both the individuals involved and the library itself are negatively affected. The greatest impact, of course, is felt by the individual who has been discharged. Studies have shown that the level of emotional stress following termination can equal the stress of being told that one is dying of an incurable disease. The individual first suffers shock and anger, followed by the certainty that a mistake has been made. After a series of mood swings, the discharged employee may experience a period of depression. Finally, self-confidence returns. The severity of these experiences differs from individual to individual, but regardless of severity, the termination makes an impact.

Coworkers may experience a mixture of shock and excitement over the news, expressing such conflicting statements as "I'm glad it didn't happen to me," "It could happen to me," "I'm sorry it happened to him," "I'm glad it finally happened to him," and "I'm angry with the person who fired him." "I wonder who's next." Employee reactions will be affected by how well the terminated employee was liked, their perceptions of the events surrounding the termination, and their opinions of the supervisor and the administration.

The supervisor of the terminated employee may experience guilt and self-pity for having to take the action, while feeling compassion for the terminated employee. Presumably the decision to discharge has been made only after the supervisor has taken every step possible to avoid the discharge. Thus, although the supervisor must be able to show compassion and empathy for the terminated employee, at the same time, he or she should feel comfortable in the correctness of the decision and of the procedures taken. It is important that the terminated employee receive whatever assistance possible in finding another position, if requested.

Every termination has its own circumstances and resulting impacts. The supervisor must be able to deal with his or her own emotions as the terminator, with the emotions of the individual terminated, and with the emotions of coworkers. A termination is successful when it is done objectively, humanely, and cleanly. It is a good termination when it can honestly be said that the result was best for all involved.

Mistakes Made in Terminations

The following mistakes made in terminations may lead to charges of discrimination or unfair treatment by persons who are terminated:

1. Documentation was lacking.

2. Performance evaluations were poorly done or not done at all.

3. The employee was unaware of the policy or that termination could be the result of his or her actions.

4. The employee was given regular salary increases, which he or she interpreted as merit increases. In some cases, merit increases may have been given.

5. The employee was treated differently from others in similar jobs.

6. The employee had not been given sufficient help to correct substandard performance.

7. The employee had not been given a definite set of performance standards.

8. The employee was given too many "second chances."

9. The wrong person was selected to handle the termination.

10. The reasons for termination were not made clear and unequivocal.

11. Possible severe emotional reactions were not anticipated.

12. Lawsuits were not anticipated.

13. The effects on remaining employees were not anticipated.

CONSTRUCTIVE DISCHARGE

To make a case that he or she was wrongfully discharged, the former employee must be able to show that he or she was in fact discharged. "Terminated," "fired," "let go," "dismissed," "discharged," and "given a pink slip" all mean the same thing: You've been fired. But sometimes the sequence of events isn't quite so clear-cut. There are cases when a court will decide an employee was fired even though the individual quit because of "constructive discharge." Constructive discharge occurs when the employer does something that makes it virtually impossible for the employee to continue on the job. For example, the court may find that an employee was constructively discharged if the employer changed working conditions, which, in turn, caused the employee to quit. The change must have been recent enough to draw a cause-and-effect relationship between the change and the resignation, and the change in working conditions has to have been so demeaning or upsetting that any reasonable person in the same situation would have quit. Being able to prove that an individual was constructively discharged is important in determining whether the former employee will receive unemployment compensation.

GROSS MISCONDUCT

Gross misconduct is one of the many just causes for termination of employees. Case law has defined gross misconduct as:

1. deliberate or negligent disregard of the employer's interest;

2. deliberate violations of reasonable standards of conduct set by the employer; and

3. behavior so careless or negligent as to amount to wrongful intent.

The court, in *Paris v. Korbel & Brothers, Inc.*, noted that inefficiency, poor conduct or performance, ordinary negligence, and errors in judgment are not enough for termination on the grounds of gross misconduct.[3]

NOTES

1. The processes specified in the Lloyd-LaFollette Act were incorporated into the 1978 Civil Services Reform Act.

2. Cleveland Board of Education v. Loudermill, 105 S. Ct. 1487 (1985), P. 1495.

3. Paris v. Korbel & Brothers, Inc., U.S. District Court, Northern California, No. C-89-1278 TEH, March 14, 1990.

BIBLIOGRAPHY

Bies, Robert, Christopher Martin, and Joel Brockner. "Just Laid Off, but Still a 'Good Citizen?' Only if the Process Is Fair." *Employee Responsibilities and Rights Journal* 6, no. 3 (September 1993): 227.

DeAgazio, Richard M. "Promoting Fairness: A Proposal for a More Reasonable Standard of Constructive Discharge in Title VII Denial of Promotion Cases." *The Fordham Urban Law Journal* 19, no. 4 (summer 1992): 979.

Dilts, David A., and Clarence R. Deitsch. "The Tests of Just Cause: What Price Predictability in Arbitral Decision Making." *Employee Responsibilities and Rights Journal* 5, no. 1 (March 1992): 13.

Documenting the Hiring Process and Documenting the Termination Process. Columbus, OH: Ohio CLE Institute, 1997.

Dworkin, Terry Morehead, and Melissa S. Baucus. "Wrongful Firing in Violation of Public Policy: Who Gets Fired and Why." *Employee Responsibilities and Rights Journal* 7, no. 3 (September 1994): 191.

Effective Interviews for Every Situation: Hiring, Performance Appraisal, Discipline, Promotion, Problem-Solving, Termination. Maywood, NJ: Alexander Hamilton Institute, 1996.

Emerging Issues in Public Sector Labor/Employment Law. Minneapolis, MN: Minnesota Institute of Legal Education, 1997.

Fox, Jeremy B., and Hugh D. Hindman. "The Model Employment Termination Act: Provisions and Discussion." *Employee Responsibilities and Rights Journal* 6, no. 1 (March 1993): 33.

Hiring and Firing. Minneapolis, MN: Minnesota Institute of Legal Education, 1997.

How to Hire Right, Fire Right: Managing Within the Law. Pittsburgh, PA: Buchanan Ingersoll Professional Corporation, 1996.

Jacobs, Carol S. "The Use of the Exit Interview as a Personnel Tool and Its Applicability to Libraries." *Journal of Library Administration* 14, no. 4 (1991): 69.

Joel, Lewin G. *Every Employee's Guide to the Law: Everything You Need to Know About Your Rights in the Workplace—and What to Do If They Are Violated.* New York: Pantheon Books, 1996.

Johnson, Kathryn A. "Constructive Discharge and 'Reasonable Accommodation' Under the Americans with Disabilities Act." *University of Colorado Law Review* 65, no. 1 (1993): 175.

Kaplan, Andrew B. "How to Avoid Wrongful Discharge Lawsuits." *Journal of Accountancy* 169, no. 5 (May 1990): 8.

———. "How to Fire Without Fear." *The Personnel Administrator* 34, no. 3 (September 1989): 74.

Kelley, Mark W. "Constructive Discharge: A Suggested Standard for West Virginia and Other Jurisdictions." *West Virginia Law Review* 93, no. 4 (summer 1991): 1047.

Klaas, Brian, and Hoyt Wheeler. "Supervisors and Their Response to Poor Performance: A Study of Disciplinary Decision Making." *Employee Responsibilities and Rights Journal* 5, no. 4 (December 1992): 339.

Kriegler, Roy. "Dismissal: Employee Rights and Procedural Fairness." *Law Institute Journal* 65, no. 12 (December 1991): 1158.

Legal Issues in Managing Difficult Employees. Walnut Creek, CA: Council on Education in Management, 1994.

McCulloch, Kenneth J. *Termination of Employment: Employer and Employee Rights.* Boston: Warren Gorham Lamont, 1996.

Morin, William J., and Lyle Yorks. *Dismissal: There Is No Easy Way but There Is a Better Way.* New York: Drake Beam Morin, 1990.

Petersen, Donald J. "The Arbitration of Fighting Cases." *The International Journal of Conflict Management* 2, no. 3 (July 1991): 201.

———. "Quits, Recision of Quits and Constructive Discharge in Arbitration." *Employee Responsibilities and Rights Journal* 3, no. 2 (June 1990): 125.

Shepard, Ira Michael. *Workplace Privacy: Employee Testing, Surveillance, Wrongful Discharge, and Other Areas of Vulnerability.* 2d ed. Washington, D.C.: Bureau of National Affairs, 1989.

Sylvia, Ronald D. *Public Personnel Administration*. Fort Worth, TX: Harcourt Brace College Publishers, 1994.

Thornton, Gene R. "Labor and Employment Review: Rights of Terminated Employees: Expanding Remedies." *Colorado Lawyer* 21, no. 8 (August 1, 1992): 1639.

"Who Says Quitters Never Win?" *Small Business Report* 19, no. 10 (October 1994): 45.

"Wrongful Discharge: Recovery for Emotional Distress Damages Caused by Discharge Based on Workers' Compensation Claim." *Law Reporter* 34, no. 2 (March 1991): 74.

Wrongful Employment Termination Practice. 2d ed. Berkeley, CA: Continuing Education of the Bar, 1997.

Youngblood, Stuart, Linda Trevino, and Monica Favia. "Reactions to Unjust Dismissal and Third-Party Dispute Resolution: A Justice Framework." *Employee Responsibilities and Rights Journal* 5, no. 4 (December 1992): 283.

Chapter Fourteen

QUESTIONS ASKED BY NEW SUPERVISORS

> *It is better to have a permanent income than to be fascinating.*
>
> —Oscar Wilde

HOW IS THIS BOOK DIFFERENT?

How is this book different from all of the other employee supervision handbooks?

1. This book is not designed for the first line supervisor in a manufacturing plant or for the meat department manager at your local supermarket.

2. This book is written for the librarian or staff member who has responsibility for the supervision of student employees.

3. This book is written by librarians with more than 50 years of experience in managing programs, staff, and student employees.

4. This book contains information basic to an understanding of supervision, student employment, and libraries and offers advice on translating management/supervision literature into usable information for library staff.

If you have read sections of this book, you will have noticed that the authors have injected suggestions, opinions, and bits of advice throughout. The authors, without giving away their ages, have over 50 years of student supervision experience. In this concluding chapter, the reader will find the authors' answers to a sampling of questions asked by new supervisors. The bibliography contains resources dealing with the future of libraries and library administration and management.

Will I Have to Change to Become a Supervisor?

Yes and no. You may have to change some of your behaviors when you become a supervisor but you will not change your basic personality. As a supervisor, you will be the same person you were before but, although you should continue to be friendly, you may become less intimate with your employees. You should continue to be relaxed, but you may have to be conscious of setting a good example for your employees. You should continue to be supportive of library goals and policies, but if you have complaints or challenges to library policy, you will take them up with your colleagues or management, not with your employees. You will know when you have made the change from employee to supervisor when you start referring to library management as "we," not "they."

Why Do Beginning Supervisors Feel Underpaid?

Many new supervisors feel that their new responsibilities are so great that the difference in pay as a worker and as a supervisor is not worth it. The change in responsibilities sometimes seems overwhelming at first, but given time, the new supervisor will gain control. Secondly, it may be that the salary difference is not enough for the work involved, but it is a price one pays to reach higher levels and salaries later. The new supervisor must take the long view.

How Much Should I
Depend on Other Supervisors?

How much you can depend on other supervisors for help and advice depends on the kind of supervisors they are. In most cases, you find that other supervisors can be of tremendous help. A good rule to follow is to seek and accept help or advice from other supervisors based on your knowledge of their skills. You are better off following your own instincts than listening to poor advice from another supervisor. Your own supervisor can be an excellent source of help but if you disagree with him or her, tactfully explain why. Ask the same question of several supervisors. You will soon learn who you can go to for help.

Where Else Can I Turn for Help?

Don't forget that you work in an ideal setting when it comes to information. There are many excellent books on supervision, many of which are listed in the bibliography of this and other chapters of this handbook. Examine the supervision books and find one that best matches your supervisory style. You will also find information on supervision in the periodical literature. Four of the best periodicals containing articles for the practitioner are *Personnel, Personnel Journal, Supervision,* and *Supervisory Management.*

How Important Is Education
to Advancement?

Formal education is the best route to advancement, so take advantage of the opportunities provided by working for a university. Watch for workshops and training sessions (offered through the university) that will improve your skills. Experience combined with strong motivation also helps you advance. Demonstrating that you have the skills for supervision will go a long way toward helping you succeed.

How Do I Cope with
Too Much Work?

There are countless demands on your time, many beyond your control. Your primary responsibility is to react calmly and keep your unit functioning while trying to squeeze in some time for planning. To maintain control, do your planning at home if you have to. That planning will eventually help you to react better to all the demands placed on you. Many supervisors of student employees also perform other job responsibilities such as cataloging, reference, selection, and instruction. Supervision may be only a portion of your job but it can consume many hours. Review the section on time management in this handbook and find a way to control your time.

How Can I Get Everything Done?

Planning is the key. Your job probably contains a combination of getting many routine tasks accomplished while trying to deal with all the unplanned-for events in the workday. First, complete those routine tasks that you must perform to free yourself for more creative work; and *delegate, delegate, delegate.* You will find it difficult at first to let go of the responsibilities you had as a worker; but let them go you must. Do not allow yourself to become bogged down with routine tasks, even though they may be what you want to do. If you can delegate them, do so.

What Should I Do When
I Get Discouraged?

If you become so discouraged with your supervisory role that you feel you should resign, go to your supervisor or someone you trust and discuss the problem openly and honestly. It is not unusual for the new supervisor to become discouraged. It happens to nearly everyone because the adjustment is more difficult than you think. Talking things over occasionally will help you survive until you get things under control and become accustomed to the supervisory role. Resigning without talking things over with someone would be foolhardy. Remember that you are not alone. All veteran supervisors have experienced many of the same feelings you have when they were just beginning to supervise.

How Can I Be Sure I Want to Be a Supervisor?

To be fair to yourself, plan to spend at least a year before making a firm commitment or asking to be relieved. Whether or not you should continue as a supervisor, you need to feel that you are performing close to your potential in the supervisory role and that you are able to cope with your multiple responsibilities. It may take longer than a year to know whether or not supervisory responsibilities satisfy your needs for a fulfilling, stimulating work experience.

Where Will I Be in Five Years?

As soon as you have become a capable supervisor, you will be able to do some career planning. As a supervisor, you have more freedom to establish and reach career goals than if you were an employee. Set realistic goals and don't become frustrated if you don't advance as quickly as you had hoped. Much will depend on circumstances and events beyond your control; but all libraries need good supervisors at all levels. Your success in the supervision of student employees will translate very well to the supervision of other staff.

How Do I Know When I Have Developed a Leadership Style?

It may take a few years to develop a leadership style that works as well as you would like. You will know you have developed a style when you feel comfortable with yourself and when those you supervise feel comfortable with you. Your department or unit will function efficiently and without turmoil. Your reputation will grow as a good supervisor; but even then, don't become complacent. There will always be room for improvement.

In a Few Words, What Is the Best Advice for Supervisors?

As a new supervisor of student employees, you should ask questions, seek advice, never stop learning, and, the best advice, "trust yourself; you know more than you think."

BIBLIOGRAPHY

Books, Bricks, & Bytes. Cambridge, MA: American Academy of Arts and Sciences, 1996.

Crawford, Gregory A. "Information as a Strategic Contingency: Applying the Strategic Contingencies Theory of Intraorganizational Power to Academic Libraries." *College and Research Libraries* 58, no. 2 (March 1997): 145–55.

Crawford, Walt, and Michael Gorman. *Future Libraries: Dreams, Madness and Reality*. Chicago: American Library Association, 1995.

Jeapes, Ben. "Digital Library Projects: Where They Are Now—Part One." *Electronic Library* 13, no. 6 (December 1995): 551–54.

Macinick, James W. "Freeway or Tollway?: The Internet and Academic Libraries." *Internet Reference Services Quarterly* 1, no. 4 (1996): 45–54.

Mayo, Diane. *Wired for the Future: Developing Your Library Technology Plan*. Chicago: American Library Association, 1998.

McCabe, Gerard B., and Ruth J. Person, eds. "Academic Libraries: Their Rationale and Role in American Higher Education." *Contributions in Librarianship and Information Science*, no. 84. Westport, CT: Greenwood Press, 1995.

Talbott, Stephen L. *The Future Does Not Compute: Transcending the Machines in Our Midst*. Sebastopol, CA: O'Reilly, 1995.

Van Gils, Wouter. "The Precarious Position Between Content and Technology: Libraries Seeking Their Future." *Electronic Library* 13, no. 6 (December 1995): 533–37.

GLOSSARY OF FINANCIAL AID TERMS ∾

The process of awarding student financial aid has grown more complex over the years and, as a result, has developed its own vocabulary. At times it may seem as though discussions of financial aid are conducted in a foreign language. To help reduce confusion for students, parents, and student supervisors, this section presents common sense definitions of many of the words used by financial aid professionals.

ACRONYMS

ACT	American College Testing Program
AFDC	Aid to Families with Dependent Children
AP	Advanced Placement
BIA	Bureau of Indian Affairs
CLEP	College-Level Examination Program
COA	Cost of Attendance
CPS	Central Processing System
CSS	College Scholarship Service
CWS	College Work-Study
ED	U.S. Department of Education
EFC	Expected Family Contribution
EFT	Electronic Transfer of Funds
ELO	Expanded Lending Option
ESAR	Electronic Student Aid Report
ETS	Educational Testing Service
FAA	Financial Aid Administrator
FAF	Financial Aid Form
FAFSA	Free Application for Federal Student Aid
FAO	Financial Aid Office
FAT	Financial Aid Transcript
FDSLP	Federal Direct Student Loan Program
FFELP	Federal Family Education Loan Program

FSEOG	Federal Supplemental Educational Opportunity Grant
FM	Federal Methodology
FWS	Federal Work-Study
GPA	Grade Point Average
GSL	Guaranteed Student Loan
HEAL	Health Education Assistance Loan
HHS	U.S. Department of Health and Human Services
HPSL	Health Profession Student Loan
IM	Institutional Methodology
IRA	Individual Retirement Account
IRS	Internal Revenue Service
ISIR	Institutional Student Information Report
MDE	Multiple Data Entry
NHCS	National Health Corps Scholarship
NMSQT	National Merit Scholarship Qualifying Test
NSL	Nursing Student Loan
PC	Parent Contribution
PCL	Primary Care Loan
PHEAA	Pennsylvania Higher Education Assistance Agency
PJ	Professional Judgment
PLUS	Parent Loan for Undergraduate Students
PSAT	Preliminary Scholastic Assessment Test
RA	Research Assistantship
ROTC	Reserve Officer Training Corps
SAP	Satisfactory Academic Progress
SAR	Student Aid Report
SAT	Scholastic Assessment Test
SC	Student Contribution
SEOG	Supplemental Educational Opportunity Grant
SLMA	Student Loan Marketing Association
SLS	Supplemental Loan for Students
SSIG	State Student Incentive Grants
TA	Teaching Assistantship
TOEFL	Test of English as a Foreign Language
USDE	U.S. Department of Education
VA	Veterans Administration

DEFINITIONS

1040 Form, 1040A Form, 1040EZ Form—The Federal Income Tax Return. Every person who has received income during the previous year must file a form 1040 with the IRS by April 15.

1090 Form—Form used by businesses to report income paid to a non-employee. Banks use this form to report interest income.

401(k)—A popular type of retirement fund. It is legal to borrow money from your 401(k) to help pay for your children's education.

Academic Year—The period during which school is in session, consisting of at least 30 weeks of instructional time. The school year typically runs from the beginning of September through the end of May at most colleges and universities.

Accrue—To accumulate.

Accrual Date—The date on which interest charges on an educational loan begin to accrue. *See also* Subsidized Loan.

Achievement Tests (SAT II)—A collection of tests that measure a student's proficiency and accumulated knowledge of specific subject areas. Different schools require different achievement tests as part of their admissions requirements. Since March 1994, these tests are now known as the SAT II tests. *See also* SAT and ETS.

Adjusted Available Income—In the Federal Methodology, the remaining income after the allowances (taxes and a basic living allowance) have been subtracted.

Admit-Deny—A practice in which a school will admit marginal students, but not award them any financial aid. Very few schools use admit-deny, because studies have shown that lack of sufficient financial aid is a key factor in the performance of marginal students.

Advanced Placement Test (AP)—Test used to earn credit for college subjects studied while in high school. They are offered by ETS in the spring. AP tests are scored on a scale from 1 to 5 (the best possible score).

Alternative Loans—*See* Private Loans.

American College Test (ACT)—One of two national standardized college entrance examinations used in the U.S. The other is the SAT. The ACT is widely used in the West and Midwest. Most universities require either the ACT or the SAT as part of an application for admission. *See also* PLAN.

Amortization—The process of gradually repaying a loan over an extended period of time and through periodic installments of principal and interest.

Appeal—A formal request to have a financial aid administrator review your aid eligibility and possibly use Professional Judgment to adjust the figures. For example, if you believe the financial information on the financial aid application does not reflect your family's current ability to pay (e.g., because of death of a parent, unemployment, or other unusual circumstances), you should definitely make an appeal. The financial aid administrator may require documentation of the special circumstances or of other information listed on the financial aid application.

Asset—An item of value, such as a family's home, business, and farm equity, real estate, stocks, bonds, mutual funds, cash, certificates of deposit (CDs), bank accounts, trust funds, and other property and investments.

Asset Protection Allowance—A portion of your parents' assets that are not included in the calculation of the parent contribution, as calculated by the Federal Methodology need analysis formula. The asset protection allowance increases with the age of the parents.

Assistantship—*See* Graduate Assistantship.

Associate Degree—The degree granted by two-year colleges.

Award Letter—An official document issued by the financial aid office that lists all of the financial aid awarded to the student. This letter provides details on their analysis of your financial need and the breakdown of the financial aid package according to amount, source, and type of aid. The award letter will include the terms and conditions for the financial aid and information about the cost of attendance. You are required to sign a copy of the letter, indicating whether you accept or decline each source of aid, and return it to the financial aid office. Some schools call the award letter the "Financial Aid Notification (FAN)."

Award Year—The academic year for which financial aid is requested (or received).

Bachelor's Degree—The undergraduate degree granted by four-year colleges and universities.

Balloon Payment—A larger than usual payment used to pay off the outstanding balance of a loan without penalty. Not all loans allow balloon payments. Simple interest loans, like many educational loans, generally do allow balloon payments.

Bankruptcy—When a person is declared bankrupt, he is found to be legally insolvent, and his property is distributed among his creditors or otherwise administered to satisfy the interests of his creditors. Federal student loans, however, cannot normally be discharged through bankruptcy.

Base Year—The tax year prior to the academic year (award year) for which financial aid is requested. The base year runs from January 1 of the junior year in high school through December 31 of the senior year. Financial information from this year is used to determine eligibility for financial aid.

Borrower—The person who receives the loan.

Budget—*See* Cost of Attendance.

Bursar's Office—(Also called Student Accounts Office) The university office that is responsible for the billing and collection of university charges.

Campus-based Aid—Financial aid programs are administered by the university. The federal government provides the university with a fixed annual allocation, which is awarded by the financial aid administrator to deserving students. Such programs include the Perkins Loan, Supplemental Education Opportunity Grant, and Federal Work-Study. Note that there is no guarantee that every eligible student will receive financial aid through these programs, because the awards are made from a fixed pool of money. This is a key difference between the campus-based loan programs and the Direct Loan Program. Do not confuse the two, even though both loans are issued through the schools.

Cancellation—Some loan programs provide for cancellation of the loan under certain circumstances, such as death or permanent disability of the borrower. Some of the Federal student loan programs have additional cancellation provisions. For example, if the student becomes a teacher in certain national shortage areas, they may be eligible for cancellation of all or part of the balance of their educational loans. Repayment assistance is available if you serve in the military; the military pays off a portion of your loans for every year of service.

Capital Gain—An increase in the value of an asset such as stocks, bonds, mutual funds, and real estate between the time the asset was purchased and the time the asset was sold.

Capitalization—The practice of adding unpaid interest charges to the principal balance of an educational loan, thereby increasing the size of the loan. Interest is then charged on the new balance, including both the unpaid principal and the accrued interest. Capitalizing the interest increases the monthly payment and the amount of money you will eventually have to repay. If you can afford to pay the interest as it accrues, you are better off not capitalizing it. Capitalization is sometimes called compounding. *See also* Unsubsidized Loans.

Collateral—Property that is used to secure a loan. If the borrower defaults on the loan, the lender can seize the collateral. For example, a mortgage is usually secured by the house purchased with the loan.

Collection Agency—An company often hired by the lender or guarantee agency to recover defaulted loans.

College Board—A nonprofit educational association of colleges, universities, educational systems, and other educational institutions. For more information, see College Board Online (CBO).

College Work-Study (CWS)—College Work-Study is simply a part-time job. This term is sometimes erroneously used to refer to the Federal Work-Study Program.

Color of Federal Forms—The FAFSA and SAR change color each year in a four-color rotation: yellow (1995–96), pink (1996–97), green (1997–98), and blue (1998–99). This will help you make sure you're filing the correct form.

Commuter Student—A student who lives at home and commutes to school every day.

Compounded Interest—Interest that is paid on both the principal balance of the loan and on any accrued (unpaid) interest. Capitalizing the interest on an unsubsidized Stafford loan is a form of compounding.

Consolidation Loan—(Also called Loan Consolidation) A loan that combines several student loans into one bigger loan from a single lender. The consolidation loan is used to pay off the balances on the other loans. Consolidation loans:

♦ reduce the size of the monthly payment by extending the term of the loan beyond the 10-year repayment plan that is standard with FFELP loans. Depending on the loan amount, the term of the loan can be extended from 12 to 30 years. The reduced monthly payment may make the loan easier to repay for some borrowers. Of course, extending the term of a loan increases the total amount of interest paid.

♦ simplify the repayment process by allowing a single payment to one lender instead of several payments to different lenders.

♦ may decrease the monthly payment without extending the overall loan term beyond 10 years, when one or more of the loans was being repaid in less than 10 years because of minimum payment requirements. In effect, the shorter term loan is being extended to 10 years. Of course, this means that the total amount of interest paid will increase. On the other hand, if you consolidate and opt to pay the same monthly payment as before, the total amount of interest paid will decrease.

Some graduate students have found it necessary to consolidate their educational loans when applying for a mortgage on a house.

Consolidation loans can sometimes result in a lower interest rate, as when a consumer loan is used to pay off credit card balances. With educational loans, however, consolidation usually results in the same or higher interest rate. The interest rate on a consolidation loan is a weighted average of the interest rates on the consolidated loans, rounded up to the nearest whole percent. (The Federal Direct Consolidation Loan is a notable exception.) Consolidation can also eliminate deferment benefits, so it is unwise to consolidate while you are still in school.

Aside from the simplification of the repayment process, consolidation is usually not in the student's best interest. Instead, students who are having trouble making their payments should consider some of the alternate repayment terms provided for FFELP loans by the Higher Education Act of 1992. Income contingent payments, for example, are adjusted to compensate for a lower monthly income. Graduated repayment provides lower payments during the first two years after graduation. Extended repayment allows you to extend the term of the loan without consolidation. Although each of these options increases the total amount of interest paid, the increase is less than that caused by consolidation.

Cooperative Education Program—A program where the student spends time engaged in employment related to their major in addition to regular classroom study.

Cosigner—A cosigner on a loan assumes responsibility for the loan if the borrower should fail to repay it.

Cost of Attendance (COA)—(Also known as the cost of education or "budget") The total amount it should cost the student to go to school, including tuition and fees, room and board, allowances for books and supplies, transportation, and personal and incidental expenses. Loan fees, if applicable, may also be included in the COA. Child care and expenses for disabilities may also be included at the discretion of the financial aid administrator. Schools establish different standard budget amounts for students living on-campus and off-campus, married and unmarried students, and in-state and out-of-state students.

Credit Rating—An evaluation of the likelihood of a borrower to default on a loan. Credit bureaus and credit reporting agencies provide this information to banks and businesses to help them decide whether to issue a loan or extend credit. Your credit rating may include your payment history, a list of current and past credit accounts and their balances, employment and personal information, and a history of past credit problems.

People who make all their payments on time are considered good credit risks. People who are frequently delinquent in making their payments are considered bad credit risks. Defaulting on a loan can negatively impact your credit rating.

A good credit rating is not required for most educational loans, with the exception of the PLUS Loan. However, students who have defaulted on previous educational loans may be required to agree to repay the loan and begin making payments before they can become eligible for further federal aid.

Custodial Parent—If a student's parents are divorced or separated, the custodial parent is the one with whom the student lived the most during the past 12 months. The student's need analysis is based on financial information supplied by the custodial parent.

Default—A loan is in default when the borrower fails to pay several regular installments on time (i.e., payments overdue by 180 days) or otherwise fails to meet the terms and conditions of the loan. If you default on a loan, the university, the holder of the loan, the state, and the federal government can take legal action to recover the money, including garnishing your wages and withholding income tax refunds. Defaulting on a government loan will make you ineligible for future federal financial aid, unless a satisfactory repayment schedule is arranged, and can affect your credit rating.

Deferment—Occurs when a borrower is allowed to postpone repaying the loan. If you have a subsidized loan, the federal government pays the interest charges during the deferment period. If you have an unsubsidized loan, you are responsible for the interest that accrues during the deferment period. You can still postpone paying the interest charges by capitalizing the interest, which increases the size of the loan. Most federal loan programs allow students to defer their loans while they are in school at least half time. If you don't qualify for a deferment, you may be able to get a forbearance. You can't get a deferment if your loan is in default.

Delinquent—If the borrower fails to make a payment on time, the borrower is considered delinquent and late fees may be charged. If the borrower misses several payments, the loan goes into default.

Dependency Status—Determines to what degree the student has access to parent financial resources. A parent refusing to provide support for a child's education is not sufficient for the child to be declared independent.

An independent student is one who is at least 24 years old as of January 1 (i.e., born before January 1, 1972 for academic year 1995—96), is married, is a graduate or professional student, has a legal dependent other than a spouse, is a veteran of the U.S. Armed Forces, or is an orphan or ward of the court (or was a ward of the court until age 18). All other students are considered dependent.

If the financial aid administrator believes that you are not an independent student they can require you to provide proof of independent status to qualify, and their decision on your status is generally not subject to appeal.

For details on what constitutes a veteran, please see *Veteran*.

See your financial aid administrator if you have any special circumstances. The FAA may be able to do an override of your dependency status on the FAFSA, if warranted by involuntary dissolution of the family or other very unusual situations. Special circumstances that are sometimes sufficient for an override include:

♦ a legal restraining order has been issued against the parents because of abusive behavior.

♦ both of the parents have been incarcerated.

♦ the parents live in another country and the child has been granted refugee status by the U.S. Immigration Service.

♦ the parents live in a country where they cannot easily leave or get money out.

A student does not qualify for independent status just because his or her parents have decided not to claim him or her as an exemption on their tax returns or are refusing to provide support for a college education. In order to override dependency status, the student must provide documentation to the satisfaction of the financial aid administrator that he or she is truly self-supporting. A few financial aid offices may require that a minimum annual income of $10,000 to establish self-sufficiency.

Several financial aid books suggest that all one needs to do for to be considered independent is to not be listed as a dependent on their parents' tax return for the past two years and for them to have earned at least $4,000 per year during the same period. This is the *old* definition of independence and is no longer valid.

Dependent—For a child or other person to be considered your dependent, they must live with you, and you must provide them with more than half of their support from another person. Spouses do not count as dependents in the Federal Methodology. You and your spouse cannot both claim the same child as a dependent. *See also* Independent.

Direct Loans—The William D. Ford Federal Direct Loan Program (a.k.a. the Direct Loan Program) is a new federal program where the school becomes the lending agency and manages the funds directly, with the federal government providing the loan funds. Not all schools currently participate in this program. Benefits of the program include a faster turn-around time and less bureaucracy than the old "bank loan" program. The terms for Direct Loans are the same as for the Stafford Loan program. For more information about Direct Loans, contact the Direct Loan Servicing Center at 1-800-848-0979.

Disbursement—The release of loan funds to the school for delivery to the borrower. The payment will be made co-payable to the student and the school. Loan funds are first credited to the student's account for payment of tuition, fees, room and board, and other school charges. Any excess funds are then paid to the student in cash or by check. Unless the loan amount is under $500, the disbursement will be made in at least two equal installments.

Discharge—To release the borrower from his or her obligation to repay the loan. *See also* Cancellation.

Disclosure Statement—Provides the borrower with information about the actual cost of the loan, including the interest rate, origination, insurance, loan fees, and any other kinds of finance charges. Lenders are required to provide the borrower with a disclosure statement before issuing a loan.

Doctorate—One of several degrees granted by graduate schools.

Due Diligence—If a borrower fails to make payments on their loan according to the terms of the promissory note, the federal government requires the lender, holder, or servicer of the loan to make frequent attempts to contact the borrower (via telephone and mail) to encourage him or her to repay the loan and make arrangements to resolve the delinquency.

Early Action—A program that has earlier deadlines and earlier notification dates than the regular admissions process. Students who apply to an early action program do not commit to attending the school if admitted, unlike an early decision program. Ivy League schools do not allow you to apply to more than one Ivy early action. Do not confuse *Early Action* with *Early Decision*.

Early Admission—A program that allows gifted high school juniors to skip their senior year and enroll instead in college. The term "Early Admission" is sometimes used to refer collectively to Early Action and Early Decision programs.

Early Decision—A program that has earlier deadlines and earlier notification dates than the regular admissions process. Students who apply to an early decision program commit to attending the school if admitted (thus, early decision can be applied to only one school). Unfortunately, this means the student has accepted the offer of admission before they find out about the financial aid package. You should only participate in an early decision program if the school is your first choice and you won't want to consider other schools. Do not confuse *Early Decision* with *Early Action*.

Electronic Data Exchange (EDE)—Program used by participating schools to electronically receive SARs from the federal processor. At some schools EDE allows students to electronically file their Free Application for Federal Student Aid (FAFSA).

Educational Testing Service (ETS)—Company that produces and administers the SAT and other educational achievement tests.

Electronic Funds Transfer (EFT)—Used by some schools and lenders to wire funds for Stafford and PLUS loans directly to participating schools without requiring an intermediate check for the student to endorse. The money is transferred electronically instead of using paper, and hence is available to the student sooner. If there is a choice of funds transfer methods, use EFT.

Electronic Student Aid Report—An electronic form of the Student Aid Report.

Eligible Non-Citizen—Someone who is not a U.S. citizen but is nevertheless eligible for Federal student aid. Eligible non-citizens include U.S. permanent residents who are holders of valid green cards, U.S. nationals, holders of form I-94 who have been granted refugee or asylum status, and certain other non-citizens. Non-citizens who hold a student visa or an exchange visitor visa are not eligible for Federal student aid.

Emancipated—To release a child from the control of a parent or guardian. Declaring a child to be legally emancipated is not sufficient to release the parents or legal guardians from being responsible for providing for the child's education. If this were the case, then parents would "divorce" their children before sending them to college. The criteria for a child to be found independent are much stricter. *See* Dependency Status.

Endowment—Funds owned by an institution and invested to produce income to support the operation of the institution. Many educational institutions use a portion of their endowment income for financial aid. A school with a larger ratio of endowment per student is more likely to give larger financial aid packages.

Enrollment Status—An indication of whether you are a full-time or part-time student. Generally the student must be enrolled at least half-time (and in some cases full-time) to qualify for financial aid.

Entitlement—Entitlement programs award funds to all qualified applicants. The Pell Grant is an example of such a program.

Entrance Interview—*See* Loan Interviews.

Equity—The dollar value of your ownership in a piece of property. *See also,* Home Equity.

Exit Interview—*See* Loan Interviews.

Expanded Lending Option (ELO)—Under ELO, some schools can offer higher annual and cumulative loan limits to students receiving the Perkins Loan. The ELO is restricted to schools with a Perkins Loan default rate of 15% or less.

Expected Family Contribution (EFC)—The amount of money that the family is expected to be able to contribute to the student's education, as determined by the Federal Methodology need analysis formula approved by Congress. The EFC includes the parent contribution and the student contribution and depends on the student's dependency status, family size, number of family members in school, taxable and nontaxable income, and assets. The difference between the COA and the EFC is the student's financial need, and is used in determining the student's eligibility for need-based financial aid. If you have unusual financial circumstances (such as high medical expenses, loss of employment, or death of a parent) that may affect your ability to pay for your education, tell your financial aid administrator (FAA). He or she can adjust the COA or EFC to compensate. *See* Professional Judgment.

Federal Direct Student Loan Program (FDSLP)—Similar to the Federal Family Education Loan Program (FFELP). The funds for these loans are provided by the U.S. government directly to students and their parents through their schools. Benefits of the program include a faster turn-around time and less bureaucracy than the old "bank loan" program. The FDSLP includes the Federal Direct Stafford Loan (Subsidized and Unsubsidized) and the Federal Direct Parent Loan for Undergraduate Students (PLUS). For more information about Direct Loans, contact the Direct Loan Servicing Center at 1-800-848-0979.

Federal Family Education Loan Program (FFELP)—This includes the Federal Stafford Loan (Subsidized and Unsubsidized), the Federal Perkins Loan, and the Parent Loan for Undergraduate Students (PLUS). The funds for these loans are provided by private lenders, such as banks, credit unions, and savings & loan associations. These loans are guaranteed against default by the federal government.

Federal Methodology—The need analysis formula used to determine the EFC. The Federal Methodology takes family size, the number of family members in college, taxable and nontaxable income, and assets into account. Unlike most Institutional Methodologies, however, the Federal Methodology does not consider the net value of the family residence.

Federal Processor—The organization that processes the information submitted on the Free Application for Federal Student Aid (FAFSA) and uses it to compute eligibility for federal student aid. There are actually two different federal processors serving specific geographic regions. ACT serves the east coast, Michigan, Wisconsin, Iowa, Alabama, Mississippi, and the Pacific Islands. I-Net serves everyone else.

People living in an area served by ACT, will send FAFSA to the following address:

Federal Student Aid Programs
P.O. Box 4001
Mt. Vernon, IL 62864-8601

People living in an area served by I-Net will send FAFSA to the following address:

Federal Student Aid Programs
P.O. Box 60001
Cahokia, IL 62206-6001

It doesn't matter which processor an individual student uses; the only difference is in the address on the envelope that comes with the FAFSA and the address on the bottom of the last page of the form.

Federal Work-Study (FWS)—Program providing undergraduate and graduate students with part-time employment during the school year. The federal government pays a portion of the student's salary, making it cheaper for departments and businesses to hire the student. For this reason, work-study students often find it easier to get a part-time job. Eligibility for FWS is based on need. Money earned from a FWS job is not counted as income for the subsequent year's need analysis process.

Fellowship—A form of financial aid given to graduate students to help support their education. Some fellowships include a tuition waiver or a payment to the university in lieu of tuition. Most fellowships include a stipend to cover reasonable living expenses (e.g., just above the poverty line). Fellowships are a form of gift aid and do not have to be repaid.

Financial Aid—Money provided to the student and the family to help them pay for the student's education. Major forms of financial aid include gift aid (grants and scholarships) and self help aid (loans and work).

Financial Aid Administrator (FAA)—A college or university employee who is involved in the administration of financial aid. Some schools call FAAs "Financial Aid Advisors" or "Financial Aid Counselors."

Financial Aid Form (FAF)—The old name for the Financial Aid PROFILE. The Financial Aid PROFILE is a supplemental financial aid form processed by the College Scholarship Service (CSS). It is not necessary to file a Financial Aid PROFILE in order to apply for Federal student financial aid; the FAFSA is sufficient. The Financial Aid PROFILE is used by many private colleges and universities for awarding institutional funds.

Financial Aid Notification (FAN)—*See* Award Letter.

Financial Aid Office (FAO)—The college or university office responsible for the determination of financial need and the awarding of financial aid.

Financial Aid Package—The complete collection of grants, scholarships, loans, and work-study employment from all sources (federal, state, institutional, and private) offered to a student to enable them to attend the college or university. Note that unsubsidized Stafford loans and PLUS loans are not considered part of the financial aid package, since these financing options are available to the family to help them meet the EFC.

Financial Aid Transcript (FAT)—A record of all federal aid received by the student at each school attended. If you have previously attended an institution of higher education and are now applying for financial aid from a different university, the university will require a FAT from each of the schools previously attended, regardless of whether aid was received or not. They are required to do this by federal law. You have to submit a FAT even if you were in high school at the time. An electronic FAT process will be in place soon which will eliminate the need for the student to submit a FAT. The FAT is not the same as an academic transcript.

Financial Need—*See* Need.

Financial Safety School—A school you are certain will admit you, and which is inexpensive enough that you can afford to attend even if you get no (or very little) financial aid.

First-Time Borrower—A first-year undergraduate student who has no unpaid loan balances outstanding on the date he or she signs a promissory note for an educational loan. First-time borrowers may be subjected to a delay in the disbursement of the loan funds. The first loan payment is disbursed 30 days after the first day of the enrollment period. If the student withdraws during the first 30 days of classes, the loan is canceled and does not need to be repaid. Borrowers with existing loan balances aren't subject to this delay.

Fixed Interest—In a fixed interest loan, the interest rate stays the same for the life of the loan.

Forbearance—During a forbearance the lender allows the borrower to temporarily postpone repaying the principal, but the interest charges continue to accrue, even on subsidized loans. The borrower must continue paying the interest charges during the forbearance period. Forbearances are granted at the lender's discretion, usually in cases of extreme financial hardship or other unusual circumstances when the borrower does not qualify for a deferment. The borrower cannot receive a forbearance if the loan is in default.

Free Application for Federal Student Aid (FAFSA)—Form used to apply for Pell Grants and all other need-based aid. As the name suggests, no fee is charged to file a FAFSA.

An electronic version of the FAFSA called FAFSA Express will be available by disk in the 1997–98 academic year. (Call 1-800-801-0576 for information about FAFSA Express.)

When filing a FAFSA, be sure to use an original form, not a photocopy. Photocopies of the form are unacceptable because photocopying alters the alignment of the forms, interfering with the imaging technology the federal processors use to process the forms.

Gapping—The practice of failing to meet a student's full demonstrated need. *See also* Unmet Need.

Garnishment—The practice of withholding a portion of a defaulted borrower's wages to repay his or her loan, without their consent.

Gift Aid—Financial aid, such as grants and scholarships, which does not need to be repaid.

Grace Period—A short time period after graduation during which the borrower is not required to begin repaying his or her student loans. The grace period may also kick in if the borrower leaves school for a reason other than graduation or drops below half-time enrollment. Depending on the type of loan, you will have a grace period of six months (Stafford Loans) or nine months (Perkins Loans) before you must start making payments on your student loans. The PLUS Loans do not have a grace period.

Grade Point Average (GPA)—An average of a student's grades, converted to a 4.0 scale (4.0 is an A, 3.0 is a B, and 2.0 is a C). Some schools use a 5.0 scale for the GPA.

Graduate Assistantship—There are two types of graduate assistantships: teaching assistantships (TA) and research assistantships (RA). TAs and RAs receive a full or partial tuition waiver and a small living stipend. TAs are required to perform teaching duties. RAs are required to perform research duties, not necessarily related to the student's thesis research.

Graduate Student—A student enrolled in a Masters or Ph.D. program.

Graduated Repayment Schedule—A schedule where the monthly payments are smaller at the start of the repayment period, and gradually become larger.

Grant—A type of financial aid based on financial need that the student does not have to repay.

Gross Income—Income before taxes, deductions, and allowances have been subtracted.

Guarantee Agency or Guarantor—State agencies responsible for approving student loans and insuring them against default. Guarantee agencies also oversee the student loan process and enforce federal and state rules regarding student loans.

    If a borrower defaults on an educational loan, the guarantee agency assumes responsibility for collecting the loan and repays the lender, usually at 98 cents on the dollar. (Legislation is pending to reduce this amount to 95 cents on the dollar). This means that guaranteed educational loans are extremely low-risk loans for the lender, despite being unsecured.

    Each state has a different guarantee agency that administers the federal Stafford and Plus loans for students in that state. There are 41 guarantee agencies for educational loans in the United States. The state guarantee agency is the best source of information about FFELP loans in your state. Although the federal government sets the overall structure of the FFELP loan program (e.g., loan limits and interest rates), each state may set additional restrictions on the loans, within federal guidelines.

For the name, address, and telephone number of your state's guarantee agency, call the Federal Student Aid Information Center at 1-800-433-3243 (1-800-4-FED-AID).

Guarantee Fee—A small percentage of the loan that is paid to the guarantee agency to insure the loan against default. The insurance fee is usually 1% of the loan amount (and by law cannot exceed 3% of the loan amount).

Guaranteed Student Loan (GSL)—(Now called the Stafford Loan.) A guaranteed loan is insured against default. In the case of guaranteed student loans, the federal government agrees to repay the loans in case of default. Each loan is charged a guarantee fee to cover the costs of defaulted loans.

Half-Time—Most financial aid programs require that the student be enrolled at least half-time to be eligible for aid. Some programs require the student to be enrolled full-time.

Health Education Assistance Loan (HEAL)—A low interest loan administered by the U.S. Department of Health and Human Services (HHS). It is available to medical school students pursuing medicine, osteopathy, dentistry, veterinary medicine, optometry, podiatry, clinical psychology, health administration, and public health. Undergraduate pharmacology students are also eligible.

Health Professions Student Loan (HPSL)—A low interest loan administered by the U.S. Department of Health and Human Services (HHS). It is now known as the Primary Care Loan (PCL).

Holder—The lender, institution, or agency that holds legal title to a loan. The holder may be the bank that issued the loan, a secondary market that purchased the loan from the bank, or a guarantee agency if the borrower defaulted on the loan.

Home Equity—The current market value of a home less the mortgage's remaining unpaid principal. It is based on the market value, not the insurance or tax value. For a conservative estimate of your home's market value, try using the Federal Housing Index Calculator. *See also* Equity.

Horizontal Equity—The principle of horizontal equity is that families with similar financial circumstances should pay the same amount, regardless of how their assets, investments, and income are defined.

In-State Student—A student who meets the legal residency requirements for the state and is eligible for reduced in-state student tuition at public colleges and universities in the state.

Income—The amount of money received from employment (salary, wages, tips), profit from financial instruments (interest, dividends, capital gains), or other sources (welfare, disability, child support, Social Security, and pensions).

Income Contingent Repayment—Under an income contingent repayment schedule, the size of the monthly payments depends on the income earned by the borrower. As the borrower's income increases, so do the payments. The income contingent repayment plan is not available for PLUS Loans.

Independent Student—An independent student is at least 24 years old as of January 1 of the academic year, is married, is a graduate or professional student, has a legal dependent other than a spouse, is a veteran of the U.S. Armed Forces, or is an orphan or ward of the court (or was a ward of the court until age 18). A parent refusing to provide support for their child's education is not sufficient for the child to be declared independent. *See also* Dependent.

Individual Retirement Account (IRA)—One of several popular types of retirement funds. It is not legal to borrow money from an IRA to help pay for your children's education.

Installment Loan—A consumer loan in which the principal and interest are repaid on a regular (usually monthly) schedule. The payments are called "installments" and are all for the same amount.

Institutional Methodology (IM)—If a college or university uses its own formula to determine financial need for allocation of the school's own financial aid funds, the formula is referred to as the Institutional Methodology (IM).

Institutional Student Information Report (ISIR)—The electronic version of SARs delivered to schools by EDExpress.

Insurance Fee—Fee passed on by the lender to the federal government as insurance against default. Insurance fees are charged as the loan is disbursed, and typically run to 1% of the amount disbursed. *See also* Guarantee Fee.

Interest—Amount charged to the borrower for the privilege of using the lender's money. Interest is usually calculated as a percentage of the principal balance of the loan. The percentage rate may be fixed for the life of the loan, or it may be variable, depending on the terms of the loan. All federal loans issued since October, 1992 use variable interest rates that are pegged to the cost of U.S. Treasury Bills.

Internal Revenue Service (IRS)—Federal agency responsible for enforcing U.S. tax laws and collecting taxes.

Internship—Part-time job during the academic year or the summer months in which a student receives supervised practical training in their field. Internships are often very closely related to the student's academic and career goals, and may serve as a precursor to professional employment. Some internships provide very close supervision by a mentor in an apprenticeship-like relationship. Some internships provide the student with a stipend, some don't.

Lender—A bank, credit union, savings & loan association, or other financial institution that provides funds to the student or parent for an educational loan. Note: Some schools now participate in the Federal Direct Loan program and no longer use a private lender because loan funds are provided by the U.S. Government.

Leveraging—If a school offers a talented student extra financial aid, regardless of need, the student is more likely to enroll. Leveraging is the controversial practice of figuring out how much it will take to attract such students and customizing aid offers to optimize the quality of the incoming class.

Line of Credit—Pre-approved loan that lets you borrow money up to a pre-set credit limit, usually by writing checks. This line of credit doesn't cost you anything until you write a check, and then you begin repayment just like a regular loan.

Loan—A type of financial aid which must be repaid, with interest. The federal student loan programs (FFELP and FDSLP) are a good method of financing the costs of your college education. These loans are better than most consumer loans because they have lower interest rates and do not require a credit check or collateral. The Stafford Loans and Perkins Loans also provide a variety of deferment options and extended repayment terms.

Loan Consolidation—*See* Consolidation Loan.

Loan Forgiveness—The federal government cancels all or part of an educational loan because the borrower meets certain criteria (e.g., is performing military or volunteer service).

Loan Interviews—Students with education loans are required to meet with a financial aid administrator before the student receives their first loan disbursement and again before they graduate or otherwise leave school. During these counseling sessions, called entrance and exit interviews, the FAA reviews the repayment terms of the loan and the repayment schedule with the student.

Master's Degree—One of several degrees granted by graduate schools.

Maturity Date—The date when a loan comes due and must be repaid in full.

Merit-based—Financial aid that is merit-based depends on your academic, artistic, or athletic merit, or some other criteria, and not dependent on the existence of financial need. Merit-based awards use grades, test scores, hobbies, and special talents to determine your eligibility for scholarships.

Mortgage—A loan of funds for purchasing a piece of property which uses that property as security for the loan. The lender has a lien on the property and will receive the property if the borrower fails to repay the loan.

Multiple Data Entry Processor (MDE)—A company that processes the FAFSA forms submitted by students. The College Scholarship Service (CSS) and PHEAA are both MDE Processors.

National Health Corps Scholarship—A scholarship program administered by the U.S. Department of Health and Human Services (HHS). It is available to medical students studying allopathic and osteopathic medicine and to students studying dentistry.

National Merit Scholarship Qualifying Test (NMSQT)—*See* PSAT.

National Service Trust—President Clinton's national community service program. If you participate in this program before attending school, the funds may be used to pay your educational expenses. If you participate after graduating, the funds may be used to repay your federal student loans. Eligible types of community service include education, human services, the environment, and public safety.

Need—The difference between the COA and the EFC—the gap between the cost of attending the school and the student's resources. The financial aid package is based on the amount of financial need. The process of determining a student's need is known as need analysis.

$$COA - EFC = Financial\ Need.$$

Need Analysis—The process of determining a student's financial need by analyzing the financial information provided by the student and his or her parents (and spouse, if any) on a financial aid form. The student must submit a need analysis form to apply for need-based aid. Need analysis forms include the Free Application for Federal Student Aid (FAFSA) and the Financial Aid PROFILE.

Need-Based—Financial Aid that is based on your financial situation. Most government sources of financial aid are need-based.

Need-Blind—Under need-blind admissions, the school decides whether to make an offer of admission to a student without considering the student's financial situation. Most schools use a need-blind admissions process. A few schools will use financial need to decide whether to include marginal students in the wait list.

Need Sensitive—Under need-sensitive admissions, the school does take the student's financial situation into account when deciding whether to admit him or her. Some schools use need-sensitive admissions when deciding to accept a borderline student or to pull a student off of the waiting list.

Net Income—This is income after taxes, deductions, and allowances have been subtracted.

New Borrower—*See* First-Time Borrower.

Nursing Student Loan (NSL)—A low interest loan administered by the U.S. Department of Health and Human Services (HHS) and available to students enrolled in nursing programs.

Origination Fee—Fee paid to the bank to compensate them for the cost of administering the loan. The origination fees are charged as the loan is disbursed, and typically run to 3% of the amount disbursed. A portion of this fee is paid to federal government to offset the administrative costs of the loan.

Outside Resource—Aid or benefits available because a student is in school and is counted after need is determined. Outside scholarships, prepaid tuition plans, and VA educational benefits are examples of outside resources.

Outside Scholarship—A scholarship that comes from sources other than the school and the federal or state government.

Out-of-State Student—A student who has not met the legal residency requirements for the state, and is often charged a higher tuition rate at public colleges and universities in that state.

Overawards—A student who receives federal support may not receive awards totaling more than $400 in excess of his or her financial need.

Packaging—The process of assembling a financial aid package.

Parent Contribution (PC)—An estimate of the portion of your educational expenses that the federal government believes your parents can afford. It is based on their income, the number of parents earning income, assets, family size, the number of family members currently attending a university, and other relevant factors. Students who qualify as independent are not expected to have a parent contribution.

Parent Loans for Undergraduate Students (PLUS)—Federal loans available to parents of dependent undergraduate students to help finance the child's education. Parents may borrow up to the full cost of their children's education, less the amount of any other financial aid received. PLUS Loans may be used to pay the EFC. There is a minimal credit check required for the PLUS loan, so a good credit history is required. Check with your local bank to see if they participate in the PLUS loan program. If your application for a PLUS loan is turned down, you may be eligible to borrow additional money under the Unsubsidized Stafford Loan program.

Pell Grant—A federal grant that provides funds of up to $2,340 based on the student's financial need.

Perkins Loan—Formerly the National Direct Student Loan Program, the Perkins Loan allows students to borrow up to $3,000 per year (5 year max.) for undergraduate school and $5,000 per year (6 year max.) for graduate school. The Perkins Loan has one of the lowest interest rates and is awarded by the financial aid administrator to students with exceptional financial need. The student must have applied for a Pell Grant to be eligible. The interest on the Perkins Loan is subsidized while the student is in school.

PhD—One of several degrees granted by graduate schools.

PLAN—An exam taken in the fall of the sophomore year in high school as practice for the ACT.

Prepaid Tuition Plan—A college savings plan that is guaranteed to rise in value at the same rate as college tuition. For example, if a family purchases shares that are worth half a year's tuition at a state college, they will always be worth half a year's tuition, even 10 years later when tuition rates will have doubled.

Prepayment—Paying off all or part of a loan before it is due.

Primary Care Loan (PCL)—A low interest loan administered by the U.S. Department of Health and Human Services (HHS). It is available to medical school students pursuing medicine, osteopathy, dentistry, veterinary medicine, optometry, and podiatry. Undergraduate pharmacology students are also eligible. To be eligible for this loan, you must commit to working in the field of primary care. It was formerly known as the Health Professions Student Loan (HPSL).

Principal—The amount of money borrowed, or remaining unpaid, on a loan. Interest is charged as a percentage of the principal. Insurance and origination fees will be deducted from this amount before disbursement.

Private Loans—Education loan programs established by private lenders to supplement the student and parent education loan programs available from federal and state governments.

Some private loan programs offer terms that are highly competitive with those of the PLUS and unsubsidized Stafford loans. Most, however, are somewhat more expensive.

Professional Degree—A degree in a field like law, education, medicine, pharmacy, or dentistry.

Professional Judgment (PJ)—For need-based federal aid programs, the financial aid administrator can adjust the EFC, adjust the COA, or change the dependency status (with documentation) when extenuating circumstances exist. For example, if a parent becomes unemployed, disabled, or deceased, the FAA can decide to use estimated income information for the award year instead of the actual income figures from the base year. This delegation of authority from the federal government to the financial aid administrator is called Professional Judgement (PJ).

Professional Student—A student pursuing advanced study in law or medicine.

Promissory Note—The binding legal document that must be signed by the student borrower before loan funds are disbursed by the lender. The promissory note states the terms and conditions of the loan, including repayment schedule, interest rate, deferment policy, and cancellations. The student should keep this document until the loan has been repaid.

Preliminary Scholastic Assessment Test (PSAT/NMSQT)—The PSAT is taken during the junior year as practice for the SAT. Scores on the PSAT are used to select semi-finalists for the National Merit Scholarship program. For more information on the PSAT, see the Kaplan Web page.

Reaching School—A school that the student would love to attend, but which isn't "guaranteed" to admit you. Every student should apply to at least one reaching school. *See also* Safety School.

Renewable Scholarships—A scholarship that is awarded for more than one year. Usually the student must maintain certain academic standards to be eligible for subsequent years of the award. Some renewable scholarships will require the student to reapply for the scholarship each year; others will just require a report on the student's progress to a degree.

Repayment Schedule—The repayment schedule discloses the monthly payment, interest rate, total repayment obligation, payment due dates, and the term of the loan.

Repayment Term—The period during which the borrower is required to make payments on his or her loans. When the payments are made monthly, the term is usually given as a number of payments or years.

Research Assistantship (RA)—A form of financial aid awarded to graduate students to help support their education. Research assistantships usually provide the graduate student with a waiver of all or part of tuition, plus a small stipend for living expenses. As the name implies, an RA is required to perform research duties. Sometimes these duties are strongly tied to the student's eventual thesis topic.

Safety School—A school that will almost certainly admit the student. The college admissions process is not predictable. Even "sure admits" are sometimes rejected. Some students are admitted to all the schools to which they apply; others are rejected by all the schools. To protect yourself against the latter scenario, you should apply to at least one safety school. *See also* Reaching School.

Sallie Mae—(Formerly known as SLMA or the Student Loan Marketing Association) The nation's largest secondary market and holds approximately one third of all educational loans.

Satisfactory Academic Progress (SAP)—A student must make this in order to continue receiving federal aid. If a student fails to maintain an academic standing consistent with the school's SAP policy, they are unlikely to meet the school's graduation requirements.

Scholarship—A form of financial aid given to undergraduate students to help pay for their education. Most scholarships are restricted to paying all or part of tuition expenses, though some scholarships also cover room and board. Scholarships are a form of gift aid and do not have to be repaid. Many scholarships are restricted to students in specific courses of study or with academic, athletic, or artistic talent.

Scholarship Search Service—A service that charges a fee to compare the student's profile against a database of scholarship programs. Few students who use a scholarship search service actually win a scholarship.

Scholastic Assessment Test (SAT)—One of the two national standardized college entrance examinations used in the U.S. The other is the ACT. The SAT (previously known as the Scholastic Aptitude Test) is administered by the Educational Testing Service (ETS). Most universities require either the ACT or the SAT as part of an application for admission.

Secondary Market—An organization that buys loans from lenders, thereby providing the lender with the capital to issue new loans. Selling loans is a common practice among lenders, so the bank you make your payments to may change during the life of the loan. The terms and conditions of your loan do not change when it is sold to another holder. Sallie Mae is the nation's largest secondary market and holds approximately one third of all educational loans.

Secured Loan—A loan backed by collateral. If you fail to repay the loan, the lender may seize the collateral and sell it to repay the loan. Auto loans and home mortgages are examples of secured loans. Educational loans are generally not secured.

Selective Service—Registration for the military draft. Male students who are U.S. citizens and have reached the age of 18 and were born after December 31, 1959 must be registered with Selective Service to be eligible for federal financial aid. If the student did not register and is past the age of doing so (18–25), and the school determines that the failure to register was knowing and willful, the student is ineligible for all federal student financial aid programs. The school's decision as to whether the failure to register was willful is not subject to appeal. Students needing help resolving problems concerning their Selective Service registration should call 1-847-688-6888.

Self-Help Aid—Financial aid in the form of loans and student employment. If every financial aid package is required to include a minimum amount of self-help aid before any gift aid is granted, that level is known as the self-help level. For example, at MIT in 1995–1996, the self-help level was $8,150 (*The Tech*, March 7, 1995, vol. 115, no. 9: 1). MIT has one of the highest self-help levels of private colleges and universities, with an average self-help level of around $5,500 at the more expensive schools.

Service Academy—The U.S. Air Force Academy, U.S. Coast Guard Academy, U.S. Merchant Marine Academy, U.S. Military Academy, and U.S. Naval Academy. Admissions is highly selective, as students must be nominated by their Congressional Representative in order to apply.

Servicer—An organization that collects payments on a loan and performs other administrative tasks associated with maintaining a loan portfolio. Loan servicers disburse loans funds, monitor loans while the borrowers are in school, collect payments, process deferments and forbearances, respond to borrower's inquiries, and ensure that the loans are administered in compliance with federal regulations and guarantee agency requirements.

Simple Interest—Interest that is paid only on the principal balance of the loan and not on any accrued interest. Most federal student loan programs offer simple interest. Note, however, that capitalizing the interest on an unsubsidized Stafford loan is a form of compounded interest.

Simplified Needs Test—If the parents have an adjusted gross income of less than $50,000 and every family member was eligible to file an IRS Form 1040A or 1040EZ (or wasn't required to file a Federal income tax return), the Federal Methodology ignores assets when computing the EFC. If you filed a 1040 but weren't required to do so, you may be eligible for the simplified needs test. Details on the eligibility requirements appear on the Simplified Needs Test Chart.

Stafford Loans—Federal loans that come in two forms, subsidized and unsubsidized. Subsidized loans are based on need; unsubsidized loans aren't. The interest on the subsidized Stafford Loan is paid by the federal government while the student is in school and during the 6 month grace period. The Subsidized Stafford Loan was formerly known as the Guaranteed Student Loan (GSL). The Unsubsidized Stafford Loan may be used to pay the EFC.

Undergraduates may borrow up to $23,000 ($2,625 during the freshman year, $3,500 during the sophomore year, and $5,500 during the third, fourth, and fifth years) and graduate students up to $65,500, including any undergraduate Stafford loans ($8,500 per year). These limits are for subsidized and unsubsidized loans combined. The difference between the subsidized loan amount and the limit may be borrowed by the student as an unsubsidized loan.

Higher unsubsidized Stafford loan limits are available to independent students, dependent students whose parents were unable to obtain a PLUS Loan, and graduate/professional students. Undergraduates may borrow up to $46,000 ($6,625 during the freshman year, $7,500 during the sophomore year, and $10,500 during each subsequent year) and graduate students up to $138,500, including any undergraduate Stafford loans ($18,500 per year). These limits are for subsidized and unsubsidized loans combined. The amounts of any subsidized loans are still subject to the lower limits.

State Student Incentive Grants (SSIG)—A state-run financial aid program for state residents. The states receive matching funds from the federal government to help them fund the program.

Statement of Educational Purpose—A legal document in which the student agrees to use the financial aid for educational expenses only. The student must sign this document before receiving federal need-based aid.

Student Accounts Office—*See* Bursar's Office.

Student Aid Report (SAR)—Report that summarizes the information included in the FAFSA. The SAR must be provided to your school's FAO. The SAR will also indicate the amount of Pell Grant eligibility, if any, and the Expected Family Contribution (EFC). You should receive a copy of your SAR four to six weeks after you file your FAFSA. Review your SAR and correct any errors on part 2 of the SAR. Keep a photocopy of the SAR for your records. To request a duplicate copy of your SAR, call 1-319-337-5665.

Student Contribution—The amount of money the federal government expects the student to contribute to his or her education and is included as part of the EFC. The SC depends on the student's income and assets, but can vary from school to school. Usually a student is expected to contribute about 35% of his or her savings and approximately one-half of his summer earnings above $1,750.

Student Loan Marketing Association (SLMA)—SLMA is the old name for Sallie Mae.

Subsidized Loan—With a subsidized loan, such as the Perkins Loan or the Subsidized Stafford Loan, the government pays the interest on the loan while the student is in school, during the six-month grace period, and during any deferment periods. Subsidized loans are awarded based on financial need and may not be used to finance the family contribution. *See* Stafford Loans for information about subsidized Stafford Loans. *See also* Unsubsidized Loan.

Supplemental Education Opportunity Grant—Federal grant program for undergraduate students with exceptional need. SEOG grants are awarded by the school's financial aid office, and provide up to $4,000 per year. To qualify, a student must also be a recipient of a Pell Grant.

Supplemental Loan for Students—Federal loans for financially independent students. This program was eliminated in 1994 with the creation of the unsubsidized Stafford Loan program.

Teaching Assistantship (TA)—A form of financial aid awarded to graduate students to help support their education. Teaching assistantships usually provide the graduate student with a waiver of all or part of tuition, plus a small stipend for living expenses. As the name implies, a TA is required to perform teaching-related duties.

Term—The number of years (or months) during which the loan is to be repaid.

Title IV Loans—Title IV of the Higher Education Act of 1965 created several education loan programs which are collectively referred to as the Federal Family Education Loan Program (FFELP). These loans, also called Title IV Loans, are the Federal Stafford Loans (Subsidized and Unsubsidized), Federal PLUS Loans, and Federal Consolidation Loans.

Title IV School Code—When you fill out the FAFSA you need to supply the Title IV Code for each school to which you are applying. This code is a six-character identifier that begins with one of the following letters: O, G, B, or E. The Financial Aid Information Page provides a searchable database of Title IV School Codes.

Test Of English As A Foreign Language (TOEFL)—Most colleges and universities require international students to take the TOEFL as part of their application for admission. The TOEFL evaluates a student's ability to communicate in and understand English. For more information, see the Kaplan Web page.

Undergraduate Student—A student who is enrolled in a Bachelors degree program.

Unearned Income—Interest income, dividend income, and capital gains.

Unmet Need—In an ideal world, the FAO would be able to provide each student with the full difference between their ability to pay and the cost of education. Due to budget constraints the FAO may provide the student with less than the student's need (as determined by the FAO). This gap is known as the unmet need.

Unsecured Loan—A loan not backed by collateral, representing a greater risk to the lender. The lender may require a co-signer on the loan to reduce their risk. If the borrower defaults on the loan, the co-signer will be held responsible for repayment. Most educational loans are unsecured loans. In the case of federal student loans, the federal government guarantees repayment of the loans. Other examples of unsecured loans include credit card charges and personal lines of credit.

Unsubsidized Loan—A loan for which the government does not pay the interest. The borrower is responsible for the interest on an unsubsidized loan from the date the loan is disbursed, even while the student is still in school. Students may avoid paying the interest while they are in school by capitalizing the interest, which increases the loan amount. Unsubsidized loans are not based on financial need and may be used to finance the family contribution. *See* Stafford Loans for information about unsubsidized Stafford Loans. *See also* Subsidized Loan.

Untaxed Income—Contributions to IRAs, Keoghs, tax-sheltered annuities, and 401(k) plans, as well as worker's compensation and welfare benefits.

U.S. Department of Education (ED or USED)—Government agency that administers several federal student financial aid programs, including the Federal Pell Grant, the Federal Work-Study Program, the Federal Perkins Loans, the Federal Stafford Loans, and the Federal PLUS Loans. For more information about these programs, please see the Student Guide or the U.S. Department of Education's home page.

U.S. Department of Health and Human Services (HHS)—Government agency that administers several health education loan programs, including HEAL, HPSL, and NSL loan programs.

Variable Interest Loan—In a variable interest loan, the interest rate changes periodically. For example, the interest rate might be pegged to the cost of U.S. Treasury Bills (e.g., T-Bill rate plus 3.1%) and be updated monthly, quarterly, semi-annually, or annually.

Verification—Verification is a review process in which the FAO determines the accuracy of the information provided on the student's financial aid application. During the verification process the student and parent will be required to submit documentation for the amounts listed (or not listed) on the financial aid application. Such documentation may include signed copies of the most recent federal and state income tax returns for you, your spouse (if any), and your parents, proof of citizenship, proof of registration with Selective Service, and copies of Social Security benefit statements and W2 and 1099 forms, among other things.

Financial aid applications are randomly selected by the federal processor for verification, with most schools verifying at least one-third of all applications. If there is an asterisk next to the EFC figure on your Student Aid Report (SAR), your SAR has been selected for verification. Schools may select additional students for verification if they suspect fraud. Some schools undergo 100% verification.

If any discrepancies are uncovered during verification, the financial aid office may require additional information to clear up the discrepancies. Such discrepancies may cause your final financial aid package to be different from the initial package described on the award letter you received from the school.

If you refuse to submit the required documentation, your financial aid package will be canceled and no aid awarded.

Veteran—For federal financial aid purposes such as determining dependency status, a veteran is a former member of the U.S. Armed Forces (Army, Navy, Air Force, Marines, or Coast Guard) who served on active duty and was discharged other than dishonorably (i.e., received an honorable or medical discharge).

You are a veteran even if you serve just one day on active duty—not active duty for training—before receiving your DD-214 and formal discharge papers. (Note: For veterans to be eligible for VA educational benefits, they must have served for more than 180 consecutive days on active duty before receiving an honorable discharge. There are exceptions for participation in Desert Storm/Desert Shield, and other military campaigns.)

ROTC students, members of the National Guard, and most reservists are not considered veterans.

Since the 1995–96 academic year, a person who was discharged other than dishonorably from one of the military service academies (the U.S. Military Academy at West Point, the Naval Academy at Annapolis, the Air Force Academy at Colorado Springs, or the Coast Guard Academy at New London) is considered a veteran for financial aid purposes. Cadets and midshipmen who are still enrolled in one of the military service academies, however, are not considered veterans. According to the U.S. Department of Education's Action Letter #6 (February 1996), "a student who enrolls in a service academy, but who withdraws before graduating, is considered a veteran for purposes of determining dependency status."

Having a DD-214 does not necessarily mean that you are a veteran for financial aid purposes. As noted above, you must have served on active duty and received an honorable discharge.

W2 Form—A record of the employee's wages and tax withheld. Employers are required by the IRS to issue a W2 form for each employee before February 28.

Work Study—*See* Federal Work-Study.

INDEX ❧

Absenteeism, 220–23, 227
Absolute format appraisals, 248, 249–50
Academic libraries, 1–2, 113, 195, 196, 228
Academic problems, student employee, 227, 229
Accountability, and supervisors, 40–44, 226
Acquisitions departments, student employees in, 3
Active learning *vs.* passive learning, 187–88
ADA. *See* Americans with Disabilities Act
ADEA. *See* Age Discrimination in Employment Act
Age discrimination, 261
Age Discrimination in Employment Act (ADEA) (1967), 153, 256–57, 261
ALA. *See* American Library Association
America Reads, 128
American Library Association, 258, 272–73
Americans with Disabilities Act (ADA), 153–54, 256–57, 259–60
Appeal processes, 267–69
Applicants, employment, 147–48, 176, 259, 283
Arbitration, 268
ARL. *See* Association of Research Libraries
Association of Research Libraries (ARL), 7
Authority, and supervisors, 40–41, 198–200, 201
Autocratic leadership, 36

Baby and Child Care (Spock), 213
BARS. *See* Behaviorally Anchored Rating Scales
Behaviorally Anchored Rating Scales (BARS), 248, 250
Benefits, work-study jobs and, 132
Boss-imposed time, 45
Brown, Montague, 57
Bryant, Anita, 258

Cataloging departments, student employees in, 3
Change, dealing with, 44–45, 228–29
Child labor laws, 168
Circulation services, student employees in, 3
Civil Rights Act (1964, 1991), 153, 256–57, 258, 262, 264
Classified employees, 284–85
Cleveland Board of Education v. Loudermill, 285
COA. *See* Cost of Attendance
Coaching, of employees, 209–10
Communication, by supervisors, 204–6
Comparative format appraisals, 248, 249
Complaints, student employees, 216
Constructive discharge, 289
Controlling, supervisors and, 12, 198
Cooperation, promoting, 208
Corrective discipline, 280, 283–84
Cost of Attendance (COA), 123
Cottam, Keith M., 6
Counseling, by supervisors, 210–13, 222–23, 227, 251

Decision-making, by supervisors, 202–4
Democratic leadership, 36–37

Development programs
  defined, 175, 179
  developmental training, 188–91
  and performance appraisals, 234–35
Developmental training, 188–91
Differentiated pay, 159–60
Dimaggio, Joe, 233
Direct Loan Program (DL), 125–26
Directions, giving, by supervisors,
  206–7
Disabled workers, 259–60
Discharged workers. *See also*
    Terminations
  and constructive discharge, 289
  and corrective discipline, 284
  defined, 279–80, 281–82
Discipline. *See also* Terminations
  corrective, 280, 283–84
  and grievances, 269
  and personality problems, 225
  and rule violation, 220–21, 223
Discrimination
  grievance and appeal process, 267–68
  hiring and, 153, 154–55
  and performance appraisals, 246
  termination mistakes and, 288–89
  in workplace, 256–62
DL. *See* Direct Loan Program
Downey, Mary Elizabeth, 4–5
Dress policies, 223

Earnings. *See* Wages
EFC. *See* Expected Family Contribution
Einstein, Albert, 195
Employee Polygraph Protection Act
  (1988), 154
Employee responsibilities, 270–71
Employee rights
  age discrimination and, 261
  appeal process and, 267–69
  and disabled workers, 259–60
  and equitable compensation, 267–70
  and grievances, 267–70
  harassment-free workplace, 263–64
  and last-resort termination, 264

national origin discrimination and,
  261–62
nondiscriminatory workplace, 256–57
predischarge, 284–85
and privacy, 264–66
religious discrimination and, 262
safe work environment, 256
and sex discrimination, 257–58
and sexual orientation, 257–58
and union participation, 266–67
and university rights, 267–70
Equal employment opportunities
  laws, 153–54
Equal Opportunity Employment
  Commission, 263
Equal Pay Act (1963), 153, 169,
  171–72, 257
Equitable compensation, 267–70
Ethics, 270, 271–74
Executive Order 11246 (E.O. 11246),
  257
Exempt workers, 163, 164–66
Expected Family Contribution (EFC),
  122–23

FAA. *See* Financial Aid Administrators
FAFSA. *See* Free Application for
  Federal Student Aid
Fair Labor Standards Act (1938)
  child labor laws, 168
  described, 163–70
  earnings defined, 163
  Equal Pay Act, 153, 169, 171–72
  exempt workers, 163, 164–66
  jury duty, 167–68
  minimum wage, 167
  nonexempt workers, 163
  overtime, 167
  volunteer labor and, 131
  wages payments, 168
Federal Consolidated Loans, 124, 125–26
Federal Direct Stafford Loans Program, 115, 124–25, 126
Federal Family Education Loans
  (FFEL), 115, 124–25

Federal Parent Loans to Undergraduate Programs (PLUS), 115,
124–25, 126
Federal Pell Grant Program, 115, 123–24
Federal Supplemental Educational
Opportunities Grant (FSEOG),
115, 127–28
Federal Work-Study Programs (FWS)
America Reads positions, 128
benefits and, 132
as campus-based aid, 127
and employee recruitment, 147
employment limitations, 130–32
funding for, 128–29
and Higher Education Act (1965), 115
job descriptions, 129–30
and National and Community
Service Act (1990), 129
non-work study employees and, 8
and rule violations, 224
student allotments under, 161–62
student eligibility for, 128–29
summer employment, 132
wages, 131–32
FFEL. *See* Federal Family Education
Loans
Financial aid
administrators, 114, 123, 128, 130
campus-based programs, 127
changes to, 114
cost of attendance, 120–21, 123
Direct Loan, 115, 125–26
eligibility determination, 115–20
expected family contribution, 122–23
Family Education Loans, 115, 124–25
independent student determination, 115–18
information via Internet, 138–41
National Early Intervention Scholarship and Partnerships, 135–36
Pell Grants, 123–24
Perkins Loans, 115, 126, 127, 134
Robert C. Byrd Honors Scholarships,
136–37
and rule violations, 224
State Student Incentive Grants, 134–35

supervisor's role in, 137–38
Supplemental Educational Oppor-
tunities Grant, 115, 127–28
Work-Colleges Program, 133–34
Work-Study, 127, 128–33
Financial Aid Administrators (FAA),
114, 123, 128, 130
Fiscal Operations Report and Appli-
cation, 127
Ford Loan Program. *See* Direct Loan
Program (DL)
Free Application for Federal Student
Aid (FAFSA), 122–23, 138
FSEOG. *See* Federal Supplemental
Educational Opportunities
Grant
FWS. *See* Federal Work-Study Programs

Glasgow, Arnold H., 35
Graphic rating scales, 248, 250
Green, Russell, 145
Grievances, 267–70
Gross misconduct, 289–90
Group effort, 206
Guaranteed Student Loans. *See*
Federal Direct Stafford Loans
Program

Handbooks, employee, 177–78,
220–21, 223, 265
Harassment-free workplace, right of,
263–64
Hawkins, Katherine W., 196
Higher Education Act (1965). *See also*
Financial aid; U.S. Depart-
ment of Education
Amendments (1986, 1992), 115,
133, 135, 136
and Expected Family Contribution,
122
Family Education Loan Program,
124–25
loan programs, 125–26

Higher Education Act (*continued*)
    Supplemental Educational Oppor-
        tunities Grant, 127–28
    Work-College Program, 133–34

Immigration Reform and Control
    Act (IRCA) (1968), 154, 261–62
Independent students, 115–19, 129
Insubordination, 229–30
Internet, 1, 138–41
Interviews
    sample questions for, 151–52
    techniques, 149–51
IRCA. *See* Immigration Reform and
    Control Act

James, Henry, 215
JIT. *See* Job Instruction Training
Job analysis, 59
Job descriptions
    features of, 60–61
    preparing, 61–63
    purpose, 59
    samples of, 63–110
Job design, 57–59
Job evaluations *vs.* performance
    appraisals, 234–36
Job Instruction Training (JIT), 184–86
Job satisfaction, 9–10, 209. *See also*
    Loyalty; Morale problems
Job security, public employee, 284–85
Jury duty, 167–68

Koopman, Harry Lyman, 4

Labor-Management Relations Act
    (LMRA) (1947), 170–71
Last-resort terminations, 264
Layoffs, 279. *See also* Terminations
Leadership, 35–40
Leadership, supervisors and, 198

Librarians, 1–2, 7, 272–73
Librarian's Conference (1853), 4
Library ethics, 272–73
Library newsletter, 227
Lloyd-LaFollette Act (1932), 284–85
LMRA. *See* Labor-Management Rela-
    tions Act
Low morale, 218–19
Loyalty, 219–20, 270. *See also* Job sat-
    isfaction; Morale problems

Management, 12, 57, 195, 196–98
Management by objective (MBO),
    248, 250
Managerial ethics, 273–74
Mediation, 268
Melnyk, Andrew, 6
Minimum wage, 167
Mistakes, 203–4
Mistakes, learning from, 51
Morale problems, 218–19. *See also*
    Job satisfaction; Loyalty
Motivation and employees, 198,
    208–10, 217

National and Community Service
    Act (1990), 129
National Defense Student Loans, 134
National Direct Student Loan (NDDL).
    See Perkins Loan Program
National Early Intervention Scholar-
    ship and Partnership Program
    (NEISP), 135–36
National Labor Relations Act (1935),
    171, 266–67
National origin discrimination, 261–62
NDDL. *See* Perkins Loan Program
NEISP. *See* National Early Interven-
    tion Scholarship and Partner-
    ship Program
Nondiscriminatory workplace, 256–57
Nonexempt workers, 163

Occupational Safety and Health Act (OSHA) (1970), 256, 264
Office of Postsecondary Education (OPSE), 115
Older Workers Benefit Protection Act (OWBPA), 261
OPSE. *See* Office of Postsecondary Education
Organizing, supervisors and, 12, 197
Orientation, 176–79. *See also* Training
OSHA. *See* Occupational Safety and Health Act
Outcome-base format appraisals, 248, 250
Overtime, 167
OWBPA. *See* Older Workers Benefit Protection Act

Paige, Satchel, 113
Paris v. Korbel & Brothers, Inc., 288–89
Participative leadership, 36–37
Participative management, 196–97
Passive learning *vs.* active learning, 187–88
Peer evaluation, 236
Performance appraisals
    absolute formats, 248, 249–50
    Behaviorally Anchored Rating Scales (BARS), 248, 250
    comparative formats, 248, 249
    and compensation, 235, 247
    confidentiality of, 246, 247
    and discrimination, 246
    follow-up to, 247–48, 252, 283
    formats of, 248–50
    frequency of, 237
    graphic rating scales, 248, 250
    management by objective (MBO), 248, 250
    meeting checklist, 241–45
    observation for, 239
    ongoing, 251
    outcome-based formats, 248, 250
    and peer evaluation, 236

performance standards of, 237, 238, 245
poor performance evaluations, giving, 243–44
preparation for, 236, 237–41, 245
reliability of, 245–46
self-appraisals, 239
structure of, 236–37
validity of, 245
vs. job evaluation, 234–36
weighted checklists, 250
written appraisal for, 240–41
Perkins, Carl D., 134
Perkins Loan Program, 115, 126, 127, 134
Personal problems, student employee, 227
Personality problems, student employee with, 225–26
Personnel, 295
Personnel Journal, 295
Planning, supervisors and, 12, 197, 219, 296
PLUS. *See* Federal Parent Loans to Undergraduate Programs
Power, defined, 41
Predischarge rights, 284–85
Pregnancy Discrimination Act (1978), 154, 257–58
Preparation departments, student employees in, 3
Privacy rights, 264–66
Probationary periods, 279, 283. *See also* Training
Procrastination, 228
Professional degeneration, 209
Progressive discipline. *See* Corrective discipline
Promotions, recognition for, 50–51

Raises, and performance appraisals, 234, 235
Recruitment, employee. *See* Applicants, employment

Reference departments, student
 employees in, 3
References, 155–56, 264–65
Released workers, 279
Relieved workers, 279
Religious discrimination, 262
Resignations, 278
Responsibility, supervisors and, 41,
 200, 201
Robert C. Byrd Honors Scholarship
 Program, 136–37
Rogers, Will, 17
Rule violations, 220–21, 223–24
Rumors, workplace, 227

Safe work environment, 256
Salaries, 163. *See also* Wages
SAR. *See* Student Aid Report
Schedules, 221. *See also* Absenteeism
SEA. *See* State Education Agency
Search policies, 265–66
Security, student employees as, 3
Select Public Health Loans, 126
Self-imposed time, 45
Sex discrimination, 257–58
Sexual harassment, 263
Sexual orientation rights, 257–58
SFAP. *See* Student Financial Assis-
 tance Programs
Shaw, George Bernard, 1
Spock, Benjamin, 213
SSIG. *See* State Student Incentive
 Grants Program
Staff, 1–2, 7, 8, 190–91
Staffing, supervisors and
 applicant notification, 156–57
 described, 12
 job description preparation, 59–63
 job design, 57–59
 as management function, 198
State Education Agency (SEA), 136
State Student Incentive Grants
 Program (SSIG), 134–35
Stress management, 48, 229
Student Aid Report (SAR), 122–23

*Student Aides in Our Library (Blessings
 and Headaches)* (Melnyk), 6
Student employees. *See also* Supervisors
 benefits for, 8
 communication with, 204–6
 counseling and, 210–13
 and discrimination, 154–55
 duties of, 2, 8
 expectations of, 9–11, 13 (*See also*
  Performance appraisals)
 as future librarians, 5–6
 grades of jobs, 62–63
 handbooks, 177–78, 220–21, 223
 hiring of, 145–57
 older, 230
 perceptions of, 4–6
 problems with, 8, 9, 215–30
 reason for working, 9–11
 recruitment of, 147–49
 referrals of, 145–47
 and regular staff, 7–8
 role of, 2–4
 as temporary employees, 279
 training of, 175–91
 work-study, 9
 workforce size, 2, 7
Student employment, history of, 4–6
Student Financial Assistance Programs (SFAP), 115
Subordinate-imposed time, 45
Summer employment, 132
Supervision, 295
Supervisors. *See also* Discipline; Student employees; Terminations
 and accountability, 40–44
 advice for, 293–98
 and authority, 40–41, 198–200
 change, dealing with, 44–45,
  228–29
 communication by, 204–6
 cooperation and, 208
 counseling by, 210–13
 and decision-making, 202–4
 defined, 18–20
 development programs and, 175
 directions, giving, 206–7

and discrimination, 154–55
education and, 295
employee opinions of, 28–30
employment, legal issues of,
    153–54
ethics for, 271–72, 273–74
expectations for, 27–28, 297
failure of, 31, 295–96
and financial aid, 113, 137–38
and grievances, 269–70
help for, 295, 296
insubordination and, 229–30
interviewing by, 149–53, 155, 157
and leadership, 35–40, 297
management duties of, 11–14
mistakes, learning from, 51, 296
motivation and, 198, 208–10, 217
negative traits of, 29–30, 52
as new supervisors, 26, 28, 294,
    296–98
and other supervisors, 295, 296
performance appraisals and, 233–52
potential for advancement, 48–53,
    295, 297
problems, employee, 8, 9, 215–30,
    283
qualities of, 20–21, 22–23, 35–53,
    213, 297
references, checking of, 155–56
report preparation, 53
responsibilities of, 11–12
and responsibility, 201
role of, 17–19, 24–25
staffing by, 145–57
and stress management, 48, 296
student employees value and, 13,
    236
and their supervisor, 52–53
and time management, 45–48
timesheets and, 223–24
training student employees (*See*
    Training)
transition from employee, 23–26,
    31–32, 294
underpayment of, 294
vs. subordinate responsibilities, 23–24

Supervisory Management, 295
Supreme Court, 261, 285
Suspensions, 283–84

Team management, 196–97
Technical services, 2
Technical services, 3
Telephone, use of, 220–23, 226
Temporary employees, 279
Terminations. *See also* Discipline
    categories of, 278–80
    corrective discipline and, 284
    documentation for, 285–86
    employee rights and, 264
    and grievances, 269
    impact of, 287–88
    insubordination and, 230
    last-resort, 264
    meeting for, 286–87
    mistakes made in, 288–89
    and performance appraisals, 235
    procedures for, 277, 285–87
    reasons for, 280–82
    violence and, 230
The University Library (Wilson and Tauber),
    5–6
Theft, 224
Time management, and supervisors,
    45–48, 296
Time policies, 223–24, 226
Timesheets, 223–24
Training. *See also* Orientation; Proba-
    tionary periods
    active learning style in, 187–88
    checklist for, 191
    developmental training, 188–91
    extended, 183–84
    implementation of, 188
    improvement of, 186–87
    Job Instruction Training (JIT), 184–86
    methodology of, 180–83, 187–88
    need for, 175, 283
    vestibule training, 180
    vs. development, 175, 179–80
Twain, Mark, 159, 175, 255, 277

Union participation rights, 266–67
University-granted rights, 267–70
University of New Mexico, 280–82
University rules, violation of, 224
Utley, G. B., 4
U.S. Constitution, amendments to,
    257, 262, 265
U.S. Department of Education
    (USDE), 113, 114, 122, 123,
    128. *See also* Financial aid
U.S. Department of Labor, 256

Vestibule training, 180
Vietnam Era Veterans' Readjustment
    Assistance Act (1974), 154, 257
Violence, by employees, 230
Vocational Rehabilitation Act (1973),
    153, 259, 260
Volunteer labor, 131
Voting time, 168

Wages
    defined, 163
    and equitable compensation, 267–70
    and low morale, 218
    minimum wage, 167
    non-work-study and, 9
    payment of, 168
    and performance appraisals, 247
    and raises, 234, 235
    work-study, 131–32
Wagner Act. *See* National Labor
    Relations Act (1935)
Warnings, 283–84
White, Emilie C., 6
Wilde, Oscar, 293
William D. Ford Federal Direct Loan
    Program (DL), 115, 125–26
Work-Colleges Program, 133–34
Work-study. *See* Federal Work-Study
    Programs